2011,01,08

DEMCO

ALSO BY BARRETT TILLMAN

NONFICTION

What We Need: Extravagance and Shortages in America's Military

Curtis E. LeMay

Heroes: U.S. Army Recipients of the Medal of Honor

*Clash of the Carriers: The True Story of the Marianas
Turkey Shoot of WW II*

The Alpha Bravo Delta Guide to the U.S. Air Force

Above and Beyond: The Aviation Medals of Honor

TBD Devastator Squadrons of WW 2

U.S. Navy Fighter Squadrons and Aces of WW II

Carrier Air War: WW II in Original Color

*Wildcats to Tomcats (with Capts. Wally Schirra,
R. L. Cormier, & P. R. Wood)*

*Pushing the Envelope: The Career of Test Pilot
Marion Carl (with M. E. Carl)*

Sun Downers: VF-11 in WW II

*On Yankee Station: The Naval Air War Over Vietnam
(with CDR John B. Nichols)*

WHIRL

The Air War Against Japan,
1942–1945

WIND

Barrett Tillman

Simon & Schuster

NEW YORK LONDON TORONTO SYDNEY

Dedicated to the memory of Jeff Ethell:
pilot, historian, colleague, friend.

"Rock your wings when we rendezvous again
and I'll join on you."

For they have sown the wind, and they shall reap the whirlwind.

—HOSEA 8:7

Contents

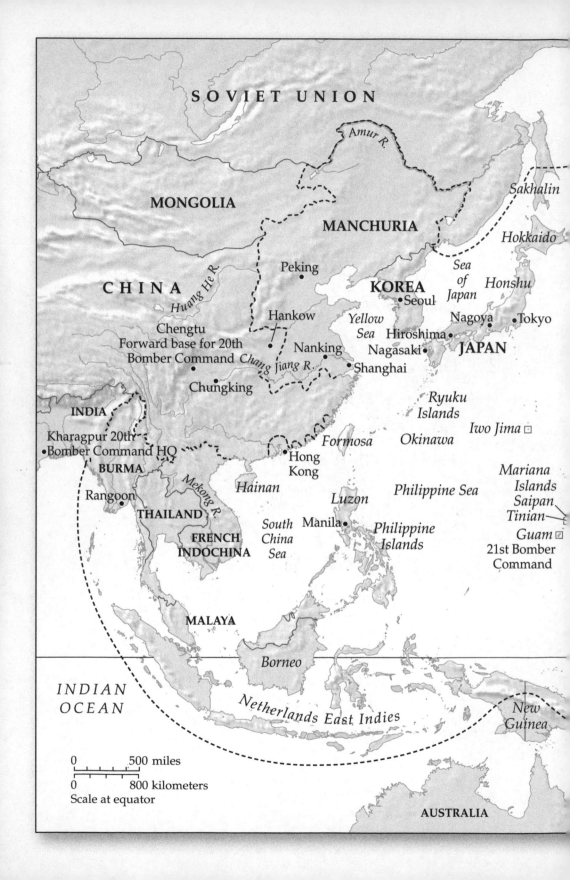

SOVIET UNION

Amur R.

MONGOLIA

MANCHURIA

Sakhalin

Hokkaido

Peking

Sea
of
Japan

Honshu

CHINA

KOREA

Seoul

Nagoya

Tokyo

Huang He R.

Hankow

Yellow
Sea

Hiroshima

Chengtu
Forward base for 20th
Bomber Command

Nanking

Nagasaki

JAPAN

Chang Jiang R.

Shanghai

Chungking

INDIA

Ryuku
Islands

Iwo Jima □

Kharagpur 20th
•Bomber Command HQ

Formosa

Okinawa

BURMA

Hong
Kong

Mariana
Islands
Saipan
Tinian

Rangoon

Mekong R.

Hainan

Philippine Sea

Luzon

Guam □

THAILAND

South
China
Sea

Manila

Philippine
Islands

21st Bomber
Command

FRENCH
INDOCHINA

MALAYA

Borneo

INDIAN
OCEAN

Netherlands East Indies

New
Guinea

0   500 miles

0   800 kilometers
Scale at equator

AUSTRALIA

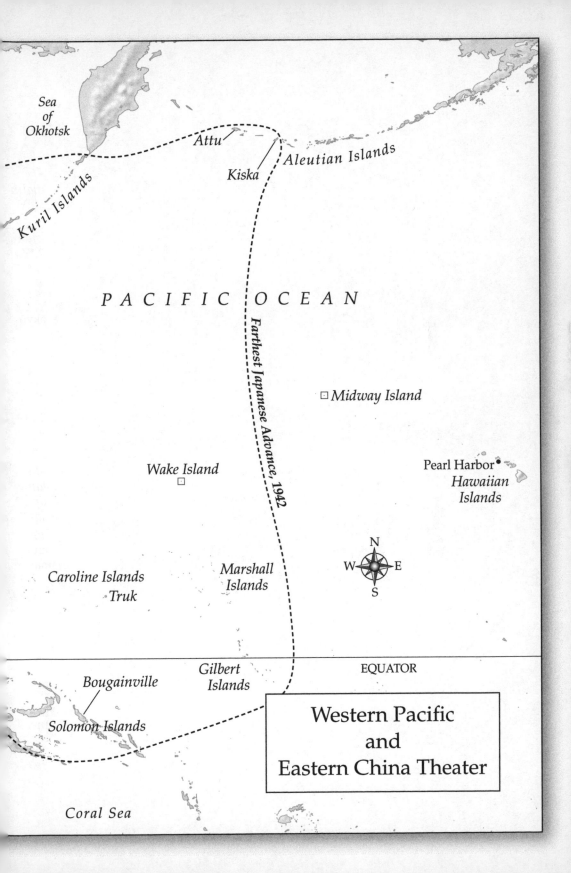

Sea of Okhotsk

Kuril Islands

Attu

Kiska

Aleutian Islands

PACIFIC OCEAN

Farthest Japanese Advance, 1942

Midway Island

Wake Island

Pearl Harbor
Hawaiian Islands

N
W E
S

Caroline Islands
Truk

Marshall Islands

Bougainville

Gilbert Islands

Solomon Islands

EQUATOR

Coral Sea

Western Pacific
and
Eastern China Theater

Preface

DURING THE LAST year of the war in the Pacific, the U.S. Army Air Forces, Navy and Marine Corps, and British Royal Navy conducted a relentless air assault against the Japanese home islands. The attacks came from around the compass: from the west out of China, southwest from Okinawa, due south from the Marianas, northeast from the Aleutians, and from almost anywhere that aircraft carriers steamed. American B-29 bomber crews razed most of the enemy's urban-industrial areas and delivered two nuclear weapons that ended the war. But there were many other significant players in the multiservice campaign: carrier-based aviators in Hellcats, Corsairs, Avengers, and Helldivers; long-range patrol bombers from the Aleutians; Mustang pilots from Iwo Jima; and almost everything in the Army Air Forces inventory from Okinawa.

Sixty-five years later, no single volume has examined the Allied air offensive against Japan in its terrible totality. Why there has been so little study of so epic a subject is difficult to explain. Certainly today, when interservice joint operations are not only common but necessary, the 1944–45 effort begs for detailed attention. Coordination of the various air forces, including land- and carrier-based Navy and Marine air groups, and integration of the British Pacific Fleet (BPF) into the American Fast Carrier Task Force, were substantial achievements on a scale never to be repeated.

The campaign was a long time coming, and a final test of some old theories of war making. As far back as the 1920s, airmen had postulated that strategic bombing could compel an industrialized enemy to surrender, thus avoiding the massive bloodletting of the Great War. But the airpower theorists reckoned from a false premise: that despotic regimes would take pity on their citizens' plight as democratic governments were expected to do. In truth, the theory worked in neither direction. In World War II, more than 60,000 Britons died in air attacks, but the U.K.'s resolve never cracked. While national resolve was mightily strained in Germany, where the death toll in bombed cities could have run half a million in five years, it held to the end. Perhaps 330,000 Japanese were killed by air attack in one-fifth that time.

The toll was terrible, but rather than fatally undermining civilian morale, bombing achieved a more subtle victory in affecting Japan's ability to resist. Moreover, airpower compelled Emperor Hirohito to surrender, sparing Japan a death count that might have grown ten-fold in an Allied invasion.

In 1942, Tokyo stood like an Asian colossus astride the sweep of the Pacific and deep into the Chinese mainland. Less than three years later Japan had lost control of its own airspace, and its cities lay open to attack on a scale the world had never seen. With its industry in ruins, Japan's chilling policy of arming women and schoolchildren with spears reminds us of the irresistible power of the concentrated Allied assault on Dai Nippon, even as it poses moral questions that persist today.

In the course of writing more than thirty previous histories, I came to know hundreds of veterans of the Pacific War, American and Japanese alike. One thing shines through: they populated a vastly different world than today. With the rise of idealistic globalism, the context in which World War II was fought is difficult for many people to fathom.

Mindful that more than 2,000 U.S. World War II veterans die every day, *Whirlwind* assembles narratives from a variety of sources: official records, published accounts, and interviews with the dwindling number of survivors. Sadly, this will be one of the last books based upon interviews with those who lived the events it describes. *Whirlwind* represents multiple stories within a story, setting in context the most devastating air campaign in history. The human drama played out in Asian skies had been divined by European visionaries three decades before, and migrated into American consciousness during the Great War. In the ensuing period an often acrimonious debate arose concerning the theory and practice of aerial bombardment. It too is part of our tale, which traces the origins of American airpower from the fledgling, controversial days of Billy Mitchell in the 1920s, through the search for an air doctrine in the 1930s to the stunning technological advances of the 1940s. The legacy remains with us in the twenty-first century. Look closely at a B-52 Stratofortress or even a B-2 stealth bomber; look beneath the sculpted perfection of an F/A-18 Hornet or an F-15 Strike Eagle. If you peer close enough, down to the cellular level, you can glimpse the long-ago silvery fleets of B-29s and the gloss-blue carrier planes that scourged an enemy who lived the biblical injunction: he who sows the wind shall reap the whirlwind.

Barrett Tillman
April 2009

Prologue

OFF HONSHU, APRIL 18, 1942

R EVENGE SPED TOWARD Japan at nearly four miles per minute, borne upon olive-drab wings.

Flown by America's finest aviator, the lone bomber approached the enemy shore at 200 feet. Three hours after taking off from the aircraft carrier *Hornet*, the forty-five-year-old pilot was determined to do something that had never been done: bomb Japan.

Piloting the twin-engine B-25 was Lieutenant Colonel James H. Doolittle, a stocky, balding flier often called a daredevil in the press but best described as master of the calculated risk. In his twenty-five years of flying he had proven both his cool head and his hot hands, winning prestigious races, setting records, and pioneering the crucial science of instrument flight. An oft-published photo showed him standing before his stubby Gee Bee racer with his Phi Beta Kappa key visible beneath his leather jacket. With a Ph.D. in aeronautics, he spoke with an engineer's precision, saying "aeroplane" and describing friends as "chaps."

Four months earlier, when Japanese carrier aircraft attacked Pearl Harbor, Doolittle had been a major conducting special projects for General Henry H. Arnold, the Army Air Forces chief. America was still reeling from Tokyo's stunning blow against Hawaii as a nonstop onslaught rolled up U.S. and Allied forces across the Pacific: from Guam to Wake Island to the Philippines, East Indies, and the Asian mainland. The nation and President Franklin D. Roosevelt called for retribution.

Thus was born the First Special Aviation Project. Oddly, it was the brainchild of a submarine officer, Captain Francis Low. He conceived the idea of launching long-range Army bombers from an aircraft carrier and proposed a daring concept: a hit-and-run raid against Japan itself, launched well beyond the limited reach of Navy carrier aircraft. If all went well, sixteen B-25 Mitchells—named for the late airpower advocate William "Billy" Mitchell—were to land in China after bombing Japan.

It was a high-risk operation, calling for volunteer aircrews who were told only that they would be "out of the country for two or three months." More men stepped forward than could be used. The crews were selected from all four squadrons of the 17th Bomb Group (Medium), the first B-25 unit. Originally stationed at Pendleton, Oregon, the group had flown antisubmarine patrols along the Pacific coast. A crew of the 17th reported sinking a Japanese sub off the mouth of the Columbia River on Christmas Day 1941, but the boat (the brand-new I-25) escaped to torpedo a tanker a few days later.

In February the group transferred to South Carolina to hunt U-boats in the Atlantic. A sub kill was claimed off the East Coast, making the 17th the first unit credited with destroying Axis submarines in both oceans.

The volunteers went to Eglin Field, Florida, to train for the special mission. Mostly they were youngsters: twelve of the sixteen pilots were lieutenants, and only five had won their wings before 1941. Fifteen of the copilots were less than a year out of flight school. Doolittle's crew was typical, with an average age of twenty-five. Besides Doolittle, merely two of the eighty fliers were over thirty: Major John A. Hilger and Technical Sergeant E. V. Scott in Lieutenant Harold Watson's number nine aircraft.

Flying a loaded Army bomber from an aircraft carrier had never been done. But during tests off the Virginia coast in February, two B-25s got off the *Hornet* without difficulty, demonstrating that fully armed and fueled bombers could operate safely. The plan went ahead.

Steaming via the Panama Canal, *Hornet* rendezvoused with her sister carrier, USS *Enterprise*, north of Midway on April 12. The task force was commanded by Vice Admiral William F. Halsey, the jut-jawed seadog who would become America's most renowned naval warrior. The "Big E," with her regular Navy air group for protection, would escort *Hornet* to within 450 miles of Japan. There Doolittle's bombers would take off, and the two carriers would turn for home. If the task force was discovered before launch, the B-25s would still take off or be jettisoned, depending on circumstances.

On the morning of April 18, ten hours before scheduled takeoff, a Japanese picket boat sighted the task force. The vessel was sunk by the cruiser *Nashville*, but American radiomen overheard the Japanese sending a warning. Doolittle conferred with *Hornet*'s skipper, Captain Marc Mitscher, and decided to launch 170 miles east of the intended point.

Doolittle lowered his flaps, stood on the brakes, revved his Wright engines, and watched the launch officer. With the carrier's bow rising in the Pacific swells, the officer's flag swept down and Doolittle released the toe brakes. Hauling the control yoke full back, he felt his bomber's wings lift fourteen tons of aluminum, steel, gasoline, ordnance, and living flesh.

He made it. He circled the ship to get his bearings, then set course for Japan, 713 miles away. The other fifteen Mitchells followed at an average of four-minute intervals. Fully loaded, each bomber had 1,141 gallons of fuel—enough for twelve hours or more of cruising at 5,000 feet. Stashed near Chuchow in China's Hunan Province were 30,000 gallons of aviation gasoline and 500 gallons of oil for the Raiders—assuming they reached their destination deep in the Asian interior.

The fliers' intended landfall was Inubo Saki, eighty miles east of Tokyo. The twenty-meter promontory with its chalky white light-house provided an excellent reference point for the navigators.

Meanwhile, advance warning of strange aircraft inbound from

the sea had been radioed to various headquarters. Many Japanese had seen the Raiders but few realized they were Americans. Some farmers and villagers waved. The noontime arrival of Doolittle's bombers coincided with a scheduled air raid practice, complete with airborne interceptors. But few defenders had any inkling of what was about to happen.

One observer who immediately recognized the unpleasant facts was Commander Masatake Okumiya, a naval officer at Kasumigaura Airbase twenty-five miles northeast of Tokyo. Glimpsing the silhouette of a B-25 skimming past his airfield, Okumiya realized that the radioed warnings had been ignored. Japan's air defense system—such as it was—anticipated conventional high-level bombers flying in formations, as Japanese squadrons did over China.

At noon local time the Americans saw three V-formations, each of three Japanese fighters—the first of scores sighted over the enemy homeland. Tokyo knew that something was afoot but lacked details.

Approaching Tokyo's north-central industrial area at barely rooftop height, Doolittle shoved the throttles forward, climbed to 1,200 feet, leveled off, and lined up a factory complex. Antiaircraft fire burst nearby, shaking the bomber's airframe, but doing no damage. Jimmy Doolittle had a clear shot at his target in good visibility.

In the glass-enclosed nose, Staff Sergeant Fred Braemer checked his makeshift bombsight, which resembled a child's toy: a protractor mounted on a stick. Mathematically accurate for a given altitude and airspeed, it could place a 500-pound bomb within blast radius of a chosen aim point. The B-25's ordnance was a mix of 500-pound M43 demolition bombs and M54 incendiary clusters, all considered "extremely satisfactory."

Braemer punched the bomb release, felt the Mitchell lift slightly, and became the first of a stream of bombardiers who would drop ordnance on Japan. His four incendiary clusters would provide a beacon for trailing bombers.

Having shed his load, Doolittle pushed on the control yoke and descended to rooftop height. America's hottest pilot was comfortable speeding at low level: he had won every air race worth entering during the 1920s and 1930s.

The Raiders' targets included petroleum facilities, ammunition stores, aircraft factories, steel mills, and the Tokyo Gas and Electric Company. Lieutenant Travis Hoover's first three-plane flight went to northern Tokyo; Captain David M. Jones's trio attacked the center; and Captain Edward J. York's the southern urban area and northern portion of Tokyo Bay. Captain Charles R. Greening's flight went for Kanagawa, Yokohama, and Yokosuka Navy Yard. He was intercepted by four fighters, two being claimed shot down by B-25 gunners. The fifth flight broke up, its planes attacking Nagoya, Osaka, and Kobe. The targets had been selected to spread the damage across fifty miles to prevent the Japanese government from denying that the attack had occurred.

Probably the most worthwhile target was a ship in Yokosuka dry dock: the 16,700-ton *Taigei*. The former submarine tender was being converted to a carrier, and it sustained a bomb hit on the bow and several incendiary clusters. Damage was light, and she would join the fleet before year end, renamed *Ryuho*. Most likely she was attacked by Lieutenant Edgar E. McElroy, with bombardier Sergeant Robert C. Bourgeois.

Antiaircraft fire was "active" but inaccurate; no bombers were seriously damaged. Doolittle's crews attacked fast and low, preventing Japanese gunners from getting a clear shot at the B-25s. Barrage balloons—as many as five or six together—forced only one plane to divert from its briefed course.

Travis Hoover bombed an arsenal from 900 feet, well below the recommended altitude, as explosions blew wreckage higher than his bomber. Some Raiders reported bombing a residential area containing factories, and inevitably some unintended buildings were hit: Tokyo reported six schools and a military hospital struck. In all, about fifty people were killed and some 400 injured, with ninety buildings reportedly destroyed.

But not everyone found a target. Lieutenant Everett "Brick" Holstrom's crew met "severe" fighter opposition. In evading the interceptors he bypassed Tokyo, proceeded to a secondary target, but was intercepted again. Frustrated, Holstrom dropped his bombs in the water and headed southwest for China.

Edward "Ski" York bombed Tokyo but knew he could not reach China. Before leaving the West Coast his carburetors had been "adjusted" by civilian mechanics. Burning 30 percent more fuel than normal, he diverted 600 miles northward across the Sea of Japan, landing north of Vladivostok in the Soviet Union.

Thirteen hours after launch, somewhere over the China coast, hundreds of miles from Chuchow, the other planes began running out of fuel. Doolittle ordered his crew to bail out, then jumped from 8,000 feet—his third parachute descent. He landed in a field fertilized with human waste.

The next morning, filthy and despondent, Doolittle sat on the wing of his wrecked bomber, pondering the failure of his mission. His gunner, Staff Sergeant Paul Leonard, snapped the CO's picture, then sat beside him and asked, "What do you think will happen when you go home, Colonel?"

"I guess they'll court-martial me and send me to prison," Doolittle gloomed.

Leonard shook his head. "No, sir. They're going to make you a general. And they're going to give you the Congressional Medal of Honor." Paul Leonard was right.

Of the eighty fliers on the mission, three died in crashes or attempted bailouts over the China coast. Eight were captured and taken to Tokyo. Four months later, they stood a mock trial in which no charges were revealed to them. All were declared guilty of war crimes, but for obscure reasons five were spared, leaving Lieutenants Dean E. Hallmark and William G. Farrow and Sergeant Harold Spatz to die. They were returned to China and, outside Shanghai one morning in October, they were made to kneel before three crosses, and were shot by Japanese soldiers. Another captured Raider starved to death in prison and fourteen others also would perish in the war.

In terms of actual damage, the Doolittle Raid amounted to little more than a pinprick. But its psychological effect was profound on both sides of the Pacific. The Doolittle Raiders had given American morale a boost unlike any other in the twentieth century. Newspapers crowed "Doolittle Do'oed it!" even while the Philippines were overrun by Japanese forces and U-boats prowled almost unmolested in American waters. Meanwhile, the Japanese Imperial Navy saw the raid as proof that the U.S. Pacific Fleet must be destroyed, adding impetus to Admiral Isoroku Yamamoto's determination to force a major engagement at Midway in June. The disastrous outcome of that battle for Japan ensured America's ability to take the offensive later that summer.

As Nationalist Generalissimo Chiang Kai-shek feared, China paid the heaviest price for the raid's success. In May the Japanese swept through Chekiang and Kiangsu Provinces, seizing Chinese airfields to prevent further missions against the homeland and scourging villages suspected of assisting the Raiders. The toll will never be known, but the Chinese estimated perhaps a quarter-million people were killed in retaliation for America's own retaliatory strike.

Metropolitan Japan would remain immune to American bombs for the next twenty-two months, until June 1944. But a terrible warning had been delivered, and a foretaste of impending cataclysm.

CHAPTER ONE

Before the Beginning

I N 1921 ITALIAN aviation visionary Giulio Douhet proclaimed, "Aeronautics opened up to men a new field of action, the field of the air. In so doing it of necessity created a new battlefield; for wherever two men meet, conflict is inevitable."

In that opening passage of *Command of the Air*, Douhet established the twin towers of his professional philosophy: evangelical aviation mated with bone-deep cynicism about human nature.

Douhet was—and remains—an intriguing character. Born in 1869, he became an artillery officer but early on grasped the violent promise of military aviation. As a technocrat—he studied science and engineering—he perceived the potential for aerial warfare almost as soon as there were Zeppelins, let alone airplanes. In 1912, a year after Italy committed aircraft against the Turks in Libya, he wrote *Rules for the Use of Airplanes in War*. It was among the first efforts to establish a doctrine for military aviation.

When the Great War in Europe erupted in August 1914, Douhet was a vigorous forty-five-year-old infantry colonel. Eagerly following aviation developments, he was primed and ready when Italy entered the fray against Austria-Hungary and Germany eight months later. Though not a pilot, he advocated building an aerial armada of 500 bombers capable of carpeting the enemy with explosives, presumably forcing capitulation without prolonged ground combat.

But Douhet was bitterly disappointed as a succession of Italian defeats and command incompetence spurred his sharpened pen and acerbic tongue. Certain that aviation technology could offset his nation's embarrassing unpreparedness, he vented his spleen in all directions, haranguing anyone who would listen, and many who would not. Inevitably such sentiments breached the tolerance of officialdom, and in 1916 Douhet was imprisoned for, among other things, "issuing false news . . . and disturbing the public tranquility."

Undeterred in his evangelism, Douhet wrote from his cell, while army commanders and government ministers remained targets for his acid ink as the war news deteriorated. Finally, in late 1917, Italy's fortunes bottomed out with the disastrous Battle of Caporetto, which produced 300,000 Italian casualties. At that dismal point Douhet was released from prison and named director of the General Air Commissariat, responsible for coordinating Italy's aviation plans and policies. However, it was too little too late. He found an ingrained bureaucracy unwilling to enact his plans, and he left in disgust in June 1918.

Following the war, the verdict of Douhet's court-martial was reversed and, remarkably, he was promoted to general. However, by then he had lost faith in Italy's government and military, and declined to return to duty.

After 1918, Douhet believed the material means of achieving his vision of airpower finally existed. His colleague Gianni Caproni had produced hundreds of large, capable bombers, some flown by Americans against targets in Austria-Hungary. Other nations also had made remarkable progress, including the firms of Vickers and Handley Page in Britain; Sikorsky in Russia; and Gotha and Friedrichshafen in Germany. Douhet was concerned that, having built an air weapon, after "the war to end all wars" Italy would neither maintain nor employ the machines as he envisioned. Consequently, he focused more on his writing, leading to publication of *Command of the Air* in 1921. Essentially, it advocated unrelenting bombing of enemy population and production centers—a two-prong attack on a nation's moral and material means of resistance. Properly conducted, Douhet asserted, such a policy could win a quick decision and save millions of lives in the long run.

High on Douhet's list of requirements was an independent air force, by 1919 a reality only in Britain. There, Douhet's opposite number was a prewar pilot, Major General Sir Hugh Trenchard, who in 1918 had belatedly espoused strategic bombardment and established a highly capable force that raided far into Germany. Unlike Douhet, Trenchard had staying power, remaining as chief of the air staff for a decade after the war.

Trenchard had already seen the reality of heavy bombers in the Great War. Though Germany's Zeppelin raids on London and environs gained most of the attention—the long, sleek dirigibles made great news copy—they proved too vulnerable to improved defenses. Instead, the kaiser had turned to an armada of Gothas and Riesen (giant) biplanes beginning in the spring of 1917. However, from 1915 to 1918 only some 300 tons of Teutonic ordnance fell on Britain, causing 1,400 deaths and nearly 5,000 other casualties. It represented barely two days' sanguinary bill at the front, but the psychological impact was enormous. The appearance of German bombers in English skies led to nearly doubling the size of the Royal Flying Corps, literally overnight. It became the Royal Air Force in April 1918.

Meanwhile, in the nexus of wartime alliances, a third airpower champion appeared. He was a French-born American, Lieutenant Colonel William L. Mitchell, known to friends and to history as Billy.

As one of the senior U.S. airmen in France in 1917, Mitchell met Trenchard and established a warm personal and professional relationship. Six years junior to the Briton, Mitchell had won his wings in 1916 and was avid in his support of aviation. Rising rapidly, he rocketed to brigadier general and directed the Allied air effort supporting the huge Saint-Mihiel offensive in September 1918. Deploying nearly 1,500 planes, Mitchell crafted a remarkably effective air-ground plan in an era when aircraft voice radio was nearly nonexistent.

In his eighteen months in Europe, Mitchell made a name for himself, and enemies as well. His fiery advocacy of aviation alienated many ground officers, and his perceived flamboyance riled some of his fellow airmen. Because America lacked a strategic bombing force, his early focus was necessarily limited to tactical airpower, but after returning to America he soon raised his sights and became a disciple of Giulio Douhet.

All three men—the Italian, the Briton, and the American—faced similar postwar problems. The greatest was public and even military indifference. Conventional wisdom held that there would be no more Great Wars, especially with the emergence of the League of Nations. Consequently, vastly reduced defense funding became the fiscal bone that army and navy dogs scrapped over. With military and naval hierarchies firmly established, the upstart airmen began at a decided disadvantage, even with Britain's Royal Air Force and then Italy's Regia Aeronautica becoming independent services in 1923.

Mitchell faced a greater challenge than Douhet and Trenchard, as America enjoyed a 3,000-mile separation from Europe, courtesy of the Atlantic Ocean. No nation in the Western Hemisphere posed a remotely serious threat to the United States, leaving congressmen and senators to ask (not unwisely) why they should appropriate scarce funds for more flying machines.

Mitchell turned the financial argument on its head, insisting that long-range bombers could defend America's shores more efficiently than a two-ocean navy. In attempting to prove his point, he finagled a series of tests pitting bombers against obsolete U.S. and captured German warships off the Virginia coast in 1921. The Navy agreed, mainly out of curiosity as to how modern naval vessels would withstand aerial bombardment. Ironically (in light of later developments) Mitchell sought participation of Navy aircraft as well.

Billy Mitchell may have been an irritating gadfly, but he meant business. He readily agreed to conduct the tests under "wartime conditions," though the target vessels were immobile. Having accepted the rules, he cheated like hell. Mitchell obtained one-ton bombs that could not easily be carried aloft, and restricted the range of any aircraft that bore them. Nevertheless, in their most spectacular test his airmen scored a major triumph by using their unconventional weapons against the "unsinkable" battleship *Ostfriesland*. The 24,000-ton veteran of the Battle of Jutland survived the first day's tests with minor damage, but the next day Mitchell launched his heavyweights, British Handley Page 0/400s. They scored two hits and four near misses that ripped *Ostfriesland*'s hull, sending her down in twenty-one minutes. The Navy was astonished—and the Army leadership embarrassed. But Mitchell's giant bombs sank other aged battleships in additional tests, even using huge 4,300-pound weapons.

The next year Mitchell met Douhet in Europe and was captured by the Italian's fervor and the depth of *Command of the Air*. Mitchell had excerpts sent to colleagues, and got banished for his trouble. Dispatched to Hawaii and then to Asia, he literally took a page from Douhet's book and spent his exile producing a tome of his own. The result was a 324-page treatise predicting war with Japan. Published in 1925, *Winged Defense* insisted that the mere threat of sustained aerial bombardment would cause a collapse of enemy willpower, and that battleships were becoming obsolete as aviation technology advanced. The fact that Mitchell reverted to colonel that year probably was no coincidence.

That was bad enough. But in September, one of Mitchell's naval counterparts died unnecessarily, following orders from nonaviators. Sent into treacherous weather over Ohio, Commander Zachary Lansdowne perished with thirteen other crew members of the dirigible *Shenandoah*. Fliers were outraged that "paddlefeet" controlled airmen's destinies. Many grumbled; Mitchell exploded. Calling a press conference, he publicly accused the leaders of the U.S. Army and Navy of professional incompetence and indicted the "almost treasonable administration of the national defense." The gauntlet had been dropped, and no one doubted that it would be retrieved and flung in the accuser's face.

In a sensational six-week trial, Mitchell exploited his court-martial to gain a public forum for his views. He received sympathetic coverage in many newspapers but the outcome was a foregone conclusion. Undeniably guilty of insubordination, in December 1925 he was suspended from active duty for five years. Rather than live with the penalty, he resigned from the Army to continue his crusade as a civilian. He died in 1936, still insisting that America's military future would be found in the sky.

Eventually Mitchell was proven wrong on many details but the concept of strategic bombardment outlived him. Almost before he was buried, the Army gave significant contracts to two leading aircraft manufacturers: Boeing in Seattle, Washington, and Douglas in El Segundo, California. Their commission was to build single examples of large, ocean-spanning bombers that could be flown and evaluated as prototypes of follow-on designs. In the words of a later generation, they were technology demonstrators.

First up was Boeing's experimental XB-15. Successfully flown by test pilot Edmund T. Allen in 1937, it featured a 149-foot wingspan and 32.5-ton empty weight. Its four 850-horsepower radial engines were reliable but insufficient to achieve tactical speeds. Nevertheless, the giant's purpose was to prove that a bomber could fly 5,000 miles, whatever the speed. Assuming a mission radius of 2,500 miles, the XB-15's 152 mph cruising speed equaled 33.5 hours airborne— the duration of Charles Lindbergh's solo flight from New York to Paris in 1927. Consequently, the ten-man crew required an automatic pilot, bunks, galley, and lavatory. With a 12,000-pound bomb load, the B-15's maximum takeoff weight was 5,000 pounds greater than that of the B-17G in World War II.

The Douglas entry, the XB-19, suffered a lengthy gestation. It represented half a generation of advancement over the XB-15, with greater size and weight, and a nose wheel configuration. With costs soaring, in 1938 the company sought to cancel the contract but the Army believed the giant (212-foot wingspan) was worth procuring. When first flown in June 1941, it had already been overtaken by advancing technology. Douglas envisioned a full crew of sixteen, including nine gunners for eleven machine guns and two 37mm cannon. There were also provisions for a six-man relief crew, acknowledging the problem of crew fatigue on prolonged missions.

Douglas lost money hand over fist on the XB-19. Paid $1.4 million, the company eventually spent nearly three times as much to complete the contract. Nevertheless, the XB-19 proved the potential for huge piston-driven aircraft, as its wingspan was seventy feet more and its seventy-ton empty weight nearly twice that of the B-29 Superfortress. However, an omen of things to come involved the troublesome Wright R-3350 engines, which proved unworkable and were replaced by 2,600-horsepower Allisons. The lone B-19 was scrapped in 1949.

Meanwhile, the Army had proceeded with a truly practical design, Boeing's classic B-17. Smaller and shorter-ranged than the XB-15 and -19, it nonetheless represented the world standard in heavy bombers when it lifted off Boeing's Seattle runway in July 1935. Later christened the Flying Fortress, it was produced in large numbers (more than 12,700 through 1945) and, perhaps more than any other aircraft, came to embody American aviation in World War II.

Other designs also were aborning, notably Consolidated's B-24 Liberator, first flown in December 1939. Even more widely built than the B-17, the Liberator is destined to hold the all-time U.S. production record with some 18,400 for the Army, Navy, and Allied nations. Between them, the Fortress and Liberator accounted for more than 60 percent of the world's heavy bombers manufactured for World War II.

Producing some 31,000 multi-engine bombers was one thing; supporting and operating them was quite another. The man responsible for making it happen was a Mitchell disciple, General Henry H. Arnold, chief of the Army's aviation branch.

Unquestionably dedicated to bombardment aviation, "Hap" Arnold was yin to Mitchell's yang. One of the Army's first two pilots in 1911, Arnold was a company man—a West Pointer in contrast to

Mitchell's rise from the ranks. But Arnold possessed vision, ability, and political skills. After overcoming the early taint of Mitchell's approval, he rose to command the Air Corps in 1938, with few policy makers doubting the need for a strong, capable air force.

There had already been some progress. In 1925 Congress established the Morrow Board (under Dwight W. Morrow, later Charles Lindbergh's father-in-law) to study military aviation. Based on that survey, barely six months after Mitchell's trial, the Air Corps Act of 1926 granted quasi-independent status to Army aviation, with representation on the general staff, and expanded the air branch.

Despite such institutional success, airpower's early high priests fared poorly—Giulio Douhet having been imprisoned and Billy Mitchell being court-martialed. Of the big three, only Britain's Trenchard survived professionally.

In Search of Doctrine

Meanwhile, the great debate about aerial bombardment continued in Europe. Trenchard in particular believed that aircraft were inherently offensive so they must be used in a policy of what he called "relentless and incessant offensiveness." But unlike Douhet, who advocated bombing enemy populations, the Briton wanted to target heavy industry because he believed that destroying the enemy's war-making potential would erode civilian morale.

Meanwhile, the U.S. Army conducted a long search for a practical doctrine of strategic bombardment. Most of the work was conducted at the Air Corps Tactical School (ACTS) at Maxwell Field, Alabama. Between the world wars, ACTS was the closest thing to a U.S. air academy. It provided courses in leadership, command, and air doctrine and strategy, though some instructors and students recognized that until proven in combat, theory necessarily remained theoretical.

When the doctrinal search began in 1920, airmen acknowledged that aviation technology would not match airpower theory for many years. In truth, two decades passed before Douhet's vision of long-range bombers delivering heavy loads became a reality. Consequently, in the first six years of discussion, ACTS's focus narrowed on the primacy of bombardment over the other aviation branches, notably reconnaissance and observation, ground attack, and fighter. Experience in the Great War had conclusively proven the worth of aircraft in reconnaissance and directing artillery fire, the great killer of the Western Front. Only the Germans deployed dedicated ground attack units, but most combatant air arms used aircraft to support the infantry.

With the primacy of bombardment aviation accepted by 1926, the Maxwell theorists next evolved the concept of the self-defending bomber, which would not require fighter escort. ACTS's second study period lasted until 1934, the dawning of the B-17 era. Though the early technological deficit was declining as more capable aircraft emerged, some important wrinkles remained to be ironed out. It is remarkable that so many knowledgeable practitioners (nearly all captains and majors) denigrated the fighter. With some exceptions, they convinced themselves that unescorted heavy bombers could not only survive but thrive in a modern air defense network. The school solution held that bombers would operate in an altitude sanctuary, well above the range of heavy flak guns and even beyond the effective ceiling of most interceptor aircraft. Among the few dissenters was a leather-faced Louisiana fighter pilot named Claire Lee Chennault, who in 1937 left the service for his heresy and took himself to China.

In truth, Chennault was not the only practitioner who recognized the importance of pursuit aviation. But as with strategic bombing, technical reality trailed in theory's slipstream. Other fliers knew that long-range fighters would be necessary to escort heavy bombers, but almost none existed before 1943. However, there was evidence from abroad for those who cared to look. The Sino-Japanese conflict (initiated in 1931; permanent from 1937) and the Spanish Civil War (1936–39) seemed to indicate the need for bomber escorts. But neither war provided many solid case studies of modern, large-scale air operations.

If the limited examples of China and Spain could be ignored, the Battle of Britain should have convinced ACTS that unescorted daylight bombing was a dead end, in both the figurative and Darwinian sense. During the four-month 1940 air campaign, the Luftwaffe lost 1,000 bombers *with* escort, proving that fighter range as well as performance was crucial to bomber survival. But Hermann Göring's Messerschmitt 109 fighters were fully extended just to cover his bombers over London from bases in northern France. His longer-ranged twin-engine Me 110 fighters, though fast and well armed, simply could not compete with lighter, more agile single-engine interceptors. Therefore, bomber escort became the question that no one dared speak. Because there were no long-range fighters, policy was tweaked to do without them. In short, the technological tail wagged the doctrinal dog.

Having spent fourteen years producing the philosophy and method of bombardment, from 1935 the next set of ACTS classes got down to bombing business: translating previous work into a viable doctrine. The process lasted until the verge of America's entry into the Second World War, being completed in 1940. It emphasized the self-defending bomber, operating in daylight (for better navigation and bombing accuracy), and attacking specific target sets: enemy industry, transport, petroleum, and other military-industrial facilities. ACTS shared Trenchard's conclusion that without specifically targeting enemy civilians, depriving them of power, water, and other services would cripple their morale and, ergo, force the hostile nation into submission. It was also vintage Mitchell, who believed "the very threat of bombing" could expel civilians (i.e., factory workers) from industrial centers. Therefore, presumably direct air attack on enemy cities would result in a shorter war and fewer military casualties.

In twenty years of discussion and study, nearly 1,100 officers graduated from ACTS. Of those, nearly two-thirds attended between 1936 and 1940, and 261 served as generals in World War II. By 1941 the technology was forthcoming, with B-17s and B-24s in the inventory, providing the second generation of American airmen with the means to conduct strategic warfare. How well theory matched reality waited to be seen.

The Nine-Day Miracle

In August 1941 the newly semi-independent Army Air Force worked a miracle, and it took just nine days to do it.

As part of the overall Army plan for U.S. entry into the European War, which had begun in 1939, the service's aviation branch was allowed to conduct its own planning. That was the good news. The bad news: the document was needed almost immediately to coordinate with British planning. Arnold tossed the hot potato to the Air Corps Tactical School.

Before Pearl Harbor, Arnold's commission to ACTS was fourfold: determine what was needed to defend the Western Hemisphere; conduct strategic operations against Germany; hold the line in the Pacific; and support an eventual American-Allied return to Occupied Europe. The overall strategy was in keeping with what would become Roosevelt and Prime Minister Winston Churchill's "Germany first" policy, announced in January 1942.

Five exceptional officers were tasked with producing what became Air War Plans Division One, better known as AWPD-1. The team included Colonel Donald Wilson, Lieutenant Colonels Kenneth N. Walker and Harold L. George, and Majors Haywood S. Hansell and Laurence S. Kuter. All would become generals. Eventually Ken Walker and "Possum" Hansell held bomber commands in the Pacific: Walker received a posthumous Medal of Honor for his combat leadership while Hansell would feature prominently in the B-29 campaign against Japan.

The planners received the go signal on the 4th of August; they delivered on the 12th.

AWPD-1 was the starting point in a series of papers describing what was necessary to conduct a strategic bombing campaign against a hostile industrialized nation. The focus was almost wholly upon Germany, as lack of targeting information prevented a similarly detailed plan against Japan. Tokyo would figure in AWPD-42, which was issued the following autumn.

Among AWPD-1's target sets were electrical power production, transportation hubs and networks, petroleum production, and enemy morale. Germany's electrical grid was dropped from first to thirteenth place in eventual priority, under the mistaken impression that it was too widespread to be crippled. In wartime, enemy industry and petroleum processing would become the major objectives, with transport and troop formations outranking power generation. However, postwar examination confirmed the planners' prescience, as the power grid was indeed vulnerable.

AWPD-1 detailed the force structure needed for a global air war: personnel, aircraft, bases, targets, and the operating doctrine to make it all work. The document's major error was the number of aircraft to be ordered, as not even the airpower acolytes predicted the enormous capability of American industry. The plan's postulated 239 combat groups (ninety-eight of them flying bombers) proved eerily close to the wartime high of 243 with 80,000 aircraft and 2.4 million men.

Well after the war, Hansell recalled the work of 1941. "In view of the world situation, the Strategic Air Intelligence Section naturally concentrated on the Axis powers. It was slow and tedious work, but ultimately we made a lot of headway with Germany and Italy. Japan, however, was a different story. The Japanese had established and maintained a curtain of secrecy that we found absolutely impenetrable. There were not even any recent maps available."

At the time, few Americans were concerned with prospects for war with Japan, considered a land of polite, smiling people who bowed much and viewed the world through Coke-bottle glasses. "Made in Japan" was stamped on cheap, imitative products of little account, and whatever mischief Tokyo conducted in Asia was far removed from the national consciousness. As Hansell wrote, "The American people simply could not believe that Japan would challenge the United States in open warfare."

Then came the events of December 7, which, as Hansell said, "in one blow destroyed the validity of all the Army and Navy War Plans. Naturally all strategic plans of any importance had embraced a major role for the United States Fleet. Suddenly the surface component of that fleet had lost its backbone. Not only were we suddenly at war but almost all the strategic planning for the conduct of our military operations had been nullified in one stroke."

Strategic airpower doctrine resembled a three-legged stool. It depended equally upon targeting (material and psychological), bombing accuracy, and the viability of the self-defending bomber. Surprisingly, AWPD-1 touched upon the desirability of long-range escort fighters but AWPD-42 did not.

Airmen such as ACTS's Kenneth Walker firmly believed in the concept of precision, daylight bombing from high altitude. The advantages were obvious: relative immunity to antiaircraft fire; the presumed difficulty of fighter interception; and better navigation and bombing accuracy than at night. However, by the time AWPD-1 was finished in 1941, the British had abandoned daytime operations over Germany, having learned that unescorted bombers could not survive in daylight. The Luftwaffe's flak and fighters made nocturnal missions costly enough: throughout the war, about half of Bomber Command personnel were killed or captured, mainly flying at night.

Theory Versus Reality

Two of the most influential figures in American bombardment aviation were immigrants: a Russian flier and a Dutch engineer. Between them, they represented the enduring pattern that strategic bombing theory usually outpaced reality by more than twenty years. They were Alexander Nikolaivich Prokofiev de Seversky and Carl L. Norden.

"Air power is the American weapon," declared Alexander de Seversky in his classic 1942 treatise, *Victory Through Air Power*. Seversky was an accomplished airman, having been taught to fly by his father at age fourteen in 1908. During the Great War the youngster joined the czar's naval air service, losing a leg but returning to duty. Loss of a limb did not prevent him from becoming the nation's leading naval ace. Appointed to a military mission to America in 1917, his stay overlapped the Bolshevik revolution in his homeland. Happy to spend the rest of his life in the United States, he quickly established relations with the aeronautic elite, including Billy Mitchell.

Seversky bore more credentials than any contemporary: naval officer, airman, fighter ace, engineer, and manufacturer. With that background he wrote widely and well—hundreds of articles appeared under his byline—and he lectured extensively. By one reckoning he addressed 100,000 military officers during his career.

Settling in New York, Seversky founded his own company in 1931 and became a factor in the aviation industry. (The surname represented a PR flack's dream: "Sever the Sky!") However, he proved a poor businessman, and in 1939 Seversky was voted out by his board of directors, who reestablished the firm as Republic Aircraft.

Nevertheless, few airmen pushed harder or more eloquently for full development of "the American weapon" than Seversky. Nearly as concerned with aviation's philosophical aspects as Douhet had been, Seversky published his "Air Power Lessons for America" in 1942. By war's end they proved about one-third accurate: among other things, he underestimated navies and aircraft carriers while overstating bombing's effect on morale. However, some of his lessons later gained credence with improved technology.

For all his success as an author and lecturer, no venue matched Seversky's bravura performance in the 1943 Disney version of *Victory Through Air Power*. Aside from the cinematic artistry, Seversky's onscreen performance mesmerized many viewers. Moving about the soundstage, his blue eyes seemingly penetrating the camera, he made an impressive appearance, reinforced by a Count Dracula voice that left audiences spellbound.

Yet for all his background and knowledge, Seversky conjured a peculiar plan. Narrating a polar view of the world, he espoused quashing Japan with long-range bombers from, of all places, the Aleutians. Whether he had ever flown there, he should have realized that the Alaskan weather factory produced arguably the worst flying environment on earth, with base construction and logistics posing enormous problems as well.

However, Seversky waged a single-minded crusade to convert his countrymen to the Mitchell vision of airpower: an all-conquering force that would turn the Army and Navy into supporting arms. Reality forced itself upon such grandiose visions, but it would be difficult to overstate Seversky's influence with the American reading public.

Meanwhile, airpower's hands-on practitioners took over from the theorists. In that regard, Seversky handed off to another émigré from even more unlikely origins.

The world's most famous bombsight was the brainchild of Carl Norden, born of Dutch parents in Java in 1880. After studying engineering in Europe he sought opportunity in America and became an industry consultant before the Great War. Impressed by his work with the Sperry Gyroscope Company, in 1920 the Navy asked Norden to develop a gyro-stabilized bombsight to replace the British and American types then in use.

Two years later Norden's design was successfully tested, and the Army took note. Despite a long rivalry, the two services had decided to standardize on some items, including a precision bombsight. The first large order (eighty Mark XI sights at $5,000 each) came in 1927, based on tests that demonstrated a mean error of 110 feet from aim point at 6,000 feet altitude.

Peering through his eyepiece, a bombardier set up his Norden for the attack with the aircraft's automatic pilot slaved to the sight so the bombardier was flying the airplane through his sight. Because accuracy depended on an absolutely level bombing platform, the Norden used two gyroscopes set to maintain wings level and a constant plumb line relative to the ground.

The bombardier had already performed a crucial task, setting values for speed, altitude, temperature, and barometric pressure. Then he consulted a thick book of mathematical tables to synchronize the sight and aircraft speeds.

As the bomber approached the target, the bombardier put his crosshairs on the desired impact point via a movable mirror that measured the changing approach angle. In his eyepiece the target appeared stationary, and the bombardier could make subtle course corrections by turning knobs that controlled the autopilot. That was important because winds aloft adversely affected a bomb's trajectory, requiring the human operator to "kill his drift" via the sight. Judging the wind was more art than science, especially since winds could be diverse at various altitudes.

Contrary to the movies, the bombardier did not press a button before shouting "Bombs away!" Rather, the exercise in three-dimensional geometry was calculated for the sight to release the bombs at the instant the plane passed through a predetermined point above the earth. Atop the sight were two parallel tracks, each with a moving pointer. One indicated the plane's progress through space; the other the bombardier's estimate of the correct release time. If the bombardier had done his job well, when the two pointers met they tripped an electromechanical switch that opened the shackles in the bomb bay, sending the ordnance on its ballistic parabola to the target.

Whatever the sight's virtues, interwar tests led to unjustified optimism about the accuracy of high-level bombing. Most of the experiments prompting unrealistic expectations had involved optimum scenarios: clear weather, no time pressure (certainly no flak or fighters), and bombers mostly flown at 10,000 feet or less. But flying straight and level at "angels ten" in the face of a well-defended target proved tantamount to suicide.

During the war, U.S. Army commanders would describe their operations as precision attacks, which in a manner of speaking fell within bounds. Flying in daylight, seeking specific aim points, the American method of strategic bombing was demonstrably more accurate than the RAF's nocturnal area attacks. But in 1942–43 the Americans fared only slightly better. The vaunted "pickle barrel" accuracy of the Norden sight mated to the B-17 and B-24 usually failed to match the brochure under combat conditions.

Nevertheless, no bombers were useful without accurate bomb-sights, and Norden's invention filled a void, becoming the world standard in its lethally esoteric trade.

Morality of Bombing

Douhet and many other airpower theorists espoused a seeming contradiction: by ruthlessly bombing civilian production centers a greater good would be realized in shortening a war, reducing the car-nage among soldiers. That dichotomy appeared rational in light of the World War I experience, but inevitably it would clash with later concerns about the morality of unrestricted bombing.

Morality was a constant factor in criticism of strategic airpower, and Britain especially rejected terror bombing, having been on the receiving end in 1915–1918. In 1938 RAF doctrine stated, "A direct attack upon an enemy civil population . . . is a course of action which no British air staff would recommend and no British cabinet would sanction."

In World War II, the Allies' moral objection to urban bombing emerged mostly in Britain, where some 60,000 civilians died under German bombs and rockets. The bishop of Chichester was a par-ticularly vocal opponent of strategic bombardment, though he sup-ported tactical air operations. He and a handful of others insisted that Britain—and, by extension, America—would lose "the moral high ground" by bombing cities.

Such philosophical concerns collided head-on with two unbending realities. First, cities were where German weapons were forged, in factories operated almost entirely by civilians, who lived in urban areas surrounding the plants. Therefore, a halt to strategic air operations on moral or any other grounds would have produced a unilateral Allied cease-fire until Anglo-American armies were landed in France. But D-Day could not have been achieved absent Allied air superiority, which was gained only by round-the-clock bombing and daylight air battles that eroded the Luftwaffe's strength.

Second, despite some airmen's assertions to the contrary, there was seldom such a thing as precision bombing. The British government was flat-out duplicitous on the matter, insisting to the end that Bomber Command only attacked military targets (amid occasional admissions that declining enemy morale was a desirable by-product). But for much of the war, the RAF could not reliably put more than one-fifth of its tonnage within damaging distance of any factory, hence the resort to area bombing. In the words of British historian Max Hastings, "It was preferable to attack anything in Germany than to attack nothing."

The airmen of all nations faced a moral and pragmatic contradiction. While few but Douhet openly advocated terror bombing, none could admit that 1940s technology and tactics mostly limited them to area attacks. It was one thing for the RAF to insist that it did not target civilians, yet another for the Americans to concede that their precision doctrine remained an ambitious goal rather than a routine reality.

To some combatants, the controversy attending strategic bombing appeared odd in the extreme. The Italian philosophy was well established, courtesy of Douhet, who died in 1930, but the Regia Aeronautica had little opportunity to test his theories by attacking major cities. The German record is checkered, from the controversial 1937 bombing of Guernica during the Spanish Civil War, to the attempt to recall the unnecessary mission against Rotterdam in 1940. However, if there was ever any discussion of the matter in Germany, there was probably none at all in Japan.

Prior to 1942 the world's most sustained, most ruthless, and bloodiest air campaign was conducted by Emperor Hirohito's bombers over China. In Tokyo's attempt to control the Asian landmass, more than fifty cities were attacked from 1937 onward. Japanese bombers killed as many as 4,000 Chinese at a time, most notably at Chungking in 1941. But faced with immense distances and an enemy army that usually refused to concentrate, the Japanese were forced into much the same position as the Anglo-Americans in 1942–44: bomb something or do nothing. The essential difference lay in each side's relative objectives: the Allies, victims of aggression, sought to cripple German industry, whereas the Japanese aggressors found precious few industrial targets and therefore resorted to an undisguised terror campaign.

Without realizing it, Tokyo's warlords handed their enemies a powerful weapon: a moral certitude that the Japanese nation and its population had earned the firestorm that lurked beyond the broad sweep of the Pacific Ocean.

The View from Tokyo

In 1941, while American planners focused their efforts on a war with Germany, the least likely enemy posed an unappreciated threat. By then Japan's 73 million people were personally and culturally inured to war in China. Based upon previous acquisitions, another 30 million subjects lived under Japanese rule, primarily in Korea and Formosa. The empire's combined population enabled Tokyo's propagandists to speak of a people 100 million strong.

Japan had largely been unified for 1,500 years and, in an astonishing national sprint, raced from essentially a feudal economy to near military parity with the Western powers in barely seventy years. Tough, disciplined, and enormously hardworking, Japanese were trained from childhood to serve the nation. Since 1890 students had been required to "offer yourselves courageously to the State."

Beginning in the nineteenth century the ages-old Bushido warrior's code had morphed into a European-style fascist ideology mated to the Shinto concept of emperor worship. The pillars of Bushido were loyalty, honor, and skill at arms, but Japan's increasingly militarist governments succeeded in displacing the moderate samurai values with far harsher attitudes. The leavening ethics of Confucianism and Buddhism were increasingly replaced, with Shintoism becoming the state religion during the Meiji era of modernization from the 1860s. However, changes under Emperor Meiji did not extend to plain speaking, ultimately with disastrous long-term results. Japanese culture still abhorred American-style candor—far better to tolerate a poor situation than to offend people, especially one's superiors.

Based on a homogenous population, the Ministry of Education touted inborn national character traits that lent moral authority to any enterprise. It was the same attitude found in the Japanese Serviceman's Code of Conduct, a rigid, brutal compulsion to obedience framed as "sublime self sacrifice." *Yamato damashi*, the Japanese fighting spirit, was exulted as mind over matter; flesh over steel.

Still, there were ironic foreign influences. The Imperial Navy absorbed the British Royal Navy's values at the cellular level, to the extent of printing some texts in English, treasuring a lock of Horatio Nelson's hair, and adopting bridge as a pastime. But more typical was Dai Nippon's contempt for Western values. A British historian quoted a Japanese army document stating that American men "make money to live luxuriously and over-educate their wives and daughters who are allowed to talk too much" (a sentiment doubtless shared by some American males). The propaganda piece excoriated the United States as a murderous land, conveniently overlooking Japanese militants who assassinated government ministers during the 1920s and 1930s.

From the early 1930s, Japan was increasingly dominated by the military, with active-duty or retired generals and admirals in the nominally civilian posts of war and navy minister. But the nation had no central command comparable to the U.S. Joint Chiefs of

Staff, and there was little coordination between diplomatic and military actions. Raised in a pervasive atmosphere of racial and cultural superiority, generations of Japanese assumed that because they dominated Asia, the same must apply globally.

Historian Dr. M. G. Sheftall notes that many ultranationalists adhered to a form of thirteenth-century Nichiren Buddhism popular in prewar Japanese literature. Their worldview was dominated by the concept of a multigenerational confrontation between East and West, climaxing in an apocalyptic victory bringing peace on earth. That view fit nicely with the ideology of "eight corners of the world under one roof."

Whatever the guiding philosophy, Japan's war policy was largely determined by the Supreme Council, known as "The Big Six," comprising the prime minister, foreign minister, army minister and chief of staff, and navy minister and chief of staff. As per the 1889 constitution, the emperor was nominally supreme commander and, though he sanctioned laws, he was not head of government. Prince Hirohito had assumed the throne as Emperor Showa (Enlightenment) in 1926, and when he died in 1989 he had been the twentieth century's longest-serving head of state.

Imperial General Headquarters had been established in 1938, responsible for overseeing the undeclared war with China. That same year the civilian population was brought more fully into the constant state of conflict with gasoline rationing and occasional rice shortages. The government tightened its control of industry; press censorship was administered by the Home Ministry; and military training became compulsory in schools.

Despite the increased war footing, Japan tangled with the Soviet giant in 1939. Tokyo controlled Manchuria but sought more, leading to a Mongolian border dispute known as the Battle of Nomohan. It ended in a decisive Russian victory after four months of fighting.

Nevertheless, Tokyo set its geopolitical sights on most of China and even India. But the army and navy had very different agendas. The army, most influential in government circles, favored not only continuing but expanding Japan's conquests on the Asian mainland. The navy, naturally more worldly, had a better concept of what lay beyond the horizon. Essentially, the navy wanted a secure source of oil to fuel the fleet. That meant the Dutch East Indies. The army wanted China. Resolving the differences took enormous effort, especially given the services' long-standing disagreements that often boiled into outright animosity. Nevertheless, the generals had their way, and 7.1 million uniformed Japanese served the cause of expanding what the Japanese termed the "Greater East Asia Co-Prosperity Sphere."

Once set upon a collision course with America and the West, Japan counted on its offensive policy to acquire a Pacific moat spanning thousands of miles. Given the immense distances involved, the state of aviation technology, and the superiority of the Imperial Navy, Tokyo's ramparts appeared safe from significant risk of attack.

It was a fatal miscalculation based upon the willing consumption of a toxic cocktail, equal parts national inferiority complex, institutional arrogance, and racial pride. A generation of Japanese would learn that a more bitter concoction had never been brewed.

CHAPTER TWO

China Skies

Bombing Japan

Serious American discussion of air attacks against Japan predated Pearl Harbor by at least two years. In January 1940 a retired naval officer delivered sensitive documents to the Navy Department for unofficial discussion. The messenger was Bruce Leighton, a former naval aviator representing Intercontinent Corporation and Central Aircraft Manufacturing Company (CAMCO), which operated in China.

Leighton met with Marine Corps Major Rodney Boone of the Office of Naval Intelligence. They proposed "an efficient guerrilla air corps" to assist China, which had been fighting Japan since 1937. The proposed American aid would go to Generalissimo Chiang Kaishek's Nationalists, as the Chinese Communists lacked the strength and alliances to field an air force.

Eight months later, in September 1940, Lieutenant Commander Henri Smith-Hutton, the U.S. naval attaché in Tokyo, reported that Japan's "fire fighting facilities are willfully inadequate. Incendiary bombs sowed widely over an area of Japanese cities would result in the destruction of the major portions of the cities." The attaché noted that the few bomb shelters also were inadequate, and he was preparing a list of "important bombing objectives," including military, government, and industrial targets. "Willfully inadequate" was an apt description. No less an authority than Billy Mitchell had noted Japan's sustained vulnerability to fire bombing seventeen years before.

During the winter of 1940–41 the Roosevelt administration approved formation of a clandestine fighter group to aid China, staffed by discharged U.S. military personnel. Anticipating eventual Allied bombing of Japan, China's Chiang Kai-shek had bomber bases constructed in the remote Chengtu area about that same time. A year passed before the First American Volunteer Group (AVG) became operational over China and Burma, entering history as the fabled Flying Tigers, led by former U.S. Army officer Major (later Major General) Claire Chennault. In the months after Pearl Harbor, the AVG's shark-nosed P-40s presented the most effective opposition to Japanese airpower on the Asian mainland.

A second AVG was formed with the intention of bombing Japan. Equipped with twin-engine Lockheed Hudsons and Douglas Bostons, the unit's 440 pilots and staff began departing the United States in November 1941. However, by the time most of the men and some of the aircraft reached Asia, America was fully at war and covert operations were unnecessary.

Other prewar plans had envisioned bombing operations against Japan from Wake Island, Guam, the Philippines, and the China coast. With those options rapidly lost in 1941–42, more ideas emerged.

In March and April 1942, the Army Air Forces sent thirteen heavy bombers to China with the mission of attacking the Japanese homeland. They were led by Colonel Caleb V. Haynes, who fetched up in India, awaiting events as his progress was barred by both the Japanese and Nationalist Chinese. The Japanese surge into Burma posed logistics problems for Haynes's unit, and Chiang Kai-shek worried that attacking Japan from eastern China would invite retaliation against the population. However, "C.V." Haynes remained in Asia, becoming Chennault's 14th Air Force bomber commander.

Meanwhile, the third plan went ahead. It was dubbed Halpro (for Halvorsen Project), led by colorful, hard-drinking Colonel Harry A. Halvorsen, who had helped develop air-to-air refueling in 1929.

Halpro's thirteen B-24 Liberators departed Florida in May 1942, winged across the South Atlantic from Brazil, and headed for China via North Africa. But they were sidetracked in Egypt, where the bombers were needed owing to pressure from the German Afrika Korps, which dominated the campaign for control of North Africa. Thus, the B-24s were sent to bomb Ploesti, a major source of Nazi oil in Romania. The mission was launched from Egypt in June 1942 with a notable lack of success. Fourteen months later a vastly larger mission was undertaken, pitting 177 Libya-based Liberators against several Ploesti refineries and incurring spectacular bomber losses.

After the Doolittle Raid, and after Haynes and Halpro faltered, the next proposal arose within China itself. In July 1942, shortly after disbanding the AVG, Chennault informed Army Air Forces chief Hap Arnold of the desire to increase the new China Air Task Force to forty-two bombers and 105 fighters supported by sixty-seven transport aircraft. Chennault claimed that with such an assembly he could drive the Japanese air force from China skies, paralyze enemy rail and river traffic in China, and bomb the home islands. Furthermore, with 100 P-47 Thunderbolt fighters and thirty B-25 Mitchell bombers, he pledged to destroy "Japanese aircraft production facilities."

Nor was that all. Three months later Chennault assured Roosevelt that with 105 of the latest fighters and forty bombers (including a dozen B-17s or B-24s) he would "accomplish the downfall of Japan . . . probably within six months, within one year at the outside." He added, "I will guarantee to destroy the principal production centers of Japan."

That a professional airman like Chennault truly believed such puffery is hard to accept. Among other things, he knew from experience that the Japanese had failed to destroy Chinese cities with far larger forces over a period of years. But however his grandiose claims were received in Washington, he remained the U.S. air commander in China for the rest of the war.

Subsequently it took hundreds of B-29 Superfortresses fourteen months to realize Claire Chennault's fantasy. In fact, when Chennault wrote Arnold that summer of 1942 the Superfortress was not yet a reality.

A Very Heavy Bomber

If any individual invented the B-29, it was Captain Donald Leander Putt. Virtually unknown today, the native Ohioan won his wings in 1929 and achieved a superior reputation as a test pilot and aeronautical engineer. Having helped develop the B-24, he was chief of the Army Air Corps Experimental Aircraft Bombardment Branch at Wright Field, Ohio, when he was brought into the next project in 1939.

The new design was to fly twice as far as the B-17 with a greater payload, hence the designation "very heavy bomber." Putt looked at what was technically feasible and produced the initial concept: a range of over 5,300 miles and a top speed of 400 mph. With Britain facing the threat of Nazi invasion in 1940, an aircraft possessing such performance appeared increasingly desirable: it might reach Germany in the absence of bases in the United Kingdom.

Actually, Boeing already had a design in mind. So confident was the firm's management that Boeing began drafting the super-bomber before government funds had been allocated. In fact, the May 1941 contract for 250 B-29s was doubled immediately after Pearl Harbor. However, the need was so pressing that the Army took the almost unprecedented step of approving volume production before the aircraft was test-flown. Boeing had orders for 1,644 B-29s before the first flight in September 1942.

Even allowing for the prewar one-off XB-15 and XB-19 (see Chapter One), there had never been anything quite like the B-29. Its size alone generated awe: a 141-foot wingspan, ninety-nine-foot length, and a towering tail reaching nearly thirty feet off the ground. Though it didn't fully match Donald Putt's vision, no other bomber equaled its 390 mph top speed and 3,200-mile combat range. More than an evolutionary step up from the B-17, the Superfortress combined several new technologies or features in one streamlined silvery shape. Unlike the B-17, the B-29 was fully flush-riveted, enhancing its speed and range. Pressurized crew spaces and remote-controlled gun turrets were even more significant features. The Superfortress boasted four remote-controlled turrets (two upper, two lower) and a manually operated tail position. Three turrets each mounted two .50 caliber machine guns while the top forward turret housed four. The central fire control (CFC) gunner and two waist gunners directed the turrets as needed, though the bombardier could control both forward turrets. The tail position originally contained two .50 calibers and a 20mm cannon but the heavier weapon proved troublesome and eventually was removed.

Upon sighting an inbound fighter, a gunner placed his illuminated sight on the target, and began tracking. The rest of the process was automatic, with the mechanical fire-control computer compensating for ballistic drop, altitude, closing speed, and deflection angle. No other bomber possessed such a capability, providing a high volume of fast, accurate defensive fire, especially in multi-plane formations.

There were bound to be numerous problems for so large, complex, and advanced a design. The remote turrets posed serious challenges, and pressurization required some work. Among the new bomber's unique features was a forty-foot pressurized tunnel connecting the front and rear of the airframe, affording fliers a shirtsleeve environment. But if an observation blister blew out, which could happen at altitude, the gunner at that position would be sucked into space, probably minus a parachute.

The B-29's main problem was the four Wright Cyclone engines. They were huge, each with eighteen cylinders producing 2,200 horsepower. (The B-17's nine-cylinder engines were rated at 1,200 horsepower.) But the twin-bank configuration caused serious cooling problems, leading to in-flight fires in the rear row of cylinders.

Since several engine components were made of virulently flammable magnesium, many fires became uncontrollable. The onboard extinguisher system proved inadequate, unable to cope with 87 percent of reported fires.

Boeing delivered the first three XB-29s in 1942, and flight-testing proceeded under the company's extremely capable chief pilot, Edmund T. Allen. Eddie Allen knew his way around big airplanes, having flown the XB-15 and other bombers and large transports. B-29 engine failures became almost routine, and he handled each incident with professional aplomb. On December 30, 1942, he landed the second "X job" with one engine streaming flames that could only be extinguished by the ground crew. The next day another Cyclone choked at 20,000 feet.

Reportedly Allen expressed doubts that so complex a machine as the B-29 could be produced in useful numbers, but he remained committed to the project. On February 17, 1943, he dealt with a serious fuel leak and landed safely.

The next day he died with his crew.

Flying the second prototype again, Allen radioed that he had a serious engine fire spreading to the main wing spar. The flames ate voraciously into the left wing as the bomber descended toward home. Not even Allen's fabled skills could retrieve the situation. The wing burned through, sending the XB-29 crashing into a Seattle meat-packing plant, killing all eleven aboard the plane and nineteen on the ground.

The setback was serious but not enough to cancel the program. The Army proceeded with thirteen "service test" aircraft designated YB-29s, the first flying four months after Allen's crash. They provided Boeing and the Army with enough Superfortresses to continue evaluation, to test improvements, and generally tweak the design before it entered production.

Meanwhile, the AAF struggled to build the immense infrastructure to maintain and deploy its B-29 fleet. A total force of twenty bomb groups was envisioned, each with 112 aircraft organized in four squadrons. Early plans to use the Superfortresses against Germany were scrapped when B-17s and B-24s were able to operate from Britain and Italy.

Two officers bearing critical influence upon the B-29 program were the project director, Brigadier General Kenneth B. Wolfe, and a surprisingly junior flier, twenty-nine-year-old Lieutenant Colonel Paul Tibbets. Wolfe possessed an extensive engineering background dating from 1920, and had worked with industry to bring new aircraft into service. In June 1943 he formed the first B-29 wing at Salina, Kansas, largely on the strength of his extensive knowledge of the aircraft and the program. Much later, General Curtis LeMay summarized the rationale for tossing the Superfortress project into Ken Wolfe's hands, citing his "splendid record in the development and procurement business." Like most AAF officers who wanted to prove themselves in combat, Wolfe would later eagerly accept the China-Burma-India (CBI) command even though his expertise was technical, not operational.

Paul Tibbets's job was essentially that of a salesman. Having flown some of the first AAF bombing missions over Occupied Europe, he possessed the credentials to make new fliers listen to him. But the word about the '29 had quickly circulated, and in some quarters it was regarded as a widow maker. Pilots heard the stories (mostly true) of in-flight fires, spectacular crashes, and an accident rate 30 percent higher than for other bombers.

Paul Tibbets had a plan.

He turned to the Women Airforce Service Pilots who ferried Army aircraft all over the country. Tibbets searched until he found two of the shortest, cutest WASPs available and taught them to fly the Superfortress. Then he went on the road, demonstrating the '29's exceptional performance to shame and educate "all those college athletes" who feared the airplane.

Even with production B-29s rolling off the first assembly line in September 1943, problems remained. Each had to be corrected (or at least addressed), leading to numerous solutions. As many as fifty fixes were required, but it took too long to interrupt production and implement the changes in the factories. Therefore, the AAF established four modification centers around the country to retrofit the changes before the bombers went to their operational units. The "mods" included fixes to engines, propellers, rudders, turrets, bomb bay doors, and radar installations.

The situation did not sit well with General Hap Arnold, a hands-on administrator who suffered four heart attacks in less than three years. In late 1943 he said, "It is my desire that this airplane be produced in quantity so that it can be used in this war and not in the next."

Clearly, the B-29 was headed for war as an immature weapon, but the need was considered urgent. Consequently, shortcuts were taken.

Crew training suffered perhaps most of all. When Ken Wolfe established the 58th Bomb Wing in Kansas during the summer of 1943, his four groups were short of everything, including B-29s. Especially B-29s. Moreover, the original ratio of combat-experienced pilots in the wing fell far short of expectations, as did those with the desired 400 hours of multi-engine flight time. Consequently, until enough Superfortresses became available some squadrons trained on Martin B-26s, fast twin-engine bombers with nose wheels and high landing speeds comparable to the B-29. Others reverted to B-17s, especially for practicing high-altitude-formation flights.

With the 58th Wing based around Wichita, "The Battle of Kansas" proceeded apace. That winter was particularly harsh, with wind-driven snow whipping across the Great Plains, freezing Army and civilian technicians alike because there were too few hangars. Most maintenance and modification was done on the tarmac, exposed to miserable working conditions.

Ready or not, the 58th Wing had a date in China, honoring a commitment that Franklin Roosevelt felt he owed Generalissimo Chiang.

Introducing "B-san"

The Japanese knew that America was developing a successor to the B-17, itself an intimidating presence in Pacific skies. In early 1943 news reports reached Tokyo of the death of test pilot Eddie Allen in the crash of "a new Boeing bomber" that February. Furthermore, American intention to mount a strategic bombing campaign against the home islands was no secret: Hap Arnold had said as much, and Domei News Service picked up information from its Buenos Aires and Lisbon bureaus in February and March.

With solid knowledge of the Boeing prototype's existence, the intelligence section of Army Air Force Headquarters was expanded to track the program. Initial assumptions of the configuration were approximately accurate: a mid-wing, four-engine aircraft with total loaded weight "in the forty-ton class." Defensive armament was estimated at four to six 20mm cannon, and bomb load at 4,500 kilograms (9,900 pounds)—about half the maximum possible ordnance load-out.

More than payload and performance, the Japanese worried about the new bomber's range. In May, Colonel Joichiro Sanada, head of the Army General Staff operations section, cited navy information that the B-29 (the designation was known by then) might reach Japan from Midway—2,580 statute miles. In fact, B-29s seldom operated more than 1,500 miles from Japan, but even that figure was cause for alarm in Tokyo.

Justifiably concerned, in early 1943 Imperial General Headquarters directed the Japanese Army Air Force (JAAF) intelligence section to determine the performance of the emerging threat, likely rate of production, and tentative combat debut. Though scattered information was gleaned from publications, consulates, and elsewhere, it was a time-consuming, often inaccurate process. Consequently, JAAF engineers were tasked with "building" a super-bomber based on known or probable capabilities of the U.S. aviation industry. An interim report issued at year end concluded that the new design would exceed the B-17 and B-24 in every category, with the range to attack the homeland from Wake Island, almost 2,000 statute miles away. Though Wake remained in Japanese hands until war's end, the Marianas were an equally obvious roost. Likely China bases included Chengtu, the actual B-29 operating area.

The Japanese reckoned top speed at 600 kph (372 mph, somewhat more than the original B-29). With an operational ceiling of 32,800 feet (an accurate figure) the JAAF correctly assumed that the bomber would have a pressurized cabin. Army Air Intelligence surmised that the Boeing had entered production that autumn, which was reasonably accurate: ninety-two B-29s were delivered in 1943.

Estimates of full-scale production led Tokyo to conclude that B-29 combat operations would begin in May or June 1944. The General Staff's Intelligence Section Six (Europe and America) and Seven (China) agreed that new Boeings would be employed against the homeland, but probably operating independently from the Pacific and China—another accurate call, if premature.

A mimeographed five-page pamphlet titled *Views on the Use of Crash Tactics in Aerial Protection of Vital Defense Areas—No. 2* was issued by the JAAF in February 1944: "Now the enemy is speeding up the mass production of powerful, extra-large bombers like the B-29 and B-32, and boasting of his intention to bomb vital areas of our empire. It is therefore a most urgent and vital task to thwart these planes by establishment of some counter policy."

The Japanese got their first look at a Superfortress when the initial aircraft landed in India in April. Therefore, Tokyo knew much about the world's most capable bomber before it appeared in Asian skies. That was the good news for Japan. The bad news: Japan could do very little to prevent "B-san" from operating wherever it chose.

Building Bases

The plan for deploying B-29s to India and China was Operation Matterhorn, originally called Setting Sun. It was approved at the Allies'

Cairo Conference in November 1943 when Chiang Kai-shek and Winston Churchill agreed to construction of heavy bomber bases in the China-Burma-India Theater. Simultaneously the Pacific Theater commander, Admiral Chester W. Nimitz, was directed to seize the Mariana Islands for the same purpose: placing B-29s within range of Japan itself.

Meanwhile, contingencies were studied to prepare operating bases for B-29s. Original plans were literally all over the map: Alaska, Formosa, the Marianas; even Siberia. But grand strategy, weather, logistics, and geopolitics narrowed the menu. For the time being, it had to be China. However, the bases needed to be located well away from the coastal enclaves controlled by the Japanese. Consequently, AAF planners decided on the Chengtu area in central China, more than 1,000 miles from the coast and 1,500 from Japanese soil.

Four locales were selected, each intended to support at least one B-29 group of four squadrons: Kwanghan, Kuinglai, Hsinching, and Pengshan. They were remote, underdeveloped, and difficult to supply, but staff studies determined that bases closer to the coast would have to be defended by dozens of new Chinese army divisions.

However, it was not enough to build B-29 bases in China. They would require enormous logistical support, including infrastructure in theater. Therefore, Arnold's headquarters in Washington dispatched an advance team to India in December 1943. The officers were to select the best Indian airfield sites and arrange for the human and matériel assets to accomplish the goal. The team settled on the Kharagpur region, sixty miles southwest of Calcutta.

Ken Wolfe was promoted from the 58th Wing to oversee the entire B-29 operation in the China-Burma-India Theater, designated XX Bomber Command. He arrived in India in January 1944, primarily concerned with base construction. It was a vast undertaking, far more complex than "merely" building eight heavy bomber bases (four each in China and India) plus others for transports and tankers. The support and supply challenges were considerable, and deeply complicated by geography.

The man who pulled it together was Brigadier General Alvin C. Welling, an engineer from the West Point class of '33. His credentials were impressive: with a master's from MIT, he had helped build the AlCan Highway across the Rockies, and the 1,000-mile Ledo Road from Assam, India, to Kunming, China.

American resources were scarce. At the time only four Army aviation engineer battalions were available for Matterhorn compared to fifteen deployed in the Pacific Theater. Work proceeded on a huge scale, largely with human labor. As many as 350,000 men, women, and children were drafted into building the Chengtu complex and perhaps as many more were employed in India. There was not enough machinery to accomplish the task, so much of the work was done manually: crushing rock, spreading it, and compacting it into usable runways.

Many Americans were astonished at the immense human effort involved in building the Asian bases—and the indifference to losses. Lacking enough tractors, GIs gawked at the sight of perhaps 550 peasants straining to tow a huge, spiked roller to compact a runway surface. Moreover, local cultural concerns occasionally infringed upon operational matters. At some bases pilots were instructed to ignore Chinese who might dash in front of a landing aircraft: peasants believing that the whirling propeller would sever "the devil" from their back. The theory held that if a prop cut a man in half, the steel blade would suffer no serious harm whereas evasive action could damage or destroy an airplane and perhaps harm the crew. As one pilot recalled, "Headquarters figured if a coolie got killed, there were plenty of replacements in the nearest rice paddy."

Construction of XX Bomber Command bases has been likened to the works of the ancient Egyptians and Mayans in that each relied heavily upon hand tools and muscle power. Yet incredibly, the task was accomplished on time. By April 1944 the eight operational bases were sufficiently advanced to accept the nascent XX Bomber Command.

Around the World to War

The 58th Wing began leaving Kansas in late March 1944, bound for Calcutta 11,500 miles and half a world away. Plans for a second, India-based wing were canceled owing to difficulty in supporting four bomb groups, let alone eight.

By the time the 58th Wing departed for Asia, Ken Wolfe had been promoted to lead XX Bomber Command, overseeing all B-29 operations in the theater. Therefore, Brigadier General Laverne G. Saunders took the wing to India. Because no fighting airman could be addressed as "Laverne," Saunders had long been called "Blondie." He was an old hand, having fought the Pacific war from December 7, 1941, into early 1943 when he was recalled to the United States. There he worked closely with Wolfe to form the wing, which he took over in March 1944.

The globe-spanning voyage was epic in every way. From the central United States the Superfortresses flew to Newfoundland, Canada, then 2,800 miles southeast over the Atlantic to Morocco, across North Africa to Cairo, then on to Karachi and finally the Calcutta area. The bombers averaged fifty hours flying time over a major ocean and three continents—a flight that would have made international headlines a few years earlier. Of 150 bombers only five were lost en route, the most frequent problems being the damnable R-3350 engines.

The first B-29 to touch Asian soil landed at Chakulia, India, on April 2, piloted by Colonel Leonard F. Harman, commander of the 40th Bomb Group. That landing represented a triumph of determination over every possible adversity. Apart from the daunting distance and weather, fewer than half the aircrews had completed the training syllabus. They were deficient in altitude and formation flying, gunnery, radar bombing, and a variety of other tasks. Furthermore, because so few combat veterans were available, most pilots and navigators had never flown outside the continental United States. It was little better with the crucial maintenance personnel, of whom perhaps half had ever worked on B-29s.

By April 19, elements of all four of Saunders's groups had touched down at their Indian fields. The largest facility, at Kharagpur, lay some sixty miles west of Calcutta; the others were seventy-five to 105 miles from that eighteenth-century city.

Upon landing at the Bengal bases, the aircrews experienced serious environmental shock. After the freezing months of a Kansas winter the fliers found themselves in the sweltering humidity and triple-digit heat of the Asian subcontinent. Three of the Indian fields had been hacked out of flat scrub land—a relatively easy task—but the 444th Group alit at Charra, the northernmost base. With a sloping runway and appalling heat, the group dubbed the place "Hell's Half Acre," and arranged a move to Dudhkundi three months later. Meanwhile, the 40th Group went to Chakulia; the 468th to Kharagpur; and the 462nd settled at Piardoba. Their sixteen squadrons were fully assembled by mid-May.

The 462nd Group commander, Colonel Richard L. Randolph, described the situation at Base B-2, Piardoba, saying, "We knew basic problems of the B-29 could not be remedied in a few days." The legacy of design defects, especially engine cooling, plagued aircrews and maintenance men alike. Mechanics tried to tweak the engines for unusually high operating temperatures but work was compounded by inexperienced technicians and frequently too few spare parts. The situation was aggravated by India's miserable climate: often no work was performed between noon and 4:00 P.M. because aluminum was searing to the touch in the 120-degree heat.

Accommodations were basic in Kharagpur, let alone at the outlying bases. (Headquarters was established in a former prison compound.) Thatched-roofed bamboo pole buildings contained interlaced hemp ropes for mattresses. Aside from the sweltering heat, the airmen remarked upon the fauna, including nine-inch centipedes and eighteen-inch lizards. Not to mention the local variety of cobra.

Another problem proved as unavoidable as the environment. It was impossible to keep secret so many B-29s arriving in India, and Tokyo quickly learned of Saunders's presence. Furthermore, Japanese agents in China could report every time the Superfortresses staged from India through Chengtu, providing hours of advance warning for the homeland. The Americans had no option but to accept that they probably would never surprise the Japanese.

Meanwhile, in Washington that April, General Arnold activated the 20th Air Force, overseeing all B-29 operations. It was a unique situation. (There were no 16th through 19th Air Forces; 20 sounded more impressive.) Arnold assumed control of the 20th, running it from the Pentagon, where headquarters would remain until July 1945. His chief of staff was Brigadier General Haywood Hansell, the same Possum who had helped draft the AAF's air war plans, AWPD-1 and -42.

Arnold had good reason for the unprecedented measure of personally running 20th Air Force. He knew that the B-29, though still untried, would prove irresistible to theater commanders from India to the Pacific. For example, one of Arnold's favorite subordinates, Lieutenant General George C. Kenney, commanding the 5th Air Force in the Southwest Pacific, had wanted B-29s early on. But when the Superfortress was limited to strategic missions, Kenney the tactical airman lost his enthusiasm, expressing doubt that the new bombers would be supportable in the Pacific. Most likely he feared that the B-29 force would siphon off men and supplies from his own operations.

Arnold sought to keep 20th Air Force headquarters close to the seat of power in Washington for geopolitical reasons. While enjoying cordial relations with his British allies, he feared that the charming, accomplished Admiral Louis Mountbatten—Allied theater commander in Southeast Asia—would try to winkle some B-29 squadrons away from American control in the CBI. Hap Arnold would have none of that—the Superfortress represented AAF doctrine, missions, and ultimately a postwar independent U.S. Air Force. Supporting one's allies was one thing; ceding them authority over the AAF's crown jewel was quite another.

Regardless of who controlled the B-29s, logistics were appalling—no surprise considering that Wolfe's command operated at the end of the war's longest supply line. Fuel was a constant worry: at least seven B-29 trips carrying gasoline from India were needed to support one combat takeoff from China. Therefore, supplies had to be flown from India over the Himalaya mountains to China.

The Himalayas stretch across six nations and 1,500 miles with 100 peaks over 22,000 feet. During the war some 450 aircraft succumbed to the climate and terrain, forming the fabled "aluminum trail" across "The Hump." Some B-29 crews logged more than thirty trips over the Himalayas, and little could be taken for granted. The 40th Group alone lost nine aircraft. Said crewman Harry Changnon, "We lost a lot of friends flying over those mountains."

To alleviate some of the strain on Superfortress engines and airframes, more than 200 B-24 Liberators were converted to C-109 tankers, each capable of ferrying 2,900 gallons of fuel. But the project dead-ended when the modified Liberators failed to perform as expected.

Japanese fighters were the least of the problems that Allied aircrews found flying The Hump. However, occasional interceptions occurred, and a peculiar legend grew up surrounding an enemy pilot. Given the unlikely moniker of "Broken Nose Charlie," he was said to prey on transport aircraft, though presumably he would tackle any lone bombers that crossed his path. However, only one B-29 was intercepted over the Himalayas and the shootout ended in a no-score tie.

On June 5, Wolfe's command launched its first combat mission: ninety-eight B-29s departing their Kharagpur bases for Bangkok. The target was Siam's major rail facility, but a heavy cloud deck prevented visual bombing. Weather and aborts reduced the strike force to seventy-seven, of which forty-eight tried bombing by radar. Results were unobserved, but sporadic antiaircraft fire and a handful of enemy fighters made no effect on the bombers cruising as high as 27,000 feet. However, six planes were lost in accidents, including one that suffered engine failure on takeoff, and three ditched in the Bay of Bengal with fifteen men killed or missing.

In the meantime, planning proceeded for strikes against Japan. Each mission to the enemy homeland would involve enormous distances, starting from the Calcutta area and flying to the Chengtu staging bases more than 1,600 statute miles northeast—some seven hours' flight time. Even from the Chinese fields, the B-29's radius of action (with a small fuel reserve) permitted missions of a near identical distance to Japan, barely nipping the northern and western parts of Kyushu, southernmost of the home islands. Consequently, one of the few Japanese targets in range was an aircraft factory at Omura, twenty miles north of Japan's eighth largest city, Nagasaki. It was as if B-29s took off from Los Angeles, refueled in Rockford, Illinois, and continued on to bomb a target in Newfoundland.

But even before the first mission to Japan, complications arose from an unexpected quarter when Chiang Kai-shek made a request of the senior American officer in China: slender, bespectacled Lieutenant General Joseph W. Stilwell. Owing to increasing Japanese pressure, the Chinese generalissimo wanted Superfortresses to support the Nationalist army with tactical missions. Stilwell, who held none too high an opinion of Chiang (whom he called "the peanut"), had no authority to divert XX Bomber Command from its strategic mission, which was exactly the reason Hap Arnold had decided to run 20th Air Force from Washington.

Meanwhile, plans continued for Mission 2: next stop, Japan.

Target Japan

In the fall of 1944 returning navy ace Saburo Sakai surveyed Tokyo with his remaining eye. "The city appeared drab and lifeless," he wrote. "Most of the stores were closed, their windows empty. The significance was clear. There were no goods to sell, and the owners were away, working in war plants. The few stores which remained open hardly resembled the colorful and well-stocked establishments I once knew. Few goods were on display, and for the most part these were crude substitutes. The Allied blockade of Japan was pinching the national stomach severely."

Sakai had returned to a nation perennially hungry. Forced to import food to sustain its growing population since the turn of the century, Dai Nippon tightened its belt, then cinched up another notch. And another. Sugar had been rationed since December 1940; rice two months later. Other commodities such as fruit, vegetables, salt, and even matches were progressively added to the list.

When general food rationing began in February 1942 the average daily intake was already less than 60 percent of most Americans. Coffee became a luxury, and a monthly fasting day was introduced. Among the few granted exceptions were miners and heavy industry workers: those who provided the steel to augment Japan's fighting spirit. Meanwhile, despite a dedicated bureaucracy to enforce food regulations, a growing black market flourished.

Faced with an American embargo in August 1941, strategic materials had been stockpiled, notably oil and iron. "Inessential driving" was banned eighteen months before Pearl Harbor, and soon thereafter production of rubber-soled *tabi* shoes was halted to save raw material.

Certainly the Japanese fabric was threadbare. After three years of unrelenting effort, the economy—one-seventeenth of America's in 1941—had reached full stretch.

It was about to be stretched further.

In ten months of operations from India and China between June 1944 and April 1945, XX Bomber Command launched forty-nine missions. Only nine targeted Japan, the first being flown the night of June 15–16. It was a harbinger of doom for Tokyo, far surpassing the pinpricks inflicted by the Doolittle Raiders more than two years before, or the more recent 11th Air Force missions from the Aleutians to the Kurils (see Appendix A). However, the campaign involved more conflict than was evident.

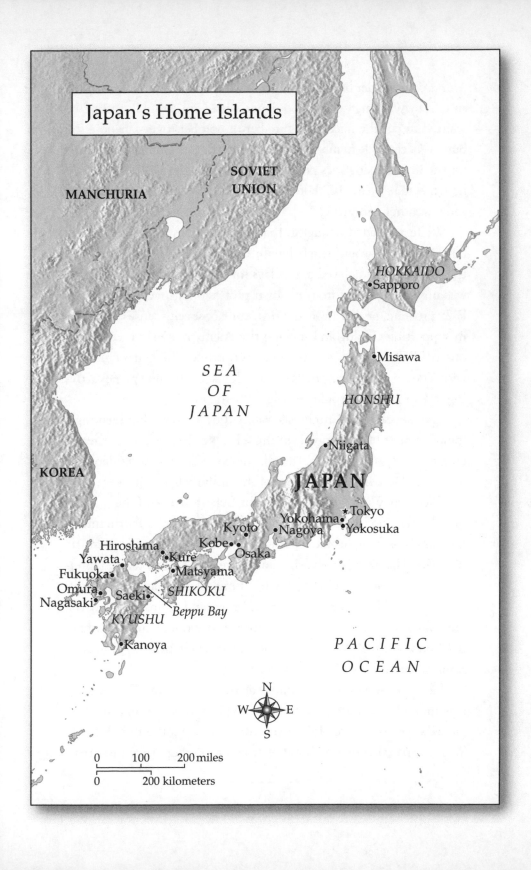

Japan's Home Islands

MANCHURIA

SOVIET
UNION

HOKKAIDO
•Sapporo

•Misawa

SEA
OF
JAPAN

HONSHU

•Niigata

KOREA

JAPAN

Yokohama
Kyoto•   •Nagoya   ★Tokyo
Kobe•   •Yokosuka
Hiroshima• Osaka
Yawata• •Kure
Fukuoka• •Matsyama
Omura• Saeki• SHIKOKU
Nagasaki• Beppu Bay

KYUSHU

•Kanoya

PACIFIC
OCEAN

N
W   E
S

0   100   200 miles
0   200 kilometers

As commander of the India B-29s, Ken Wolfe felt constant pressure from Washington. In accordance with Hap Arnold's wishes, he wanted to put the maximum number of bombers over Japanese soil but an "acceptable number" was problematical. Seeming to care little for the immense logistics problems inherent to the CBI, Arnold said he expected at least 100 bombers to be dispatched "on or before 15 June, weather permitting."

Wolfe advised Washington that ninety planes might leave India but barely half would reach Japan; the situation might improve if the mission were delayed a few days for extra maintenance. Arnold was unyielding: aside from his own professional investment in the B-29 program, he was aware of President Roosevelt's sense of urgency in supporting Chiang and striking the enemy homeland. Following orders, Wolfe sent ninety-two bombers north to Chengtu on June 13, with a dozen aborts and one loss. That left seventy-nine planes arriving in China; fewer would be able to fly the mission.

The takeoff from China was watched by a crowd that seemingly included most of the generals in the CBI. Not least was U.S. theater commander "Vinegar Joe" Stilwell, the bone-deep infantryman who seemed dubious about the utility of the military flying machine.

The 58th Wing put up sixty-eight Superfortresses (one crashed on takeoff), confirming Wolfe's skepticism to Arnold. Furthermore, targeting was complicated by the fact that from Chengtu even the B-29 could barely reach Kyushu, and there existed only limited intelligence on Japanese facilities. Flying at night helped avoid detection but also complicated navigation and bombing. Consequently, the Superforts went after one of the known industrial plants, the Imperial Iron and Steel Works at Yawata, identifiable near Shimonoseki Strait separating Kyushu from Honshu.

Tactics were necessarily simple at that early date. The Boeings flew individually, forming a lengthy bomber stream similar to RAF procedure over Europe. Taking another page from the British book, Wolfe dispatched two pathfinders from each group, timed to arrive about five minutes ahead of the main force and mark the target with incendiaries.

Only forty-seven bombers reached the primary target, and they straggled overhead for nearly two hours in an altitude band extending from merely 8,000 feet up to 21,000, depending on pilot preference. Penetrating the night sky over northern Kyushu, they released 221 tons of bombs, inflicting marginal damage on Yawata. Nine B-29s, unable to reach Japan, attacked other authorized targets.

Weather proved a far greater problem than the Japanese. The challenge was immense: trying to bomb visually at night, through a five-tenths cloud deck above a blacked-out target. Only fifteen bombardiers felt confident enough to toggle their 500-pounders visually, the others relying upon radar. The results were beyond disappointing: one bomb struck the steelworks.

Deprived of daylight, the defenders were forced to rely upon their scanty night fighter organization. The Japanese Army Air Force's 4th Sentai, or regiment, put up six flights of four twin-engine Nick fighters, with no option but to rely upon the regiment's partly trained aircrews.

Among the interceptors was First Lieutenant Isamu Kashiide, an ace from the 1939 Manchurian clash with the Soviets. Glimpsing a silvery streamlined shape in the glare of searchlights, he gaped at the sight. "I was scared! It was known that the B-29 was a huge plane, but when I saw my opponent it was much larger than I had ever expected. There was no question that when compared with the B-17, the B-29 was indeed the 'Superfortress'!"

Few Nicks got close enough to shoot at the bombers, and just one pilot scored. Warrant Officer Sadamitsu Kimura found a B-29 coned in a searchlight pattern and throttled his twin-engine fighter to near collision range. His target was *Limber Dugan* of the 468th Group, four months out of the factory at Omaha.

Peering through his gunsight, Kimura squinted at the glare reflecting off the bomber's aluminum skin. Apparently the crew thought that the fighter was going to ram, as Captain Dushan D. Ivanovic pulled up abruptly. Kimura pressed the triggers, slamming 20mm and 37mm shells into the huge airframe. He pulled away, glimpsing a piece tumbling from the tail as his victim spun into the darkness below. Then he went hunting for more.

In two hours the 4th Sentai claimed seven kills, three by the intrepid Kimura. In truth, *Limber Dugan* was the only loss to fighters, with no survivors. However, five other B-29s were lost in accidents and six more sustained flak damage. Another bomber with engine problems landed at Neihsiang Airdrome well northeast of Chengtu and vulnerable to attack. The Japanese, vigilant to an opportunity, bombed and strafed the sitting duck to destruction.

In all, fifty-seven American fliers and a war correspondent were listed killed or missing.

The first homeland mission had demonstrated the problems inherent to XX Bomber Command. Hitting Yawata used up the fuel stockpiled at the Chengtu fields, forcing a delay of further missions until more gasoline could be ferried over The Hump.

However, the Superfortress's debut in homeland skies could not help but make an impression on individual Japanese. An author, Masataka Kosaka, would write of "the sight of a glistening B-29 trailing white vapor high in the sky." It engendered an eerie mixture of fascination and fear, comparable to the emotion that American sailors would shortly experience in watching kamikazes. But the Superfortress represented something more. Kosaka declared, "its beauty and technological perfection . . . came to symbolize the superior strength and higher civilization of the United States."

The military view was expressed by Lieutenant Commander Mitsugu Kofukuda of the Sixth Air Corps: "By the time the B-29 Superfortress appeared . . . we had achieved great strides in increasing the firepower of our fighters and interceptors. However, even these steps came too late, for the B-29 represented a remarkable advance over the tough B-17, and we were unable to keep pace with American engineering developments."

*　　*　　*　　*　　*

On July 4, Ken Wolfe was recalled to Washington for a session on Arnold's carpet. Despite his avuncular demeanor, Hap was not a happy warrior. Officially he lauded Wolfe but behind the scenes he was testy and impatient. Some 20th Air Force office politics only exacerbated the situation. The chief of staff, Haywood Hansell, expressed displeasure with Wolfe's attitude, which was considered pessimistic. Though having few friends at court, Wolfe saw his view as realistic: his command had been committed to combat prematurely without adequate training or support. In truth, Wolfe probably did the best he could at the time. His role in bringing the Superfortress into service merited more recognition than condemnation.

Nevertheless, Wolfe was out after only three missions, the second to Japan occurring while he was in Washington. Learning that he had been "promoted" to overseeing B-29 production and training, he cabled the 58th Wing that he would not be returning and that a new commander would be named. That could only be Major General Curtis LeMay, America's foremost bomber commander, just returned to the States from England. Meanwhile, wing commander Blondie Saunders would remain in caretaker status until returning stateside for a new assignment.

Years later, Curtis LeMay blamed the higher-ups (by inference, Hap Arnold) for the gremlins dogging the B-29 and unfairly treating Ken Wolfe: "People sat around a table and said, 'Let K.B. [Wolfe] take it out there. He'll be able to do it.'" As an unexcelled operator, LeMay recognized that Wolfe the engineer had been handed a near impossible task.

Three weeks passed before enough supplies could be stocked to support the second Empire mission, and it left much to be desired. On the night of July 7—the day after Saunders temporarily took over from Wolfe—just seventeen Superfortresses were sent to bomb Sasebo, Omura, and Tobata. Three diverted to secondary and "last resort" targets around Hankow, China. The mini-mission cost two planes, including one from the 40th Group that burned from an elec-

trical fire on the ground. Another, from the 462nd, ditched with
three of the crew drowned. The Omura plant was untouched and
other damage was light.

On the 29th, the 58th Wing launched against the steel works
at Anshan, Manchuria. One plane was ganged by fighters; one succumbed to flak and another crashed near Likiang. But the mission
was noteworthy in that one B-29 was lost forever when it landed
at Vladivostok with flak damage. *Ramp Tramp* thus became the first
Superfortress retained by America's Soviet allies, being reverse-engi-
neered after the war to produce the Tupolev Tu-4 "Bull," Russia's first
nuclear-capable bomber.

The third B-29 mission to Japan was flown on August 10–11,
nearly two months after the first. Two dozen bombers attacked individually in the Nagasaki area. More significantly, that same night
thirty-one bombers staged through Ceylon to attack a Japanese refinery in Sumatra, Dutch East Indies. Other Superfortresses dropped
mines in the river near the city of Palembang on Sumatra. From
Ceylon to Palembang and back was an eye-watering 3,900 miles, the
longest unrefueled mission of the war. Only one aircraft was lost, suffering fuel exhaustion. The B-29 still had its share of gremlins, but
the Superfortress had truly stretched its legs.

On August 20, Blondie Saunders led seventy-five bombers from
Chengtu, flying with Colonel Howard Engler of the 468th Group,
aiming to restrike the Yawata steel works. As usual, Japanese agents
had ample time to send word of the takeoff, and radar provided warning of the sixty-one bombers that reached Kyushu. At 4:30 P.M.,
Japan's Western Air Defense Command scrambled four army fighter
regiments, which put up eighty-nine aircraft, while the Imperial
Navy launched elements of two air groups for a total of more than
100 Japanese interceptors.

Flying in threes and fours, the bombers began their run-in, brack-
eted by heavy flak between 20,000 and 26,000 feet. The enemy
ground gunners hit one of Engler's planes, knocking *Ready Teddy* out
of the pockmarked air, and damaged eight others.

Each Superfortress released its six 500-pounders. Then, free of the flak zone, the bombers turned for home just as the fighters rolled in.

Leading the attack was the 4th Sentai's Lieutenant Isamu Kashiide, who had first seen B-29s on the initial Yawata strike in June. Flying a Nick, Kashiide initiated a head-on attack against the 468th, targeting the flight led by Colonel Robert Clinkscales, previously General Douglas MacArthur's personal pilot. Kashiide's wingman was Sergeant Shigeo Nobe, who radioed his intention to ram a "B-san." No one ever knew if his gunner shared his enthusiasm.

Clinkscales's *Gertrude C*, named for his mother, was closing its bomb-bay doors when the two Nicks attacked. Nobe made a quick turn, lined up the leading bomber, and rolled into knife-edge flight, wings vertical. His upraised right wing smashed into the B-29's left wing.

Onlookers—Japanese and American—watched in appalled fascination. Some witnessed the suicide as if in slow motion. The impact ignited a fireball from the bomber's wing tanks as the Nick's shattered airframe tumbled onward through the diamond formation.

Burning wreckage flashed past the next bomber, which emerged unharmed. However, the tail-end Boeing could not avoid all the debris. Captain Ornell Stauffer hauled *Calamity Sue* into an abrupt climb that nearly cleared the worst of Nobe's wreckage. But enough of the Nick remained intact to sever one of *Sue*'s horizontal stabilizers. As she dropped into a death spiral, only one crewman bailed out.

Exultant, the Japanese pilots claimed twelve B-29s destroyed, nine by the 4th Sentai alone. One of Kashiide's squadron mates, Master Sergeant Tatsuo Morimoto, was credited with three kills and four damaged, and received a rare citation.

In the four-mile-high shootout, Saunders's gunners claimed seventeen Japanese planes plus thirteen probably destroyed. But twelve Superfortresses were lost—a galling 22 percent of the bombers that reached the target. In exchange, ninety-six tons of bombs wrecked two coke ovens.

It was a poor bargain.

Back in China, 20th Air Force analysts consulted their debriefing notes. In addition to Clinkscales of the 468th, the 462nd Group lost Colonel Richard H. Carmichael. Continued loss of senior leaders could not be sustained for long.

From the American perspective the Japanese fighters had been relatively ineffective. It looked as if five B-29s were lost to enemy action, including one to flak. Half a dozen crashed in China and one crew bailed out in Russian airspace.

Meanwhile, some important administrative changes occurred that month. On August 28, Possum Hansell assumed command of the new XXI Bomber Command at Colorado Springs; he was succeeded as 20th Air Force chief of staff by Brigadier General Lauris Norstad.

The next day in India, Major General Curtis E. LeMay took over XX Bomber Command.

The Ice Man Landeth

Curtis LeMay was living proof of the Jungian concept of synchronicity—"meaningful coincidences" that put the right man in the right place at the right time. Once committed to combat, LeMay rocketed up the promotion ladder so fast that he outranked two of his prewar squadron commanders.

LeMay had won his commission through Army ROTC in 1929 and spent his early years as a fighter pilot. But he saw the budding potential of bombardment aviation and got the assignment meant for him: Langley Field, Virginia. When he arrived there in 1936 he was already an expert pilot and accomplished navigator, exactly the kind of talent that the 2nd Bombardment Group needed to bring the new B-17 into service. LeMay navigated the group's silvery Boeings to headline status on record-setting flights to South America and pinpoint interceptions of ships hundreds of miles at sea. Along the way, he taught himself everything worth knowing about the Norden bombsight.

As a professional airman, LeMay had very few peers, if any. Possessing an intimate knowledge of his craft mated to an icy intelligence, he left his mark wherever he landed.

In early 1942, LeMay was a newly minted lieutenant colonel who found himself in command of a green-as-grass bomb group. He built the 305th literally from the ground up: trained it according to his own rigorous standards, took it to England, and rewrote the manual on bomber tactics. His innovations included straight and level bomb runs to improve accuracy, a box formation to maximize defensive firepower, and lead crews with navigators and bombardiers specializing in selected targets.

Promoted to wing commander, LeMay still flew "the rough ones," including the epic August 1943 double strike against Regensburg and Schweinfurt. Losses were appalling—sixty bombers and 600 men written off in a day—but LeMay stood out. His reputation soared as his command achieved new heights: he pinned on his first star in September, and five months later, at thirty-seven, he became the youngest major general since Ulysses S. Grant. Beyond that, LeMay was five years younger than his nearest counterpart in any of the armed services.

To staff officers such as General Lauris Norstad, LeMay was the ultimate operator. Stocky, terse, and blunt, he spoke little and listened much. Inevitably he is described as "cigar-chomping" though he preferred a pipe (tobacco alleviated the effects of an infection contracted during a prewar posting in Panama). But beneath the hard-as-nails exterior, the foreboding edifice that would earn him the postwar epithet "caveman in a bomber," Curtis Emerson LeMay wrestled his own demons. He had risen so far so fast that he realized he barely grasped the essentials of one job before tackling the next. Consequently, he maintained an open-door policy. He was receptive to any suggestion that seemed to increase efficiency, and therein lay the key to Curt LeMay: he was about results, and hang the regulations.

Upon LeMay's return from England in 1944 there was only one place to send him: the China-Burma-India Theater. But he refused to go until he learned the Superfortress inside out. He said, "If I'm going to command a bunch of airplanes that are strange to me, I'm going to learn to fly one of them first." Even for a fast study like LeMay, that took time.

When he arrived in India in August 1944, Curt LeMay was warmly received by Blondie Saunders, an old flying school classmate. But the new commander had barely stowed his bags at Kharagpur when Saunders disappeared on a farewell flight in the local area. The next day LeMay himself helped locate the crash and directed rescuers to the site; Saunders survived with the loss of a leg.

LeMay was appalled at what he found at Kharagpur. His sympathy for his predecessor only increased, as LeMay described the logistics as "utterly absurd" and declared that Wolfe "had been given an impossible task."

LeMay chafed under the restriction imposed by 20th Air Force that prohibited him from flying missions. Finally he wangled permission for a one-time good deal, riding on a major strike against Anshan, Manchuria, on September 8. The perfectionist was not pleased with what he saw: incompletely trained crews, loose formations, and poor bombing. He resolved to do better and sent his sixteen squadrons back to school. He stood down the command for remedial education: improving operating techniques, standardizing procedures, and identifying potential lead crews in all four groups. Among other things, he ditched the four-plane diamond in favor of squadron-size formations of up to twelve Superfortresses, making better use of their formidable firepower.

The stand-down was no loss to operations. Because of perennial logistics problems, the 20th had only flown two missions per month since June. LeMay used the three weeks after Anshan to teach his air force his way of flying, and slowly the results began to show. Fuel management improved, permitting greater ordnance loads, and bombing accuracy began tightening up. With designated primary bombardiers an entire formation could "drop on lead," taking advantage of the most skilled operators available.

Perhaps LeMay's greatest success was achieved on the ground. He restructured maintenance by disbanding the dedicated support units, spreading the most knowledgeable mechanics and technicians throughout the bomb groups, and streamlined groups from four squadrons to three. It worked. Before he left China in January 1945, LeMay had nearly doubled the monthly sorties, reduced the aborts, and raised bomb tonnage on primary targets by 300 percent and on all targets by 250 percent.

But problems persisted. There was never enough information: not on weather, maps, or targets. Some charts were demonstrably wrong, leading LeMay to resort to the old airmail pilot's formula: add 2,000 feet to every mountain for oneself and 3,000 more for the wife and children.

As if those complications weren't enough, in September, Japanese forces overran several Allied airfields in southern China and threatened areas slated for the construction of other B-29 bases. The wisdom of building the remote Chengtu complex loomed larger: China's best defense was its enormous size.

While LeMay and company struggled with the CBI's myriad problems, events pushed forward in the Pacific. In October the advance echelon of Brigadier General Emmett O'Donnell's 73rd Wing landed on Saipan and logged XXI Bomber Command's first mission, hitting the Caroline Islands on the 28th. Four weeks later, O'Donnell's Superfortresses struck Japan from the Marianas for the first time.

The message was clear: the B-29's future lay in the Central Pacific, not on the Asian mainland.

With a harbor and airfields, the city of Omura remained XX Bomber Command's destination of choice in Japan. The target most often attacked was the "aircraft plant," actually part of the 21st Naval Air Arsenal. It was a relatively minor facility that mainly produced small quantities of second-line fighters, floatplanes, and engines. Nevertheless, that was the target on October 25.

The fifth homeland mission began inauspiciously when a 40th Group aircraft crashed on takeoff in China, killing all aboard. Of the other seventy-seven Superfortresses, fifty-nine struck the primary and eleven found targets elsewhere. Nevertheless, for once the bombardiers had a shot at their briefed objective in decent visibility. Hunched in the nose of each B-29, peering through their rubber-lined eyepieces, bombardiers twisted the knobs of their Nordens, compensating for wind drift as well as they could while the sight's twin pointers ticked toward one another in their tracks and the contact points finally touched. Green lights extinguished on the armament panel as each bomb was released.

In contrast to the initial Omura strike in July, the October mission did the job; the B-29s left the aircraft plant a wreck.

But over the island of Kyushu the 40th Group's *Heavenly Body* was shot up by fighters. The flight deck suffered explosive decompression; "Damage to the plane was severe. In general, the whole right side was a mess," recalled the aircraft commander, Captain Jack C. Ledford. He had been severely wounded when a heavy bullet ripped a six- by two-inch gash in his right side, clipping his spine and leaving him without control of his legs. Additionally, the bottom of his parachute was shredded. Nonetheless, he was concerned about Master Sergeant Harry Miller, the flight engineer, comatose from a head wound. Ledford turned over control to First Lieutenant James V. DeCoster and ordered himself moved to the engineer's station to manage fuel and power settings—the right inboard engine was dead. He refused morphine for nearly an hour in order to keep a clear head despite continuing blood loss. All the while, *Heavenly Body* limped toward China.

With the *Body* losing fuel from battle damage, it was not possible to reach Chengtu. Therefore, Ledford ordered a bailout over central China. The crew tied a shroud line to Miller's ripcord and dropped him successfully, as his parachute opened. Fitted with a spare chute, Ledford was released through the nose wheel well. He fell perhaps 5,000 feet before pulling his own ripcord. He alit in a rice paddy where he was found by friendly Chinese. The crew regrouped in a nearby village, where a Norwegian missionary informed them that Miller had died. En route to base, the crew was hosted by a hard-drinking Chinese general who asked the Americans for tennis balls. He had rescued another 40th Group crew, which had promised to deliver the balls and he expected payment.

The *Body*'s crew members remained together and named their next B-29 in honor of Harry Miller. Captain Ledford recovered stateside, received the Distinguished Service Cross for his extraordinary heroism, and retired as a brigadier general in 1970.

The next homeland mission was launched on Armistice Day twenty-six years after "the war to end all wars." Nearly 100 bombers departed the Chengtu complex for Omura again, but weather forced an abort. However, twenty-nine planes never received the recall message and continued on to make a radar attack above a cloud deck. The results were described as "negligible." Forty more bombers diverted to Nanking and other Chinese alternates, without significant effect. The effort cost four B-29s destroyed. Another, damaged over Omura, was unwillingly delivered to the Russians—a 468th Group aircraft named *The General H. H. Arnold Special*, after the Air Forces chief.

The seventh homeland mission was XX Bomber Command's largest: 109 Superfortresses launched against the usual target, Omura's air arsenal, on November 21. Sixty-one bombers reached the objective, releasing nearly 200 tons of bombs. Meanwhile, a baker's dozen hit Shanghai and some others attacked targets of opportunity. Seven Superfortresses were lost plus one that diverted to Vladivostok, the last of three B-29s retained by the Soviets. In January the crew of *Ding How* and the other interned B-29s were permitted to "escape" through Persia.

The 58th Wing's gunners submitted claims for twenty-seven kills but the American losses were heavy. One plane was wiped out in a runway collision while another crashed on takeoff, killing all but one of the crew. The 444th Group wrote off two planes including one in a crash landing; five men perished. Actual mission losses on the 21st included a 40th Group bomber whose crew bailed out over China, while a 462nd aircraft crashed in the China Sea with its entire crew.

The 462nd Hellbirds also lost a plane in combat. Returning near Hankow, Captain Richard McMillan's aircraft was shot up by a skillful Japanese pilot. With two engines out, McMillan rang the bailout bell at 13,000 feet and four men jumped safely. Of the others, the central fire control gunner's parachute was damaged and no spare was available. The remaining crewmen stayed aboard, attempting a belly landing alongside the Hankow–Peking railroad. The crippled bomber drew heavy ground fire that killed three men including McMillan. The badly wounded copilot, First Lieutenant Vernon Schaefer, was pulled from the wreckage and recognized his three remaining companions. Unable to move, he was thrown into a filthy cell and left untended by the Japanese. Surprisingly, he recovered and survived.

The Japanese took the others into brief captivity. The flight engineer, radar operator, and primary gunner were paraded in Hankow and publicly abused by Japanese masquerading as Chinese in a propaganda effort to discredit the Nationalists. Then secret police strangled the exhausted fliers and ordered their bodies cremated. But instead of dumping the ashes in a lake as directed, the Chinese buried the remains, knowing that eventually friendly forces would return. In 1946, eighteen Japanese military, police, and Hankow civic officials were indicted for war crimes, including the major general who ordered the sham parade and executions. He and three others were executed.

Meanwhile, the four who had bailed out were picked up by Communist leader Mao Tse-tung's guerrillas and returned to safety, beneficiaries of LeMay's cordial relations with the Communist leader.

That night of the 21st the Japanese sent bombers against Chengtu Airdrome, damaging a grounded B-29 named *Typhoon McGoon III*, but American night fighters were up. In an hour of nocturnal stalking, a P-61 Black Widow claimed one raider confirmed and one probably destroyed.

*   *   *   *   *

If there existed any doubt about Washington's view of LeMay's methods, it vanished with arrival of a letter from Arnold, dated November 17. The AAF chief's "Dear Curt" message was effusive, saying that he was passing around 58th Wing strike photos from Formosa and Japan, and had endorsed LeMay's methods to Possum Hansell in the Marianas. Arnold added that Hansell had admitted "he would have to push his people pretty hard to stay in the same league with your Command."

That same month Hansell's XXI Bomber Command launched its first attack against Japan from the Marianas—further proof that the B-29 campaign had turned a corner. But in December came disquieting news: in addition to the enemy thrust northwest from Liuchow in south-central China, aerial reconnaissance showed 100 Japanese transport aircraft on fields in the Hankow area, 600 miles east of Chengtu. The latter seemed to fit with "persistent reports of several thousand Jap paratroops in enemy held China." Consequently, XX Bomber Command admitted the "very definite possibility of a Japanese paratroop attack on the B-29 bases."

Meanwhile, missions continued. On December 19, the 58th Wing launched a "minimum effort" against Omura. Thirty-six bombers took off but weather permitted just seventeen to hit the primary target, an aircraft factory. Thirteen were unable to reach Omura and unloaded over Shanghai, 500 miles short of Kyushu. Three planes never returned: two 40th Group crews abandoned ship with mechanical problems over China, and a 468th aircraft was rammed by a Japanese fighter over Mukden. The latter's crew was listed as missing; the others found their way to safety.

China Farewell

As LeMay had predicted upon arrival in India, XX Bomber Command was burning a short candle. In October 1944, with additional B-29 bases being completed in the Marianas, the new American

CBI commander, Lieutenant General Albert Wedemeyer, asked that LeMay's organization move to the Pacific. At least from that same month, policy advisers in Washington had expressed serious doubts about continuing the CBI Superfortress operation.

Since his command could barely sustain itself, with no room for growth, LeMay had already declined the 73rd Wing when offered to him. Consequently, America's military high priests bowed to the gods of war. In mid-January the Joint Chiefs issued a warning order, directing consolidation of all 20th Air Force operations in the Central Pacific. LeMay was to move his entire operation to the Marianas by mid-April while conducting some farewell missions. Actually, he flew to Saipan in January, leaving Brigadier General Roger Ramey to close up shop.

The command's ninth and last mission against Japan was a disappointment. On January 6, 1945, forty-nine Superfortresses winged away from Chengtu, aiming at the Omura urban area generally and the naval aircraft plant in particular. Only twenty-eight bombers reached the briefed objective. Thirteen more attacked an alternate target at Nanking and six others found targets of opportunity. One B-29 was lost against claims of four Japanese fighters downed.

The impending end of CBI operations did not guarantee safety. At Chakulia on January 14, 1945, the 40th Group anticipated a concert by conductor Andre Kostelanetz and soprano Lily Pons. Around noon the 44th Squadron was ordered to download cluster bombs from two standby aircraft. However, the ordnance crew was concerned about handling the notoriously sensitive M47s, which were armed. The armament officer suggested expending the weapons in a practice mission but the orders stood.

In removing a cluster from the first B-29, one of the bands securing the bundle worked loose, allowing a weapon to fall. It exploded on impact. Nine men were killed, twenty-one wounded, and another B-29 was damaged beyond repair.

Minutes later a message arrived from the Army ordnance office in New Mexico, declaring the M47 unsafe and ordering its immediate retirement. Said Captain Frank Redler, group armament officer, "The barn door was locked, but too late."

On January 27, the first Chengtu Superfortresses headed for India to begin the long trek to the Central Pacific. Kharagpur to Tinian in the Marianas is a straight-line 3,832 miles or seventeen and a half hours by B-29. It equaled the distance from Seattle to the Panama Canal.

In late February and early March the groups began preparing for the journey by air, land, and sea. Meanwhile, XX Bomber Command closed out its mission log on the night of March 29, attacking oil storage facilities at Singapore. During April the 444th and 462nd Groups departed India, followed by the 40th and finally the 468th. The wing was reunited at West Field, Tinian, during the first week in May.

The nine homeland strikes had been a tiny portion of XX Bomber Command's total effort. In attacking Omura five times, Yawata twice, and a few miscellaneous targets, the B-29s' Kyushu missions represented one-sixth of the command's total sorties and less than one-tenth of the bomb tonnage dropped. Significant damage was limited to the naval aircraft plant. Meanwhile, in all operations XX Bomber Command lost 125 B-29s, but only twenty-nine to enemy action.

In retrospect LeMay remained disgusted at the convoluted scheme for operating B-29s in China. Twenty years later he wrote, "I've never been able to shake the idea that General Arnold himself never believed that it would work."

If the B-29 operation in Asia left a legacy, let it be this: XX Bomber Command operated the world's most complex but technically immature aircraft at the end of the war's longest supply line, over the world's highest terrain in some of the worst weather, with half-trained crews and mechanics living in an oppressive climate on primitive bases.

Nevertheless, the nascent Superfortress grew into a fully fledged weapon in China skies. During his Asian odyssey Curtis LeMay learned what he needed to know about turning the '29 into a truly strategic weapon, one that would have a greater effect upon the Pacific War than anything in the AAF inventory.

The wind that began flowing out of China would grow to cyclonic force in the Pacific.

CHAPTER THREE

From the South

THE STRATEGY WAS known as island hopping, and it worked. But it required what Winston Churchill called "triphibious operations"—the melding of sea, land, and air forces into a nearly seamless entity focused on seizing islands from the enemy, each one representing another step on the long road to victory.

The process had begun eight months after Pearl Harbor when U.S. Marines landed at Guadalcanal in the Solomon Islands. Nearly two years later their seven-league boots splashed ashore in the Marianas, 2,000 miles northwest and more than half the distance from "Guadal" to Japan.

However, each leap of the triphibious frog was limited by the range of available airpower. Because air superiority ensured that no amphibious operation failed in the Pacific War, the success rate among all major landings in World War II ran over 99 percent.

Fortunately for the Allied cause, America had invested early and heavily in development of aircraft carriers. In June 1944 the U.S. 5th Fleet brought fifteen fast carriers to the Marianas, resulting in the greatest flattop duel in history. Three of Japan's nine carriers were lost, and with them most of its carefully hoarded cadre of trained aircrews. The battle went into legend as "The Great Marianas Turkey Shoot," and the ensuing victories ashore provided B-29 bases within range of Tokyo.

Masatake Okumiya, the Imperial Navy officer who had glimpsed some of Doolittle's Raiders skimming the rooftops in 1942, recognized the Superfort's potential. He recalled, "There was good reason to believe that the Marianas conflict might give the enemy the final advantage necessary to defeat Japan. Should American troops successfully occupy the islands, then the Japanese homeland itself would fall within the effective bombing range of the U.S. Army Air Force's new B-29 bomber, which could well cripple our production."

Between June and August 1944 the Americans seized three Japanese-held islands in the Marianas, 1,500 miles south of Tokyo. Saipan, Guam, and Tinian were remade by incredibly efficient engineers, providing runways, housing, and support facilities for the 20th Air Force's growing bomber fleet. The Army and Navy both fielded engineering and construction crews, though the sailors got by far the most ink. The Navy Seabees were so popular that they featured in a John Wayne movie; nobody ever made a film about the Army's aviation engineers.

The Pacific Theater was the largest of World War II. It dwarfed any conflict before or since, not merely in size (3,800 miles from Honolulu to Tokyo; more than New York to Paris) but in unprecedented challenges. For airmen it was especially daunting, requiring the routine reliability of a commercial airline for lengthy combat missions, new operating procedures, and unerring navigation on flights spanning hundreds of miles over open water.

The Pacific also required more bases than had ever been built. In less than four years Army aviation engineers and Seabees provided more than 100 airfields in that vast expanse, from Hawaii to New Guinea to the Marianas to Okinawa. The preferred runway material was asphalt, but Pacific Theater engineers encountered the conventional wisdom that blacktop was unsuited to the hot, humid climate. Until that was disproven, the construction crews managed with packed dirt, coral, gravel, and PSP: pierced steel planks. As always, solutions placed a premium upon innovation, and the engineers never lacked that invaluable commodity.

MANCHURIA

SOVIET
UNION

KOREA

SEA
OF
JAPAN

CHINA

JAPAN

★Tokyo

Hiroshima
●

Nagasaki ●

Okinawa

Ryukyu Islands

Formosa

☐—Iwo Jima
P-51 Fighter Base

PACIFIC OCEAN

N
W ⊕ E
S

Mariana Islands

Philippine
Islands

Saipan
Tinian
Rota

Guam
**B-29 Bomber
Bases**

From the Marianas
to Japan

Palau

0   100   200   300 miles

0   200   400 kilometers

Airbase construction represented as great an advantage to the United States as aircraft production. Commander Mitsugu Kofukuda wrote, "A world of difference existed between the ability of the Japanese and Americans to construct air bases in combat theaters. Basically, we relied upon primitive manpower to clear jungles and pound out airstrips for our planes, while the Americans literally descended in a mass mechanical invasion on jungle, coral, and rock to carve out their airbase facilities. This difference . . . undeniably and seriously affected the air operations of both belligerents, much to the benefit of the Americans."

The U.S. Army and Navy arrived at similar structures for their construction units. A typical aviation engineer battalion included a headquarters company and three engineer companies. The first two battalions, formed in 1940, each numbered twenty-seven officers and 761 enlisted men operating an astonishing array of equipment. The gear included 146 vehicles plus 220 other items: air compressors, asphalt and concrete pavers, bulldozers, cement mixers, graders, pumps, rock crushers, rollers, mechanized shovels, scrapers, trucks, and tractors. There were also small arms to repel enemy attacks and machine guns for air defense.

Most Seabee battalions included a headquarters company and four construction companies, each with platoons specializing in construction, maintenance, road blasting and excavation, waterfronts, and tanks and pipes.

Construction units of either service were always in short supply. In December 1944, Hap Arnold sent two engineer battalions to the Marianas before either had completed training. But even that was insufficient. From January to June 1945, twenty-one more battalions were hurriedly shipped to the Pacific. Consequently, individual and unit training frequently suffered; the constant, increasing worldwide demand simply overwhelmed the Army's ability to get battalions through a full training cycle.

From June 1944 to August 1945 some fifteen Army engineer battalions (six "colored") worked on Saipan alone. At least two—the

34th and 152nd—landed before the island was secure. Most passed on to other jobs, especially on Okinawa, but on V-J Day four were still needed on Saipan.

Whether construction crews or aircrews, everyone lived in the same oppressive environment. Most of the Marianas lie within 15 degrees of the equator, and one veteran recalled, "It would rain for a brief, heavy downpour and usually about four times a day followed by bright sunshine. The temperature never varied more than 15 degrees the year round (from 70 to 85) and the humidity stayed so high all the time we had ear and feet fungus and everywhere else fungus. Dengue Fever was rampant and could lay you low."

Most men lived in tents; the fortunate ones enjoying a wood floor to reduce the mud. Sixty years later, veterans of the Pacific Theater of Operations still grind their teeth over the cinematic images of a balmy climate, Quonset huts, and decent food.

The Saipan invasion began on June 15, and Army aviation engineers went ashore the next day, starting to improve the captured Aslito airstrip on the island's south coast. Previously a Japanese fighter base, Aslito was renamed in honor of Commander Robert Isely, a naval aviator killed in the conquest of the Marianas. However, due to a clerical error, the field became "Isley" and remained so throughout its existence.

Not counting smaller airfields, the engineers had to shoehorn six B-29 bases with eleven runways onto three islands with a total area of 297 square miles. When work began at Saipan, Guam's first bomber field was six months from completion; Tinian's last runway was eleven months downstream.

On Saipan the construction process began by leveling two coral mountains and crushing the material with bulldozers. Then the coral was loaded into 100 trucks, each carrying four tons, shuttling repeatedly from the "quarry" to the airfield site. There the longest runway in the Pacific was laid out, awaiting the expertise of engineers who relished the challenge of doing what some said could not be done.

Though stateside experts insisted that asphalt could not be used in an equatorial climate, the aviation engineers paid no heed. They shipped in drums of hardened asphalt and, like their Seabee counterparts, got on with the job. Some GIs found an abandoned sugar boiler and set about rebuilding the Japanese facility. They welded a tall smokestack from empty oil drums and built their own asphalt melting plant. It proved an inspired idea: the plant provided 700 tons of liquid asphalt a day for the final runway surface over the coral base.

Guam

If Saipan was a big job—and it was—Guam was bigger. After the initial landings on July 21, a three-week slogging campaign was conducted with far better Army-Marine cooperation than on Saipan. When the island was declared secure on August 10, hundreds of Japanese stragglers remained at large, occasionally harassing the Americans but more often seeking food. According to one popular tale, an uncommunicative soldier wearing a mismatched set of fatigues made it through a darkened chow line but was apprehended when he bowed in appreciation.

Meanwhile, construction continued apace. North and Northwest Fields became operational in January and April 1945, while Depot Field housed a heavy maintenance facility. Depot was renamed for Lieutenant General Millard F. Harmon, commander of U.S. Pacific Air Forces, who disappeared over the Pacific in February 1945.

Recreational facilities were scarce at first but the Yanks provided their own amusement. On Guam the shore was mostly ringed by rocky cliffs, though Tumon Bay offered a sandy beach where some improvised boats were fashioned from discarded aircraft fuel tanks. However, the tropic scenery could prove deceptively inviting, and Americans soon learned to spend no more than twenty minutes in the water to avoid serious sunburn.

Eventually, living conditions improved for many airmen who moved from tents into Quonset huts. On Guam there was a post exchange (PX) offering familiar items such as Hershey bars and Pep-sodent toothpaste sold by "some matronly ladies who worked there," recalled William R. Thorsen, a seventeen-year-old Seabee. Some men augmented chow hall and PX fare with bananas and coconuts from the remaining jungle, though most carried weapons on such expe-ditions, knowing of Japanese stragglers. Thorsen said that he never went anywhere without his M1 rifle and a bandolier of ammunition.

The real currency was liquor, especially whiskey. Enterprising air-crews stuffed their planes with as much liquid barter as they could manage before leaving the States or Hawaii, anticipating a scandal-ous profit in the Central Pacific. Their entrepreneurial foresight was universally proven. Among the most popular was Schenley's Black Label, which went for $40 or more a fifth. For a case of good (or at least acceptable) booze, almost anything was available, from an ice machine to a personal jeep.

Tinian

The obscure island of Tinian—just south of Saipan—became per-haps the least appreciated engineering feat of the twentieth century. The island was destined to host six runways, the largest aviation complex on earth.

The Seabees went ashore practically cheek by jowl with the invad-ing Marines in late July 1944. In order to accomplish the task, the Navy formed the 6th Construction Brigade, eventually comprising three regiments each with multiple Seabee battalions. Most of the actual airfield work was completed by the 30th Construction Regi-ment while the 29th provided vital support infrastructure including roads, housing, public works, and fuel and ordnance dumps.

Tinian required nearly everything involved in constructing Pacific island airfields: clearing jungle and cane fields, uprooting large trees, leveling hills, filling ravines, moving and crushing coral. But that was just the preliminary work before actual runway construction could begin. All the while, Seabees dug and scraped and drilled and blasted and rolled and paved their way to completion.

The enormity of the job was summarized in the statistics: 11 billion cubic yards of dirt and coral went into the six fields: enough to fill a line of dump trucks stretching the 940 miles from Washington, D.C., to Kansas City. The grind never let up, as crews went through twelve tons of dynamite and nearly 5,000 blasting caps every day.

Seabee officers computed that the construction material equaled three Boulder Dams. That much work required 770 cargo and dump trucks, 173 wheeled pans, 160 tractors, sixty graders, eighty power shovels, forty-eight rollers, ninety drill rigs, and dozens of water wagons, welders, cranes, and other heavy equipment. Men and gear toiled twenty hours a day with two crews working ten-hour shifts, leaving only four hours for maintenance and repair.

After the surface was scraped clear and the runway beds established, the compacters went to work. Huge rollers were run up and down the 8,500-foot lengths and 400- to 500-foot widths, chuffing smoke and crushing coral into ever denser packs. Then the Seabees called upon their hand-built asphalt plant that provided 700 liquid tons a day. For each runway they poured a layer of asphalt two and a half inches thick. Finally they rolled that layer, compressing it to two inches to accept the bulk of Superfortresses taking off and landing.

However, it wasn't just about laying a long, wide strip across the island: in the tropic environment rain was ever present, and drainage was a critical factor. Engineers carefully computed the proper gradient for each runway—the crest of a 500-foot-wide strip could be four feet higher than the sides, with drainage ditches dug and maintained to handle the runoff.

Aside from the enormous size of the job, the greatest tribute to the Seabees' "Can Do" motto was that, with one exception, every field was completed on schedule or earlier, none in more than fifty-three days. West Field's second runway took twenty days longer because the plans were altered partway into the project, doubling the size of the job.

Early on, some Easterners insisted that Tinian's shape resembled Manhattan. (Only vaguely; at thirty-nine square miles, Tinian was 70 percent larger and nowhere as skinny.) A New Yorker—Captain Paul Halloran, skipper of the 6th Seabee Brigade—christened the main north–south road Broadway; an east–west thoroughfare became 42nd Street; and others were Fifth Avenue and Riverside Drive. Before long the north end of the island was being called the Bronx while the southern portion was the Battery. ("The Bronx is up and the Battery's down.") Those familiar names might have eased a bit of homesickness among construction crews, but the best they could do for Central Park was a bomb dump in the middle of the island.

When the Tinian complex was completed in May 1945, North Field had four bomber runways while West Field had two more. But that was only part of the job. Before all six runways were finished, the construction crews produced eleven miles of taxiways and hardstands for some 450 Superfortresses. That did not include the roads, housing, and storage facilities that a modern air force required.

About 15,000 Seabees had produced the world's largest airport but the chore was ongoing. When the first B-29 took off from North Field in January 1945, some Seabees expected to move to other islands. But the enormous facility required regular maintenance, and several battalions remained on the islands for the rest of the war.

Regardless of their duty, for island-bound soldiers and sailors, morale often turned on mail. Any contact with home was avidly received, but there were hitches. Officers could censor their own mail while enlisted men and noncoms had to submit correspondence for security review. Clashes were inevitable. In just one instance a thirty-three-year-old sergeant had been rebuked by a twenty-two-year-old lieutenant for the steamy contents of a graphically composed love letter. Said a squadron mate, "The lieutenant was infuriated and offended because the sergeant had gone into lengthy, minute, explicit, meticulous, specific and exquisite detail." When the ninety-day wonder demanded an explanation, the sergeant asked, "Why not? She's my *wife!*" The letter was forwarded as written.

Targeting

With B-29s in range of Honshu, the main island, Japan belatedly began dispersing its industry much as Germany had done. With major factories in Tokyo, Nagoya, and Ota, the centralized nature of Japan's aviation industry invited attack, as Nakajima built 37 percent of the country's combat aircraft, trailed by Mitsubishi's with 23 percent. Nobody else was close.

Meanwhile, in November 1944 American targeting priorities had been established by the Joint Chiefs of Staff: four principal aircraft engine factories, then five airframe manufacturers and assembly plants. Secondary and "last resort" targets included major ports followed by thirteen urban-industrial areas. By concentrating first upon the aircraft industry, American planners expected to defeat enemy airpower in its nest—a prerequisite for the expected invasion.

Looking back, Commander Masatake Okumiya said, "The Americans chose their targets wisely, for [Tokyo and Nagoya] were the most critical centers of the entire nation. Nagoya was Japan's aircraft manufacturing center, one great factory at Daiko-cho alone produced 40 percent of all our aircraft engines, and the sprawling plant at Ohe-machi assembled 25 percent of our aircraft. Tokyo, of course, was our military and political center. The incessant raids rapidly disorganized internal functions, and government activities practically reached a standstill."

The Japanese army leadership agreed. Lieutenant General Masakazu Kawabe, inspector-general of aviation and de facto chief of the Japanese Army Air Force, stated: "One of the biggest things leading to the surrender was the bombing of industrial cities. . . . Your bombing of small industrial cities and the use of fire bombs was very effective."

Defensively, Tokyo was hopelessly slow off the mark, waiting until after the first Marianas-based strike in November 1944 to take serious measures. Attacks on airframe and engine plants in Nagoya convinced Japanese planners of a severe dilemma: they needed to increase aircraft production but under present conditions their industry could be crippled or even destroyed in a short time. Though dispersing the factories would necessarily reduce production for several months, it was preferable to losing the facilities entirely. The government opted for dispersal, beginning with Mitsubishi. The company physically separated the engineering division from manufacturing while spreading production facilities to a dozen or more sites on Honshu. However, establishing factories in outlying areas incurred the disfavor of residents and evacuees from other cities who had been displaced by air raids.

Mitsubishi designer Jiro Horikoshi explained, "Many a factory that went through the time-consuming steps of dispersing its most important machine and assembly lines now found itself no better off than before dispersal. The B-29s relentlessly and literally tracked down every move; no sooner had the new factory sections settled down in their new locations than the bombs showered down. The plant managers searched frantically for new sites, and sought refuge in factory buildings surrounded by steep mountains, or placed their vital machines within emergency caves drilled into the sides of hills. Eventually the dispersal plan proved to be a complete failure. At the time when we most desperately needed production, our industrial personnel scrambled in the hills for new machine sites. Devastation in Japan mounted daily."

The 73rd Wing Arrives

As the Pacific part of the 20th Air Force, the Marianas operation was designated XXI Bomber Command. Its chief was well known to American airmen.

Brigadier General Haywood "Possum" Hansell was a soft-spoken forty-one-year-old Virginian who had been flying since 1929. His cockpit credentials included Claire Chennault's aerobatic team that had performed at the Cleveland Air Races. He served a stretch with air intelligence, including observer status during the Battle of Britain in 1940. His stellar work at Maxwell Field, helping produce the 1941 air war plan, had marked him as one of Hap Arnold's favorites. Subsequently, Possum led an 8th Air Force wing in Britain during the rough days of 1942–43, and he did well enough to earn command of the Marianas B-29 operation in August 1944.

On October 12, XXI Bomber Command welcomed its first B-29, though no bomber fields were yet fully operational. Greeted by two P-47s, Hansell landed his pet Superfortress, which he had wanted to christen *The Pacific Pioneer*. However, the crew had its own preference: *Joltin' Josie*. The impasse was broken in an unmilitary compromise, and thus did the famous B-29 become *Joltin' Josie, the Pacific Pioneer*.

Hansell's subordinate was Brigadier General Emmett O'Donnell, commanding the 73rd Wing. "Rosie" was a blue-eyed New York Irishman who had played halfback at West Point, class of '28, and later coached the Cadets. A 1939 graduate of the Tactical School, he was well versed in the theory of bombardment aviation and a noted practitioner. In September 1941, as a major, he had led the first "mass flight" (nine B-17s) from Hawaii to the Philippines. He flew missions from Java until the Japanese seized the Dutch East Indies, then served in India before returning home to advise Hap Arnold and subsequently learn the B-29 trade.

One of the things that Hansell and O'Donnell had in common was Hap Arnold's willingness to give them a chance to fail. That was about all that the AAF chief ever offered, even to favored subordinates. Though both commanders wore brigadier's stars, Hansell was three years older and tended more toward the school solution. O'Donnell, having seen how badly plans could turn to hash in the Philippines and Java, was more open to unorthodox methods. But apart from philosophical differences, they were simply birds of differing feathers: the Southern gentleman and the rollicking Yankee.

It took a while for the 73rd Wing's four groups to settle in, but the command logged its first mission before month's end. On October 27, the 497th and 498th Groups launched eighteen bombers on a "local" warm-up mission to Truk Atoll in the Carolines, 600 miles southeast of Saipan. Four aborted, including Hansell's aircraft, but no planes were lost. Bombing results against a submarine base were assessed as poor. Five more practice missions followed, averaging twenty planes each prior to the first strike against Japan in November.

A New Kind of War

The Marianas B-29 operation was history in the making. For the first time ever, bombers would routinely fly transoceanic combat missions. Until then, XX Bomber Command had flown almost 600 miles over water from the China coast north of Shanghai to reach northern Kyushu—a record-setting distance in mid-1944. But from the Marianas to Japan was 1,500 miles one way; about fifteen hours round-trip. Nothing remotely comparable had ever been attempted. Hansell's *Joltin' Josie* and her stablemates truly were Pacific pioneers.

With 3,000 miles of saltwater below them, Marianas B-29 crews literally entrusted their lives to their navigators. The ordinary concern that airmen feel when flying beyond sight of land was eased by having four engines, but even when the irksome R-3350s performed well, there was always the worry of getting lost or running short of fuel. And rescue was never certain for those lost on a wide, blue sea.

Ironically, nocturnal navigation held more advantages than daytime. At night, with weather permitting, navigators could use sextants to "shoot the stars" with more accuracy than sun angles, and electronic methods were more efficient. Radio aids performed best after sunset owing to better atmospherics, and LORAN (LOng RAnge Navigation) beams could be tracked 700 miles from base during day and upward of 1,000 at night—a huge advantage when flying overcast skies.

Nevertheless, navigators remained second-class citizens in some pilots' eyes. It says a great deal about the Air Force culture that its World War II figures show exactly 191,654 pilots trained from 1941 to 1945 versus approximately 45,000 bombardiers during the war and some 50,000 navigators from 1943 to 1945. Presumably the 1942 figures are unavailable.

Once Saipan dropped astern, the B-29ers would be on their own. If anything went seriously wrong, the best they could hope for was a controlled ditching in the ocean, for no friendly shore lay within reach. The only noteworthy land between the Marianas and Japan was the Japanese-held Bonin Islands. Largest of the Bonins was Iwo Jima, nearly eight square miles of ashy, sulfurous sand resembling "a large, gray pork chop." With its fighters and bombers, Iwo posed a problem for XXI Bomber Command, including the advance warning it could give Tokyo every time B-29s passed overhead.

Bombers could not perform their function without target information, just as Possum Hansell had noted in drafting AWPD-1 before Pearl Harbor. Therefore, photoreconnaissance versions of the B-29 also began arriving in October. Designated F-13s, the spy planes of the 3rd Photographic Reconnaissance Squadron were equipped with six or more cameras to detect enemy installations.

On November 7, an F-13 was not only the first Superfortress over Tokyo but the first American aircraft since the Doolittle Raid thirty-one months before. The intruder drew immediate attention. The single silvery shape high in the thin air over Honshu was the target of nearly 100 Japanese fighters, only two of which got anywhere near the Boeing droning along at 32,000 feet.

The next day the Marianas command sustained its first loss during a mission to Iwo Jima. Though a Zero fighter dropped a phosphorus bomb on the American formation without serious consequences, a 498th Group aircraft was forced into a water landing with mechanical problems. Only two men survived.

Meanwhile, B-29 crews grew more accustomed to their environment. Guam's North Field was probably the trickiest in the Marianas. Takeoffs were usually made to the northeast, into the prevailing trade winds that had benefited eighteenth- and nineteenth-century merchant sailors. Though the first 2,000 feet or so of runway ran slightly downhill, the latter portion was somewhat uphill, causing some heavily loaded bombers to stagger into the moist tropical air, engines howling and propellers biting in low pitch.

The critical phase of a takeoff came immediately after becoming airborne. Between the end of the runway and the cliff that plunged to the sea was half a mile of "terrible coral." Once the world fell away beneath a B-29, pilots could nudge their control yokes slightly forward, descending to use some of the 500 to 600 feet above the ocean to accelerate to a safe flying speed. Thrust overcame inertia and lift defeated gravity, elevating sixty-five tons of aircraft, fuel, ordnance, and human souls. Then, with landing gear raised and wing flaps milked up a few degrees at a time, the burdened bomber became a craft of the air.

Yet there were rewards despite the dangers. Amid the hours of tedious routine, and the languorous time spent listening to the pulsing drone of four powerful engines, there were moments of sublime compensation. The glory of a Pacific sunrise, when sea and sky turned from gray-black to vivid golden hues, or the vertical grandeur of a backlit thunderhead cresting 30,000 feet was worth the entire fifteen-hour trip.

After the warm-up period there ensued a maddening time of waiting for the Marianas' first bombing mission to Japan. Each day aircrews arose, ate, dealt with their pre-mission jitters, and went to briefing. But poor local weather canceled the big event for a solid week: every day from November 17 to the 23rd. Tension rose with each stand-down; some fliers alternated between joy and gloom, all the while knowing that one day they would fly.

On the 24th the bombers went to Tokyo.

Defending Tokyo

Even after the Doolittle Raid, Japan largely ignored what loomed just over the horizon until far too late. The pulsing, throbbing engine of

American industry, fueled by rage as much as petroleum, droned an insistent hum that should have been audible across the far expanse of the Pacific. But Tokyo's ears were deaf to noise; its brain immune to logic.

Combat losses from 1942 onward had badly depleted Japan's cadre of prewar aircrew, carefully trained fliers who had thoroughly mastered their weapons and their trade. With more squadrons needed to defend the homeland, some of the deficit was made good by withdrawing units from overseas. But inevitably, partly trained rookies were pushed forward to fill available cockpits. The youngsters (some teenagers) were motivated and generally eager, but could not begin to compare with the skill and experience of their increasingly numerous enemies.

Once B-29s and carrier planes began operating almost at will over Japan, every man was needed to defend the home islands. When the draft age was raised to forty-five many men were accepted into military service who never would have been considered previously. The declining standards were brought home to Prince Higashikuni of the General Defense Command in late 1944 when, visiting an antiaircraft site, he found that gun crews included men with physical debilities and even one eye.

The best known example of physical handicap was navy ace Saburo Sakai, who had destroyed or damaged more than fifty Allied aircraft in 1941–42. He lost the use of his right eye over Guadalcanal but returned to combat at Iwo Jima in 1944 and remained active in the home islands.

The army retreads included Burma veterans such as Captain Yohei Hinoki, who had lost a leg to an American fighter in 1943, and Sergeant Yukio Shimokawa, half-blinded by a B-24 that same year. Other veterans, worn out from years of combat, were put to use as instructors or ferry pilots.

Tokyo lagged badly in the material realm as well as the human. Japanese aircraft production simply could not match attrition. From an average wastage of 500 per month in early 1942 the number quadrupled by the fall of 1944. From 1941 onward Japanese factories turned out nearly 70,000 airplanes but losses reached 50,000, more than half in accidents.

In comparison, throughout the war U.S. forces lost 27,000 planes in the Pacific, one-third on combat missions. At the end America produced 11,000 planes in August 1945, almost exactly the number of Imperial Navy aircraft lost to all causes from April 1943 to March 1945.

Japan's unexpected dilemma called for exceptional measures. In October the JAAF's 10th Flying Division formed dedicated ramming flights with fighters stripped of guns and armor plate. Thus lightened, the Kawasaki Tonys could reach B-29 operating altitudes. The 244th Sentai's "special attack" unit debuted on December 3 when two pilots collided with bombers but the rammers survived. In all, the 10th Division claimed two other ramming successes among five B-29s lost to all causes.

The Imperial Navy's premier air defense unit was the 302nd Air Group (Hikotai) established in March 1944. From Atsugi the 302nd's fighters could reach Tokyo in about fifteen minutes, and equipment reflected the growing concern for combating "B-san." At the time of the first U.S. carrier strikes in February 1945 the group's squadrons flew seventy Zekes, Jacks, Irving night fighters, and six generally ineffective twin-engine Franceses. There was also a reconnaissance squadron. The most potent were the Jacks, rugged single-seaters with four 20mm cannon; and the twin-engine Irving night fighters with radar and four cannon.

A few Irving crews claimed spectacular success, despite their mount's slower speed than the B-29. One was Lieutenant Sachio Endo, credited with eight victories. At age twenty-nine Endo was unusually experienced; since 1933 he had been a carrier aviator and fought in China. After three years back in Japan he was sent to Rabaul, New Britain, where he was mated with the *Gekko* but without success. Following that unproductive tour he reported to Omura in 1944, training more night fighter crews. There he hit his stride.

He began scoring by night and day, and was transferred to Atsugi in November, in time for the first Marianas B-29 missions.

During an interception on January 14, 1945, Endo piled into a 73rd Wing formation and attacked two Superforts. One was thought destroyed; the other damaged. However, in the running battle his Irving was riddled by .50 caliber rounds that ignited the fuel. The observer bailed out, apparently while Endo kept their burning aircraft under control, then he jumped. But he was too low; both men died in the attempt to save themselves. It was doubtful that either would have survived their burns.

Superfortresses over Tokyo

The November 24 mission was a historic event: the first B-29 attack on Tokyo. Leading from the front, as expected of the flying generals, was Rosie O'Donnell in *Dauntless Dottie*. Across the throttle console from him was Major Robert K. Morgan, famous throughout America as the pilot of the B-17 *Memphis Belle*. Having survived his 8th Air Force tour in 1943—a feat statistically unachievable at the time— Morgan had stepped up to Boeing's next bomber for the Pacific half of the war. By then he had married and named his new bomber for his bride.

Following O'Donnell and Morgan were 110 other Superforts rising from Guam's runways on the mission code-named San Antonio 1. Seventeen never reached Japan, aborting with mechanical (mostly engine) problems. Six more lined up a target in their Norden sights but could not release their bombs.

Buffeted by terrific winds and bedeviled by clouds, only twenty-four planes found the primary target, the Nakajima Company's Musashino aircraft factory. Most of the other Superforts went after port facilities and urban-industrial areas while five had to settle for targets of last resort. All fought a battle with the 130 mph jet stream that prevailed at bombing altitudes up to 32,000 feet, in some cases resulting in astonishing ground speeds of 440 miles per hour.

Though the 3rd Photo Squadron sent F-13s ahead of the main force, dropping aluminum strips that clogged Japanese radar scopes, some stations detected the approaching raiders. Thus, the defenders had nearly eighty minutes' notice, permitting about 125 interceptors to take off.

Some Japanese pilots proved suicidally brave. Anticipating B-29s from the Marianas, Major General Kihachiro Yoshida had ordered his 10th Fighter Division to form dedicated ramming units that flew fighters without guns or armor plate. Thus lightened, the fighters stood a better chance of reaching the B-29s' altitude.

Among the first Japanese to reach the formation was Corporal Yoshio Mita, flying a stubby Nakajima fighter the Americans called Tojo. He selected a 497th Group aircraft flown by Captain Sam P. Wagner. Pressing a run from behind, Mita ignored the .50 caliber fire that struck his Tojo. About 200 yards out he rolled almost inverted and slashed into the bomber's tail, ripping off the elevator and right horizontal stabilizer. Mita's plane fell away burning and exploded in midair.

Wagner and his copilot struggled with their crippled plane—ironically, it was named *Lucky Irish*—but the damage was fatal and it spun down offshore, crashing inverted. Another bomber had to ditch in the Marianas, its fuel tanks holed by AA fire, but the crew was saved.

B-29 crews reported downing seven interceptors (actually they got five) but the American gunners accidentally shot up three Superfortresses in addition to the eight damaged by Japanese flak. Despite the loan of a naval fighter group, General Yoshida's command had failed to dent the first B-29 strike on the capital. He responded by doubling the number of ramming aircraft.

The Americans also studied the first Tokyo mission. Almost from the start, Possum Hansell and Rosie O'Donnell had differed over the best way to attack Japan, with Hansell favoring AAF doctrine of high-altitude precision bombing while his subordinate wing commander inclined toward more flexible tactics. In any case, later study showed that merely forty-eight of 240 bombs dropped on Musashino had struck the target, including three that failed to explode. Intelligence analysts assessed damage at one percent of the factory buildings.

Retaliation was not long coming.

On November 27, the Japanese launched a long-range attack of their own. Two night-riding Mitsubishi Bettys from Iwo Jima attacked Isley Field, Saipan, reducing a B-29 to rubble and damaging eleven more before getting away cleanly. But that was just the preview. That morning, led by two navigation aircraft, a dozen Zeros left Iwo for Saipan, flying more than three hours literally at sea level. One damaged its propeller on the waves and diverted to Pagan, north of Saipan, where it was downed by prowling Thunderbolts. Meanwhile, the other eleven swept over Isley Field, achieving complete noontime surprise.

Brigadier General Hansell had a front-row seat to the drama, even as mission San Antonio 2 was winging to the Musashino factory. While the Zeros strafed, torching three B-29s, Hansell sped to the scene in his jeep with his operations officer, Colonel John B. Montgomery. But one Mitsubishi bored in low, well positioned to kill the head of XXI Bomber Command. Hansell bailed out of his jeep and threw himself beneath it, only to find the smaller, more agile Montgomery already there. Then Hansell looked up with unbelieving eyes as the Zero passed overhead, wheels coming down. The Japanese pilot landed, braked to a stop, and jumped out. Pistol in hand, the enemy flier picked a gunfight with GIs on the flight line until killed in a hail of rifle fire.

None of the intruders survived, so the name of Hansell's heroic assailant remained unknown. But if nothing else, the suicide raid on Saipan was testament to how much the Superfortresses threatened Japan.

For sheer distance the little-known "battle of the islands" had no precedent—720 statute miles one way. There had been previous interisland air battles, but the 1941–42 aerial siege of Malta was conducted by Axis aircraft from Sicily only fifty-five miles away. Far greater distances typified the Solomons campaign of 1942–43, when Japanese bombers flew 650 miles down the chain from New Britain to Guadalcanal. However, the longest stretch between those islands was 180 miles, and most lay within fifty miles of one another.

There was almost nothing between Saipan and Iwo Jima.

The industrious Japanese observed December 7 with another surprise attack. Mitsubishi Bettys from Iwo Jima staged two raids on Saipan: one at four in the morning and the second ten hours later. The raiders did more strafing than bombing, but that was bad enough. Though six Bettys were downed, they destroyed three B-29s and badly damaged three more. Obviously something had to be done—and it was.

The next day more than sixty B-29s joined 100 7th Air Force B-24s in Sledgehammer 1 to smother Iwo's three airfields beneath 800 tons of bombs. The Liberators carried most of the weight during the ensuing campaign, though the Christmas Eve Rockcrusher mission added thirty more Superfortresses. Three more B-29 missions in January and February knocked out one field and further damaged the remaining operational base.

Providentially, no Superforts were lost during the preventive efforts against Iwo, though a few B-24s succumbed. The Bonin Islands were among the worst places for Americans to be captured: at least one Liberator crewman who survived his shootdown was killed by Japanese who used him for bayonet practice.

Meanwhile, on December 3, Hansell put up eighty-six Superforts for the third Tokyo mission, again hitting Target 357, the Musashino plant. Though 85 percent of the attackers attempted to bomb the primary target, just 2.5 percent hit it.

Many of the Japanese interceptors concentrated on the 500th Group led by Colonel Richard T. King in the *Rosalia Rocket*. Major

Robert Goldsworthy's plane was shot down with just three survivors, including Colonel King, a prize catch for Japanese intelligence.

Lieutenant Hugh Mcnamer's unnamed plane was running in to the target when it was swarmed by interceptors. They hit the bomber repeatedly, causing the landing gear to extend and the bomb bay doors to open prematurely. The crippled aircraft drew unwanted attention—as many as fifty Japanese pilots smelled blood, making pass after pass. They shot large pieces off the sturdy B-29, which was unable to drop its bombs. Nevertheless, Mcnamer and his crew shoved up the power and slowly outpaced their tormentors. At length the bombardier salvoed his load and the crew began lightening ship. After dumping everything not fastened down, the crippled bomber reached Saipan, making an emergency landing on the B-24 runway.

The mission lost five bombers and most of four crews, including those that ditched from battle damage or fuel shortage.

In early December O'Donnell convened a meeting of his brain trust to discuss progress of the 73rd Wing's operations. The 200 or more airmen included his squadron and group commanders plus the lead crews. Despite their cautious relationship, O'Donnell also invited Hansell and some of his staff officers to attend.

Sitting quietly, Hansell listened with growing disbelief at Rosie O'Donnell's rosy assessment of the wing's performance to date. When O'Donnell invited his boss to address the assembly, Possum Hansell unloaded both barrels of his verbal shotgun.

"I'm in sharp disagreement because in my opinion you people haven't earned your pay over here," he began. "Unless you do better, this operation is doomed to failure."

Hansell's bluntness shocked those who knew him as a good-humored optimist. However, aside from his doctrinal differences with O'Donnell, he had previously declared his dissatisfaction with results to date, acknowledging that there was still much to learn. Now, openly contradicting his subordinate merely broadened the two leaders' differences, but it was hard to disagree with Hansell. In the first three major missions to Japan, no more than moderate damage was inflicted. Largely that was because merely one-third of the sorties attacked primary targets. Though only nine B-29s had been lost, the 19 percent abort rate was distressing—and it was not improving. Perhaps at that point Hansell began rethinking his previous insistence to Arnold that Ken Wolfe be replaced after only three China-based missions.

On December 27, O'Donnell tried again to deliver a knockout blow against the Musashino complex. The 73rd Wing put up seventy-two bombers in the command's last mission of the year, another daylight effort. However, the abort rate went through the hangar roof—a staggering 28 percent. For those crews that reached Japan, low clouds and the jet stream conspired once more to thwart their effort. As usual, the Japanese had plenty of warning and positioned four fighter regiments to intercept, plus one naval group flying a menagerie of single- and twin-engine types.

Some B-29s got above the interceptors, climbing to nearly 34,000 feet. But altitude ruined accuracy, and the bombing was miserable—only six hits within 1,000 feet of the aim point. Furthermore, the fifty-two attackers trickled into the target area for more than an hour, diluting the bombers' defensive firepower against some 270 fighter passes.

The Americans were lucky to escape with just three losses, two operationally. All were from the 498th Group, whose *Uncle Tom's Cabin* fell to savage fighter attacks. The beleaguered Boeing went down fighting, having been rammed twice. Other interceptors pursued the crippled bomber, hammering away with cannon and machine gun fire. Finally Major Thomas Krause's plane spun into Tokyo Bay. Three of the crew bailed out, and though all survived captivity, Major William Walker died one day after liberation.

*　　*　　*　　*　　*

XXI Bomber Command had launched five missions to Japan in December, totaling 415 sorties with nineteen losses. That equaled a 4 percent casualty rate, which was acceptable for B-17s and B-24s but was heavy for the much costlier Superfortresses. Bombing results were assessed as "good" on only two occasions, both against the Mitsubishi plant in Nagoya. In the eight homeland missions since November 24, no target had been destroyed.

Almost every major mission cost Superfortresses lost at sea, and back in Washington Hap Arnold took note. In 1944 a B-29 cost $605,000, nearly three times a B-17, and the noncombat loss rate was a constant concern. Consequently, Arnold wrote Hansell, "In my opinion the B-29 cannot be treated in the same way we treat a fighter, medium bomber, or even a Flying Fortress. We must consider the B-29 more in terms of a naval vessel, and we do not lose naval vessels in threes and fours without a very thorough analysis of the causes and what preventive measures may be taken to avoid losses in the future." Hansell certainly knew that his efficiency was subject to close scrutiny, and likely suspected that his command was at stake.

A New Year

While cynical GIs rhymed that they would see "The Golden Gate in '48," Hansell's command struck Japan four times in the first nineteen days of January 1945, beginning on the 3rd. Mission 17 sent the B-29s to Nagoya's port and industrial area, but of ninety-seven dispatched, a disappointing eighteen aborted—nearly one in five. Dropping through six-tenths cloud cover, the bombing was rated "fair" as reconnaissance showed 140,000 square feet of docks and urban area destroyed, and crews reported seventy-five fires throughout the area—the product of an increasing proportion of incendiary bombs. Though the Japanese were far more active than before with 346 fighter attacks, they only downed one bomber while B-29 gunners claimed fourteen kills. Three other bombers went missing, cause unknown.

One flier survived a horrifying experience. Japanese fighters attacked the 497th's *American Maid*, wounding the tail gunner and shooting out the left side blister at 29,000 feet, where the pressure differential sucked the waist gunner through the portal. Only Sergeant James B. Krantz's improvised safety harness saved him from a nearly six-mile fall. Dangling in the 200 mph slipstream at nearly the height of Mount Everest, exposed to frigid temperatures, he spent a punishing fifteen minutes slamming against the fuselage, unconscious from lack of oxygen. Two gunners were unable to haul him inside until the copilot and radar operator lent their weight to the struggle. Krantz was retrieved and, though suffering broken bones and frostbite, survived to return to Kentucky.

Meanwhile, early in January LeMay made a quick trip to survey the Marianas operation, as he knew that his XX Bomber Command eventually would transfer there. While on Guam—headquarters had recently moved from Saipan—he consulted with Hansell and Lieutenant General Lauris Norstad, the 20th Air Force chief of staff from Washington. LeMay and Norstad had a professional relationship, largely devoid of warmth. After serving together in Hawaii in the 1930s they had taken separate tracks, Norstad as a staff man, LeMay as an operator. Now Norstad dropped a verbal bomb on LeMay and Hansell: the entire B-29 operation would fall under the umbrella of XXI Bomber Command, and holding that umbrella would be Curtis LeMay.

Obviously, Hansell was on the way out. By all accounts Hap Arnold respected Possum, especially as one of the miracle workers who had produced AWPD-1 in nine days in 1941. But despite Arnold's pixieish appearance and cheerful demeanor, he could be a ruthless throat cutter, often impatient to a fault. (His expectations for the immature B-29 in the primitive China Theater and Wolfe's precipitous dismissal were but two examples.) LeMay hastened back to India, bearing orders to return to Guam in about two weeks.

In LeMay's absence Hansell continued operations, targeting Tokyo's Musashino aircraft plant by night on the 9th and Nagoya's

Mitsubishi factory by day on the 14th. Neither mission accomplished much, largely due to poor weather over the targets. However, Musashino's searchlights made an impression on the fliers. A navigator wrote, "About 50 lights—some on us momentarily. Pretty lonely up there all by ourselves." The two missions cost eleven B-29s, mostly through ditchings.

Meanwhile, the new 313th Bomb Wing arrived at Tinian's North Field in mid-January. Brigadier General J. H. Davies, a two-tour veteran of the Southwest Pacific, arranged for his groups to fly four warm-up missions before tackling Japan in early February. The Marianas bomber command was stretching its wings toward maturity.

Among Davies's four groups was the 9th, which included a pilot who granted unusual recognition to his ground crew. While most bombers displayed the names of the airmen assigned to each aircraft, those who "kept 'em flyin'" were seldom acknowledged. An exception was recalled by Sergeant Chester Ziel, who worked on a B-29 named *The B.A. Bird*.

Upon seeing their first B-29, Ziel's friend Gerald Vining had remarked, "Boy, that's a big ass bird." Ziel added, "When we got to Tinian with all those other big ass birds and our flight crew hesitated to give our plane a name. . . . Jerry and Ray Snyder took it upon themselves to approach Captain Wendell Hutchinson, aircraft commander of the unnamed plane." Hutchinson agreed to have his bomber called *The B.A. Bird*. More than that, however, the name of each engine mechanic was lettered on the appropriate cowling with names of wives and sweethearts. "As far as I know, we were the only ground crew so honored," Ziel said.

Official recognition of ground crews also was rare, though citations were issued to mechanics with outstanding records. A case in point was Sergeant William J. Owens, who kept the 6th Group's *Gravel Gertie* flying. His citation said, "Sergeant Owens was crew chief at a base in the Marianas Islands supervising the maintenance of a B-29 aircraft. Working under adverse conditions which frequently involved new problems never before faced in aircraft maintenance, he directed the ground servicing of his plane so effectively that it completed 22 combat missions without a mechanical malfunction necessitating early return. Displaying indefatigable zeal, he devoted exceptionally long hours to keep the plane operational, sometimes leading his crew in repairing battle damage suffered in one raid while simultaneously readying the bomber for its next mission."

Under New Management

Curtis LeMay returned to Guam on January 19 and, in pilot talk, "shook the stick" to signal "I've got it" the next day. He landed in an awkward situation, relieving an old and valued friend, but he was senior to Hansell and had already proven himself a rare innovator. In a well-meaning but unworkable gesture, Arnold tossed Hansell a bone, offering him a slot as LeMay's deputy, but the Possum declined to chew it. As he later said, LeMay "didn't need any 'assistant commander' and I . . . would not be content to stay completely in the background."

LeMay asked Hansell to remain awhile to help with the transition, and he agreed to stay for several days. Fortunately, Hansell's chief operations officer was well known to LeMay: Colonel John Montgomery, one of the early B-17 fliers from Langley Field, Virginia, in 1937–38. LeMay was pleased to have his old colleague onboard; they would work closely in the months to come.

On January 19, the day LeMay arrived from China, Hansell launched Mission 20 against the Kawasaki aircraft factory at Akashi, on the coast west of Kobe. Of eighty Superforts dispatched, sixty-two bombed the primary target and nine opted for alternates. An abort reduced the 499th Group's deception force (drawing attention of enemy radar) to just two planes, which drew twenty fighter attacks. One navigator confided, "This was a nail biter for us."

Flying in decent weather for a change—less than three-tenths cloud cover—the B-29s inflicted serious damage on the plant with nearly 40 percent of the complex's roof area totally or partially destroyed. Furthermore, all the bombers returned—the first time that had happened since operations began almost two months before.

However, the success of the 19th proved short-lived. The next mission, four days later, was the first flown under LeMay's aegis, and it did not please him. Eradicate No. 3 targeted the Mitsubishi factory at Nagoya, and only twenty-eight of seventy-three planes attacked the primary from above a nearly solid undercast. Despite extremely heavy fighter opposition—nearly 700 fighter passes were counted— only one bomber was lost to enemy action and one operationally. (B-29 gunners claimed thirty-three kills for their biggest day so far.) But the greater concern was the abort rate and negligible damage to the engine plant. With 18 percent aborts and fewer than half the effective sorties bombing the designated target, Curt LeMay reckoned that he had much to do.

The January 27 mission produced more drama with a two-tiered battle against the weather and the defenders, in that order. Two B-29s provided advance information on conditions over Musashino and Nagoya, deeming the best chances were offered by Target 357— the resilient Nakajima plant at Musashino. However, by the time the main force of some sixty planes arrived an hour later, the clouds had closed in with a ten-tenths carpet. There was no option except radar drops on the Tokyo urban area, with no bomb strikes observed.

Meanwhile, nobody had trouble seeing Japanese fighters, which were up and waiting. In addition to a huge increase in interceptor sorties, there were also more ramming attempts, some of which succeeded. Attacking between 24,000 and 30,000 feet, the B-29s had lost much of their previous altitude sanctuary as crews counted a jaw-dropping 984 fighter attacks.

On each Superfortress, central fire controllers handed off turrets to waist gunners and bombardiers, depending upon the direction of the threat. Gunners swung their controls, placed their sighting reticles on each fighter in turn, and opened fire as far out as 800 yards— nearly half a mile. The .50 calibers chattered incessantly, spewing a stream of half-inch slugs that arced away in their ballistic trajectories at 2,700 feet per second.

In an aerial gunfight lasting nearly an hour, five bombers were chopped down while the Superforts' claims were pegged at sixty, nearly twice the previous record.

Amid the flak and fighters one pilot swore, "If I ever get out of this one I'm through flying—and at that moment I really meant it."

Nine B-29s were lost, including two destroyed in collisions and perhaps a third. Taking the brunt of the defenses was the 497th Group, with one squadron led by Lieutenant Colonel Bob Morgan of *Memphis Belle* fame. In the formation was Lieutenant Lloyd Avery's *Irish Lassie*, which was selected for destruction by a flock of Tojos. *Lassie's* gunners threw out a .50 caliber barrage at the misidentified Zeros, claiming three for starters, but the Japanese pilots were suicidally motivated. Elements of the JAAF's 244th Regiment bored in, and one fighter survived the bomber's gunfire to crash the left wing behind the outboard engine, puncturing a fuel cell. Moments later Captain Teruhiko Kobayashi dived in from astern, trading gunfire with tail gunner Sergeant Charles Mulligan. Grimly determined, Kobayashi drove his Nakajima into *Lassie's* tail, clipping the left stabilizer. The impact knocked him unconscious but he recovered to bail out, confident he had destroyed his prey.

Lassie's perforated airframe quickly lost pressurization, exposing the crew to subzero temperatures. Mulligan was trapped in the mangled tail, suffering severe frostbite before his friends could extract him. They stripped off his frozen clothes and piled on anything available to protect him as the pilots dived to denser, warmer air.

Irish Lassie shook off the effects of two collisions and repeated gunfire hits to return to Saipan. Barely controllable, she smashed down hard and collapsed on the runway, a write-off, but her crew prevailed. Chuck Mulligan lost both his frozen hands and radar operator Walter Klimczak sustained serious injuries to his pelvis, back, an arm and leg. Nevertheless, both men survived thanks to the Superfortress's tough airframe.

That battle had been won in the B-29 factory in Omaha.

Three other 497th crews were less fortunate. *Shady Lady* fell to suicide pilots and *Haley's Comet* was shot down by a navy night fighter, which likely succumbed to the defenses in turn. *Were Wolf* blew in two, possibly when gunfire detonated part of its bomb load. Seven men bailed out but only three survived, apparently because four parachutes malfunctioned.

Fighters hacked down the 499th's *Rover Boys Express*, flown by Lieutenant Edward "Snuffy" Smith. A twin-engine Nick executed a devastating pass just before bombs away, knocking out three engines, killing a gunner and wounding two more fliers. The crew abandoned ship amid other fighter attacks but navigator Raymond Halloran stopped to gulp part of a sandwich, uncertain when he might eat again. Knowing that Japanese pilots often killed parachutists, he fell for about 23,000 feet before pulling the ripcord. Dangling beneath his canopy at about 3,500 feet, "Hap" Halloran was thinking about his landing when he heard aircraft engines. Looking up, he saw three Japanese planes—fixed-gear trainers—closing in. With nothing to lose, he waved. Two of the planes broke off but the other circled protectively, the pilot tossing a salute.

Fifty-five years later Halloran shook hands with his guardian angel, Corporal Hideichi Kaiho, who had declined to use his machine gun on the helpless American. Kaiho explained that his commanding officer had insisted that his men abide by the traditional Bushido code of chivalry rather than the militarist version that regarded enemies with murderous contempt.

Halloran was extremely fortunate; one *Rover Boys* crewman was murdered by civilians and another disappeared into prison camp, never to emerge. Halloran found himself displayed in Tokyo's Ueno Park Zoo. He was kept naked in a tiger cage, vacant since the government had killed or starved the animals to death to prevent their escape in a bombing.

Typically, both sides thought they did far better than the facts allowed. Against nine B-29s lost to all causes, the Japanese celebrated twenty-two kills, while the bomber gunners downed about fifteen fighters—one-quarter of the Americans' claim. Still, it had been a bitter, hard-fought battle that boded ill for the near future. Sixty B-29 crewmen had been killed or captured.

By month's end Hansell was gone. Ironically, he was replaced at a time when he was making progress: placing greater emphasis on crew training; improving weather information; and eliminating unnecessary aircraft weight. In establishing a school for lead crews, he had taken a page from LeMay's European Theater book, but the concept also had proven itself in China. Nonetheless, Haywood Hansell sidled from airpower's center stage and faded from history's front lines. Subsequently he commanded a training wing in New Mexico and finished the war with Air Transport Command in Washington. He was medically retired in 1946, but was recalled during the Korean War and finished his career as a major general. Nevertheless, it is safe to say that his greatest contribution was achieved in that sweltering Alabama summer of 1941 when he and four colleagues wrote the AAF's plan for fighting World War II.

"If You Don't Succeed . . ."

Officially, Curtis LeMay's professional neck was on the chopping block amid some professional choppers. Later he paraphrased a message from Norstad: "If you don't succeed, you will be fired. . . . If you don't get results it will mean eventually a mass amphibious invasion of Japan, to cost probably a half a million more American lives."

However, to LeMay's ears Norstad's threat probably rang as hollow as an empty fuel drum. It was far from clear who might replace LeMay were he fired. Apart from his unexcelled background, no one had his experience operating the B-29 in combat, let alone duplicating his results in the CBI. With Wolfe and Hansell already sidelined, Arnold would have to reach far down the roster to summon another field captain, and nobody came close to LeMay's winning record.

Because it is inconceivable that Norstad's message was delivered without his chief's approval, it bespoke Arnold's desperation. He had staked not only his own reputation and the AAF's biggest program upon the Superfortress, but also his cherished vision: an independent air force in the future.

Norstad was correct about one thing. Though he surely exaggerated the likely toll of American dead, an invasion of Japan could only be averted by massive violence applied from the air. Even then it was uncertain that Tokyo would capitulate under the weight of B-29 bombs, but no other option applied. Therefore, thirty-eight-year-old Curtis LeMay accepted the enormous burden upon his shoulders, shrugged off the threat, and got on with the war.

However, it was a two-front war and the opposition included the U.S. Navy. When LeMay obtained back-channel information on the host service's priorities, he found XXI Bomber Command somewhere on the fifth page, after tennis courts, interisland boating docks, and the fleet recreation center. Perhaps uncharitably, he inferred that Admiral Chester Nimitz, commanding the Pacific Theater, believed that B-29s bombing Japan did nothing to enhance the Navy's public image.

In January the command grew with arrival of the 314th Wing on Guam. The commander was Brigadier General Thomas S. Power, an intelligent, competent officer almost totally lacking in people skills. At age thirty-nine he was well experienced, having flown B-24s in the Mediterranean Theater before standing up the 314th. He would become one of LeMay's most trusted subordinates.

In the eleven weeks before LeMay took over, the command had logged seventeen missions, averaging one a week to Japan. Of the 950 sorties, 170 (18 percent) had failed to bomb a primary, secondary, or alternate target, and no target had been destroyed. It was a wasted effort that LeMay could not abide. Regardless of the threat hanging over him from Washington, he was determined to find a better way. True to form, he reverted to basics, focusing upon "a real training job once more."

Frustrated that the wizardry of radar was not being fully exploited, LeMay collared his resident electronics specialist, Dr. King Gould, "a capable scientific type" from MIT. LeMay told him, "Pick out a couple of the stupidest radar operators . . . and Lord knows that's pretty stupid." LeMay designated a point on Guam's coast and asked Gould to determine whether subpar operators could distinguish it from the surrounding water. The chief was not being entirely uncharitable, as radar had come late to the B-29 program and many extraneous gunners had been assigned the duty with little interest and insufficient training.

After some test flights, "Doc" Gould reported back, allowing as how some of his guinea pigs might become tolerable technicians if provided ample training. Gould uttered the magic word—training. True to form, LeMay established a radar school for current operators as well as new crews, featuring both classroom lectures and airborne training.

Apart from remedial education, LeMay had to juggle several administrative balls at once: Allied, inter- and intraservice politics; supply and logistics; intelligence and targeting; maintenance; and personnel concerns. The latter included the all-important aircrew rotation policy. In Europe the twenty-five-mission tour for bomber crews had been increased to thirty owing to reduced losses in 1944, then to thirty-five. That same figure was applied to XXI Bomber Command, but a comparison of the two theaters was incompatible. From Guam to Tokyo and back took fourteen to fifteen hours flying time versus less than nine hours round-trip from England to Berlin. Therefore, during thirty-five European missions a B-17 crew might log 300 combat hours, whereas its B-29 counterpart could expect 500 hours, nearly all over water.

XX Bomber Command's loss rate from June through December had averaged 5 percent, and the XXI's first three months in the Marianas ran 4.1 percent. However, more pertinent to aircrews was that in LeMay's first six homeland missions, losses among effective (nonabortive) sorties ran 5.6 percent. That was not a cheerful number.

Extrapolated over a thirty-five-mission tour, it meant that B-29 crews lived on borrowed time after eighteen sorties. Nonetheless, morale held as the actuarial figures improved and the first crews to reach thirty-five missions rotated home in May.

Another problem was facilities for the new units. When the 314th Wing arrived in January, Guam's North Field was largely completed but had precious few accommodations. LeMay was living in a tent at the time, in vivid contrast to Guam's admirals, who entertained him in hilltop houses and even on a yacht. Through most of its existence XXI Bomber Command slept under canvas, which was semitolerable, but some engine components and most electronic systems needed indoor spaces, away from blowing dirt and excess moisture.

Under LeMay's direction, the Marianas command launched six major missions from January 23 to February 19, totaling 646 sorties with eighty-eight aborts (13 percent), a measurable improvement owing to LeMay's more efficient maintenance policies. But results were mixed: the portion of planes bombing the primary target ranged from zero to 70 percent, mainly depending upon weather. Overall, just one in three bombers attacked the primary—a galling figure to LeMay, whose standard of acceptability was target destruction. Losses were generally light, though the strike against Ota's aircraft plant on February 10 cost a dozen Superforts, only one directly attributable to enemy action. (One crashed on takeoff; two collided; seven ditched; and one disappeared.) The 505th Group was particularly hard hit, losing five planes operationally. Nevertheless, with the new 313th Wing's four groups, 118 sorties on the Ota strike represented the largest B-29 mission of the war to date.

Whatever the statistics showed, one inescapable fact stared Curt LeMay in his impassive face: he had destroyed no more targets than Possum Hansell. Something had to change.

The most obvious factor affecting the command's performance was totally beyond its control: the weather. The alliance of Pacific currents and frigid winter winds from the Asian landmass produced almost perennial clouds over Japan. Bombardiers could not hit what they could not see, even with radar, which was largely used for navigation. Better equipment was forthcoming, but meanwhile there was another inescapable problem—the damnable jet stream. Little known before the war (it had been discovered by Japanese scientists in the 1920s), the stream's hellacious winds strewed bombs far and wide when dropped from the doctrinal 27,000 to 30,000 feet. Though a few targets had been hard hit, those missions were the result of unusual circumstances: manageable winds aloft and rare days of good visibility, which occurred perhaps five days a month. Operations analysts computed that 400 B-29s were necessary to destroy an industrial target via high-altitude bombing but LeMay had not yet been able to launch 200. Even if he had more, many were always down for maintenance or repair.

What to do?

LeMay put his brain trust to work. The staff sought all manner of information, especially target intelligence, enemy order of battle, and weather data. The latter was hard to come by, and at one point the AAF tried to decipher coded Soviet weather reports, as the Russians seldom shared information with their allies. In any case, cryptanalysis was only marginally useful because, in LeMay's mind, the Kremlin changed its codes "with diabolical frequency."

In China, more than two-thirds of the bombs loaded in B-29s had been high explosives. That figure had remained fairly steady in the first three months of Marianas operations, but in February LeMay and some staffers began questioning the conventional wisdom. He knew that incendiaries had proven unexpectedly effective in the December strike that razed Hankow, and that Tokyo's construction was much the same—mainly wooden structures.

Firebombing Japan had been discussed as far back as Billy Mitchell's heyday in the 1920s and confirmed by prewar attaché reports (see Chapter One). If in fact 90 percent of Tokyo consisted of wood buildings, the entire city was vulnerable to incendiaries.

After consulting his subordinates, LeMay approved a change of tactics. Small-scale fire raids had been flown against Nagoya (fifty-seven planes on January 3) and Kobe (sixty-nine bombers on February 4). Results were encouraging enough to warrant a bigger test: Mission 38 was scheduled for February 25: the largest incendiary raid yet launched from the Marianas.

Somehow, the Japanese learned of the forthcoming mission in astonishing detail. The female radio personalities collectively known as Tokyo Rose had long provided unwitting entertainment to American servicemen, but in February the airmen got a shock. Rose astonished the 313th Wing by welcoming one of the 6th Group fliers by name: Captain Edgar McElroy, assuring him a warm welcome from Japan's finest fighter pilots.

McElroy was unique in the 20th Air Force in that his first Tokyo mission from Tinian would be his second to the enemy capital. He had flown the Doolittle Raid in 1942 and sustained a serious back injury but returned to flight status. After a practice mission to Truk, McElroy realized that he might be unable to stand fifteen-hour homeland missions but he refused to be put off by Tokyo Rose. The Texan holstered his pearl-handled .45 automatic and prepared to fly Mission 38.

The command's three wings established a new record on February 25: 231 Superforts in a daylight high-altitude attack. At the assembly point off the enemy coast, fliers gawked at the sight of so many B-29s inbound, representing an aerial cavalcade of kinetic destruction aimed at the Tokyo urban area. Here was Giulio Douhet's vision embodied in chilling reality: an unstoppable air fleet aimed directly at the core of the enemy homeland.

In all, 202 bombers unloaded 454 tons of fire bombs, including thirty planes that attacked alternate targets. The result surpassed most expectations as nearly one square mile of the capital was razed in an unchecked conflagration. The incendiaries fell upon snowy ground throughout the target area, destroying nearly 28,000 structures and leaving 35,000 people homeless. Even the sacrosanct Imperial Palace was violated, with damage to guard barracks, a library, and staff apartments.

The saturation attack overwhelmed the defenses. Flak was described as "meager" and fighters were "nil." American casualties were astonishingly light, though the oft-battered 497th Group sustained all three losses. Ed McElroy, the Doolittle Raider, survived his second flight to Tokyo and, still nursing his strained back, soon was rotated stateside.

The previously unmatched success of Mission 38 proved a turning point in the air war against Japan. It marked almost the hour and minute when XXI Bomber Command turned from high explosives to firebombs as the means of destroying Tokyo's industry.

LeMay often is credited with the decision to switch to incendiaries but he later acknowledged that several others in the Marianas and Washington made contributions. Shortly before Hansell left, Norstad had urged Arnold to support "a test incendiary mission" to assess the value of a fire raid on Tokyo.

But incendiaries were only part of the equation. Planners had recognized the doctrinal importance of mass, with a large enough bombing force to maximize the effects of the fiery weapons. That meant building up the B-29 wings and stockpiling enough ordnance for a sustained effort to overwhelm the defenses for a period of several days.

The decision to switch from explosives to incendiaries implied a change in targeting: from the first-priority aircraft industry to urban areas. Norstad himself addressed that concern in early January, insisting to Arnold that the test mission represented not so much a targeting shift as "a necessary preparation for the future." The implication was obvious: once Japan's aircraft industry was destroyed, the next target set would involve the greater urban-industrial areas and the cottage industries that supported other major manufacturers.

Another factor in the evolving plan was bombing altitude.

LeMay's operations officer, John Montgomery, already had endorsed "low-level" night missions, though still above 20,000 feet. Others such as wing commanders Rosie O'Donnell and Tommy Power pushed for even lower altitudes, while at least a few in Arnold's Washington circle later made similar claims. But regardless of who else supported the departure from the doctrine of high-altitude bombing, it was LeMay's call. Without giving away his intentions, he queried Norstad, "You know General Arnold. I don't know him. Does he ever go for a gamble?"

Curt LeMay was playing the game. Knowing the immense pressure Arnold felt to make a success of the B-29, LeMay wanted to keep his chief removed from the line of fire as much as possible in case the gamble went awry. Norstad was noncommittal—he had his own chips on the table—but apparently did not ask specifics. LeMay came away with the impression that "being a little unorthodox was all right with Hap Arnold."

In truth, LeMay was thinking far beyond "a little unorthodox." He was thinking of not merely throwing away the AAF's playbook, but burning it to cinders—along with Tokyo.

After concurring with some trusted acolytes, in late February LeMay gave serious thought to a low-level nocturnal fire raid on the enemy capital. However, his concept of low level was totally outré.

Two decades before, as an Ohio State ROTC cadet, LeMay had studied artillery. He had taken his old manuals with him to England in 1942 and used the tables to compute rough values for the effectiveness of German antiaircraft cannon against bomber formations. Now he dug out his books again and applied that same icy analysis to Japan. The mathematics, combined with his extensive flying experience, told him what he intuitively suspected. A low-level night attack, compressed into minimum time, would present enemy flak gunners with only fleeting targets, speedily ghosting through the dark. At altitudes below 10,000 feet, the heavy guns would be unable to track the bombers that they did see. In that respect, the B-29s would be flying "under the guns."

That left light flak, and it worried him. Like all airmen, LeMay retained a healthy respect for the Luftwaffe's 20mm to 37mm flak guns. Expertly manned and scientifically arrayed to destroy whatever crossed their sights, they took a fearsome toll of Allied aircraft from 1940 onward. But almost nothing was known about Japan's light AA weapons: neither numbers, locations, nor capabilities.

Undeterred, the bomber chief got down to details as small as intervalometer settings for spacing bombs from various heights, and came to a conclusion. Nobody had ever thought of flying four-engine aircraft over an enemy city at low level—at night. Therefore, the defending gunners would never expect it. As for night fighters, LeMay was dismissive. The few that Japan possessed were nowhere as numerous or as effective as Germany's practiced bomber killers.

Still, it remained a major gamble. If he was wrong, LeMay stood to lose a sizable portion of his force, and with it his position, his repu-tation, and—worst of all—hundreds of his airmen who relied upon his judgment for their survival. But even that paled next to the loom-ing specter of an invasion of Japan, with hundreds of thousands of American lives at stake.

Curt LeMay pondered the odds and thought deeply one more time. Then he rolled destiny's dice.

CHAPTER FOUR

From the Sea

BENEATH LEADEN GRAY skies, skirting squall lines and snow showers, the Hellcats and Corsairs crossed the Honshu coast, cruising at high speed toward Japanese airfields. The pilots had been briefed to expect the biggest air battle of the war, a significant warning considering the scale of the largest previous tangles with enemy fliers: more than 300 Japanese had been shot down on June 19 off the Marianas and well over 200 on October 24 at Leyte Gulf.

Anticipating large, confusing swarms of friendly and hostile aircraft, the Americans had painted yellow bands on the noses of their carrier planes for quick identification. Aircrews were only informed of operation plans in four-hour increments, limiting the information they could impart if captured.

As the first fighter sweep crossed the coast with master armament switches on and gunsight rheostats turned up, the F6F and F4U pilots scanned the cloudy skies, searching for dark green planes bearing rust-red Hinomaru suns. The flattop aviators expected to shoot their way into Tokyo.

The presence of American carrier planes in Japanese airspace on Friday morning, February 16, 1945, signified far more than met the eye. The U.S. Navy's debut over the home islands provided strategic cover for one of the most important amphibious operations of the war: the impending Iwo Jima invasion.

Sixty miles off Honshu the greatest assemblage of naval power on the planet stood by to launch follow-up strikes. Tokyo was about to confront the challenge of American carrier aviation—at once the Army Air Forces' partner and rival in the air war against Japan.

Building an Air Navy

Thirty-four months after the Doolittle Raid, America's huge industrial capacity had produced the Fifth Fleet, dwarfing to insignificance the pinprick attack launched from USS *Hornet* (CV-8) in April 1942. The fleet's striking arm, Task Force 58, counted sixteen fast carriers (all capable of more than 30 knots) plus eight battleships, fifteen cruisers, and seventy-seven destroyers under Vice Admiral Marc Mitscher.

Mitscher's 116 warships totaled 975,000 combatant tons with some 1,200 aircraft—probably more striking power than could be deployed by the earth's other navies combined. Nearly all the ships were new: more than eight in ten had been commissioned since Pearl Harbor.

The fast carriers—marvels of concept, design, and construction—represented more than two decades of argument and experimentation, trial and error. But the challenge of building them was no clean-cut engineering problem to be solved solely with drafting boards and slide rules. The task required an evangelic commitment by a generation of aviators, and some of those evangelists left their blood on narrow wooden decks in proving their beliefs.

The Navy had at least as much institutional investment in carriers as the AAF did in heavy bombers. But there were profound differences. For example, navies nearly always opposed other navies whereas strategic air forces sought to destroy enemy cities. For another, navies tend toward an evolutionary progress—sometimes spanning centuries, as with the ship of the line—whereas air forces are by definition revolutionary. In the forty-two years between Kitty

Hawk and Hiroshima, the most significant change in navies was due to aviation.

Shipboard takeoffs and landings had been demonstrated in America in 1910–11 but only the Royal Navy had developed a workable if rudimentary system in 1917, launching from platforms erected on battle cruisers. The first true aircraft carriers with flight decks unimpeded by superstructure appeared with His Majesty's Ship *Argus* (1917), United States Ship *Langley* (1922), and His Imperial Japanese Majesty's Ship *Hosho* (1923).

The timing in Japan and America was not wholly coincidental. In 1921–22 the Five-Power Naval Treaty among the United States, Britain, France, Italy, and Japan limited the tonnage (and therefore, numbers) of capital ships. Since carriers were still an unknown quantity, and not deemed major combatants, the conferees allowed conversion of battleships and battle cruisers to flattops. The United States and Japan especially made use of that exception.

Dating at least from 1906, American strategists anticipated conflict with Japan, and produced a succession of contingencies. They became War Plan Orange, which envisioned a battle of the dreadnoughts in mid-Pacific. Orange evolved into Rainbow Five, the plan current in December 1941. Aircraft carriers had been gradually folded into the plans, evolving from merely scouting into active combat roles.

The task facing the naval airmen was twofold: to develop a viable means of operating shipboard aircraft for attack missions, and to gain a place at the nautical table amid the resistance of "the gun club," the battleship traditionalists who envisioned any future sea war as a replay of Jutland in 1916. The rivalry was compounded by vastly reduced peacetime budgets, especially in the Depression years of the 1930s.

Institutionally, naval aviation's biggest problem was a lack of seniority. Though the first naval officers had earned their wings in 1911, thirty years later very few had risen high enough to set policy. In fact, the two leading advocates of carrier development were products of the pre-aviation Navy.

Rear Admiral William A. Moffett established the Bureau of Aeronautics in 1921. He had graduated from Annapolis in 1890, eight years before the Spanish-American War. He fought at Manila Bay and received the Medal of Honor for action in Mexico in 1914.

Blessed with uncommon vision, Moffett grasped the potential of naval aviation as a battleship captain in World War I. He took note when Billy Mitchell's fliers rocked naval orthodoxy to the keel by sinking the captured German *Ostfriesland* in 1921. Though a soft-spoken Carolinian, Moffett's tough-minded attitude gained him recognition as the father of naval aviation. He secured control over not only technical matters and acquisition, but also personnel. Moffett proved indispensable, remaining as chief of BuAer until 1933, when he died in an airship disaster.

The other major influence in naval aviation was slender, bearded Joseph M. Reeves, an Annapolis athlete credited with inventing the football helmet. Four years junior to Moffett, Reeves also went the battleship route, seeing action against the Spanish at Santiago Bay.

Between 1914 and 1923, Reeves commanded a cruiser and two battleships, establishing himself as a card-carrying member of the gun club. But after attending the Naval War College he was drawn to flying. In 1925, at the advanced age of fifty-one, he completed the aerial observer's course, qualifying him for aviation leadership. Later that year, as commander of the Pacific Fleet's air component, he flew his flag in USS *Langley*, America's first flattop.

Probably no one did more to develop carrier tactics than "Billy Goat" Reeves. With his white Vandyke he was instantly recognizable to fliers and sailors alike. His four years with *Langley* were seminal; he experimented with procedures and techniques that would become standard in World War II. More embarked aircraft, faster operating tempos, and offensive missions rather than scouting all evolved on his watch. By the time he transferred out in 1931, the carrier navy was well on its way with two 33,000-ton giants, *Lexington* (CV-2) and *Saratoga* (CV-3). Reeves retired as a vice admiral in 1936 but was recalled to duty in 1940, serving in Washington throughout the war.

Naval airmen spent the 1920s and 1930s determining how best to integrate carriers into surface fleets, optimizing the roles of reconnaissance, observation, and attack. Eventually the world's navies hit upon four basic roles for tailhook aircraft: scouts, torpedo planes, dive bombers, and fighters. The institutional differences were most notable in Britain, where the Royal Air Force retained control of naval aircraft until 1937. In contrast, American and Japanese naval aviators were fully integrated into their fleets.

In the 1930s, U.S. naval aviation's seniority problem became so acute that older officers were run through flight training to fill the expanding number of aviation billets. The JCLs or Johnny Come Latelys included William Halsey and John S. McCain, both fifty-two when they pinned on their wings. More senior was Ernest J. King, a sour but formidably capable officer qualified in both submarines and aviation, who became chief of naval operations in 1942.

At the time of the Japanese attack on Pearl Harbor the U.S. Navy had seven large carriers, four of which were sunk in 1942. But America's vast industrial base began making up the deficit even as the battles roiled around islands called Midway and Guadalcanal.

Arguably the most nearly perfect instrument of sea power was the Essex class carrier, eleven being ordered in 1940's massive naval budget. The name ship, designated CV-9, was commissioned in December 1942, setting the pattern for all her twenty-three sisters. She displaced 27,100 tons, carried eighty to 100 aircraft, and could make 32 knots. Cruising at 15 knots, she had fuel for 15,000 nautical miles, affording a fast, long-ranged offensive punch almost ideally suited to the Pacific Theater. The United States could not have successfully prosecuted the war without the Essexes, and for longevity the American taxpayer probably never got a better bargain.

Apart from the Essexes, American shipyards worked overtime to turn out smaller fast carriers. Nine light cruiser hulls were hastily modified to produce the Independence class CVLs, all delivered in 1943. At 10,600 tons displacement, they embarked some thirty-five aircraft and were capable of 31 knots. Shorter ranged than their

CV stablemates, the Independences could cruise 13,000 miles at 15 knots. Though in combat from 1943 onward, and despite frequent battle damage, only one was sunk—testament to the soundness of the design.

In February 1945 the industrial miracle of the American home front manifested itself on Tokyo's doorstep, with promise of more to come.

The Tailhook War

The Fifth Fleet was in the calm, capable hands of Admiral Raymond A. Spruance, victor at Midway in 1942 and Philippine Sea in 1944. But the hand on the helm of Task Force 58 was Vice Admiral Marc A. Mitscher, who had been flying since 1916. Just turned fifty-eight, he was a small, slight officer with a soft voice and almost diffident manner. He had made a hash of his tenure as first captain of *Hornet*, even allowing for her role in the Doolittle Raid. His tendency toward cronyism and inattention to detail nearly cost his career after the Battle of Midway, but he had already been selected for promotion, and he rebounded nicely.

By 1945, "Pete" Mitscher was the world's most experienced—and most successful—carrier admiral. With few interludes he had led the Fast Carrier Task Force since January 1944, gaining significant victories from the Central Pacific westward. His greatest triumph had been won in June 1944, the lopsided victory known as the Great Marianas Turkey Shoot. The seeds of that victory sprouted ashore, producing B-29 bases before year's end.

For all his success, Mitscher needed hand-holding. Even his admirers conceded that "He wasn't real bright," and he proved surprisingly reluctant to try new equipment or techniques—an ironic turn for a pioneer naval aviator.

The task force staff worked hard to fill in what the admiral often omitted. Much of the credit went to his chief of staff, Captain

Arleigh Burke, an extraordinarily astute "black shoe" surface officer who had made his reputation as a destroyer skipper in 1943. But he won over the sometimes parochial aviators who sported brown shoes as a badge of honor and became known as "Thirty-one Knot Burke" for his press-ahead style of leadership.

Task Force 58 was organized into five task groups, typically each with three Essex class carriers and an Independence class light carrier. Riding those sixteen flattops off Honshu were 1,187 airplanes: 895 Hellcat and Corsair fighters, 201 Avenger torpedo planes, and ninety-one Helldiver dive bombers.

In order to provide more fighters to repel kamikazes, *Bennington*, *Bunker Hill*, *Essex*, and *Wasp* each received two Marine Corsair squadrons. It was a last-minute decision, and fitting into Navy air groups took some comradely adjustment. As one marine ruefully noted, "We were invited to one of their poker sessions and didn't even have time to warm up the chairs before we were flat broke!"

Short on instrument flight time and carrier experience (one marine went to war with one shipboard landing in his logbook), the leathernecks nonetheless took the inevitable losses as part of the steep learning curve inherent to tailhook aviation.

The Pacific Fleet's two oldest carriers—the battle-wise *Enterprise* and *Saratoga*—represented a capability unique in all the world's navies. Led by Rear Admiral Matthew Gardner, they fielded specially trained night-flying air groups. Gardner, previously skipper of the Big E, had the potential of keeping carrier aircraft over Japanese bases around the clock, and he intended to prove it with his ninety-six fighters and thirty-nine bombers.

On February 10, Task Force 58 had departed the fleet anchorage at Ulithi Atoll in the Caroline Islands, nearly 550 miles southwest of Saipan. With an immense lagoon covering 200 square miles, it was a natural base, fully developed after U.S. forces landed in September 1944. Ulithi lay 1,700 miles south of Honshu, putting naval airpower within range of Tokyo itself.

*   *   *   *   *

Most carriers provided a supportive environment for their air groups. One of the best examples was contained in the end-of-cruise report from the commander of Air Group Six aboard Captain Robert F. Hickey's *Hancock*. "During the period 9 March 1945 to date, while Air Group Six was aboard . . . it is the opinion of the squadron commanders and the air group commander that nowhere could one find a closer feeling than existed between the ship's officers and enlisted men and the air group. The air group felt that the *Hancock* was their ship just like in peace time days."

That report was submitted by Commander Henry L. Miller, who had taught the Doolittle Raiders everything they needed to know about carrier takeoffs in 1942.

Some others were not as supportive, and the new *Shangri-La*, under Captain James D. Barner, was certainly among the worst. Recalled one veteran, "The relationship between the ship and the air group was not a good one. It may have been one of the worst in the Pacific." The feud began during the ship's shakedown cruise when the executive officer was outraged to discover liquor aboard. He confiscated all the bootleg booze, declaring that anyone who wished could reclaim it—and stand court-martial. Thereupon the devil's brew was taken to the fantail where "it was publicly smashed and dumped over the side." Relations between the senior ship's officers and the air group continued downhill from there.

To Japan

As Task Force 58 pounded north through roughening seas, Spruance took advantage of the poor weather to shield his approach from the Japanese. During the twelve-hour run-up to the launch point, carrier aircrews sorted out their equipment, and many donned long underwear against the North Pacific weather. Half of the air groups were new to combat, and Pete Mitscher had taken pains to prepare them as well as possible. His staff had issued notes on tactics and operational procedures, including the latest information on Japanese defenses.

Though of mixed quality, intelligence had come a long way since the Doolittle Raid. One pilot recalled, "The maps were good geographic and strategic target aids, but most recent tactical info was sparse and not very accurate."

Some old Pacific hands had waited a long time for a look at Tokyo. They included Lieutenant Commander Fritz E. Wolf, flying off *Yorktown*. A prewar Navy pilot, he had joined Claire Chennault's Flying Tigers and returned home credited with downing four Japanese planes. Unlike most of the naval aviators in the Tigers, he reentered his parent service and wangled another combat assignment. He assumed command of Fighting-Bombing Squadron 3 a week before his twenty-ninth birthday.

Commander Charles Crommelin, skipper of Air Group 12 on *Randolph*, had been chasing "meatballs" since 1943. The Pacific War was a family affair for him and his four brothers, all of whom not only served in the Navy, but graduated from Annapolis (1923–41), an all-time record.

A few pilots had seen the other half of the global war, like Fighting Squadron 4's Lieutenant Dean Laird. Flying a Wildcat, the lanky Californian downed two German planes off Norway in October 1943. Lieutenant Donald A. Pattie, commanding *San Jacinto*'s bombers, had been the first American to land in Vichy-occupied Morocco in November 1942.

On the evening of the 15th at least one carrier prepared to load napalm bombs for use against the Imperial Palace and surrounding area, "but plans were aborted at the last minute." Later the squadrons were told that the palace had no military significance, though a few aviators grumbled at what they considered a missed opportunity.

Veterans or rookies, pilots manned aircraft around 0600 the next morning, groping in the flight decks' predawn blackout to find their designated aircraft. They were appalled at the weather, which a *Hor-*

net (CV-12) pilot called "dark and icky." On occasion the carriers' radio masts were obscured by the low-lying scud.

On rain-swept decks, launch officers judged each carrier's motion in the spume-capped waves. As the bow began to rise, a checkered flag dropped abruptly and the first pilot off each ship released his toe brakes, kept a stiffened arm against the throttle, and began his take-off roll.

Gloss-blue Hellcats and Corsairs lifted off at fifteen-second intervals, rising into the chilling gloom with running lights shining from wingtips and tails, providing essential reference for pilots joining their two-plane sections and four-plane divisions.

Thus began almost eleven hours of continuous flight operations.

Thanks to the weather, Spruance's intent for an unannounced arrival was fulfilled. An Imperial Navy officer later stated, "The attack of the 16th was a complete surprise to our homeland defenses."

Surprise was important to the Americans' plans. Their initial goal was air superiority—beating down Japan's airpower—which was best accomplished by destroying enemy aircraft on the ground. Once the tailhookers gained control of enemy airspace, they would devote more attention to the pinpoint targets that B-29s seldom hit in high-altitude attacks: specific aircraft and engine factories that contributed directly to Tokyo's air defense.

Therein lay the striking contrast between Army and Navy aviation. Faster than many enemy fighters and possessing powerful defensive armament, the Superfortress was capable of operating unescorted in hostile airspace, usually shrugging off interceptors while delivering massive bomb loads. Carrier-based aircraft were far more vulnerable. In order to bomb any target effectively, they had to descend into the teeth of the defenses, releasing their ordnance below 3,000 feet where the light antiaircraft fire was thickest and most accurate. Nor could Avengers or Helldivers outrun most Japanese fighters. Therefore, carrier bombers relied upon close escort of Hellcats and Corsairs to run interference for them. It was an unavoidable tradeoff: the range and power of land-based bombers versus the mobility and relative precision of carrier aircraft.

First blood was spilled at the southernmost tip of the Chiba Peninsula, twenty miles south of Yokohama. Five *Essex* Hellcats spotted a cigar-shaped Mitsubishi Betty and pounced. A Louisianan, Lieutenant (jg) E. J. "Nic" Nicolini, won the race. He shot down the twin-engine bomber at 0800, beginning nine hours of almost uninterrupted combat.

Lieutenant Commander Herbert N. Houck, leading twenty of his own *Lexington* Hellcats with twenty more from *Hancock* and *San Jacinto*, was an old hand, having led Fighting Squadron 9 since December 1943. Moreover, it was one day short of a year since his last combat: the frantic hassle over Truk Atoll in February 1944. In worsening weather, his pilots shifted targets, opting for Katori Airfield near the coast. Minutes later Houck's formation piled into a half-hour combat.

The dogfight spread as if by cyclonic action, drawing outriders into its vortex as Zekes arrived from Mobara and Katori. Several carrier pilots got repeated opportunities: Lieutenant (jg) Henry K. Champion fired at seven bandits in succession, claiming a kill and two probables. Lieutenant Commander W. J. "Pete" Keith, leading *Hancock*'s Fighting Squadron 80, became an ace in a day, claiming five victims. So did one of his division leaders, Lieutenant William C. Edwards, who had flown dive bombers in 1942. Unusually old for a combat pilot, "Bulldog" Edwards was a week short of his thirty-first birthday.

By the time the cloudy sky cleared of aircraft over Katori, the Americans had claimed forty-eight Japanese planes destroyed. Though the results were exaggerated, the outcome was American control of Japanese airspace. But it could be a tough education: *Bunker Hill*'s virgin Air Group 84 launched its initial combat sorties just twenty-one days out of Alameda, California. At some targets the flak was described as "pedestrian" because, in the words of one squadron commander, "you could get out and walk on it."

From the best-known dogfight of the day emerged the legend of Kaneyoshi Muto. With eight years of experience, the diminutive warrant officer was described by no less an authority than leading ace Saburo Sakai as "a genius in the air." Yet on the ground he was "a friendly and cheerful ace who was liked by everybody."

Breaking into combat in China in 1937, Muto returned to Japan and became a tactics instructor. From 1941 he increased his victory log in the Philippines and Java, later leaving his mark in the Solomons and New Guinea. He survived Iwo Jima's Darwinian summer of 1944, cementing his reputation as "the toughest fighter pilot in the Imperial Navy." Now he flew with the Yokosuka Air Group's operational evaluation unit at Atsugi.

On February 16, the twenty-eight-year-old Muto was awaiting news of the birth of his child when word came of Grummans inbound. The noontime scramble pitted seven *Bennington* F6F Hellcats against ten or more Zeros, Mitsubishi Jacks, and Kawanishi Georges led by Lieutenant Yuzo Tskuamoto. Muto revved his George into the air to intercept the Hellcats.

The Americans were well trained but inexperienced, entering their first combat against some of the elite of the Imperial Navy. It was a shattering initiation: two *Bennington* pilots were lost and two captured. In the frantic low-level dogfight Muto used his four 20mm cannon to good effect, claiming multiple victories. Almost as soon as he landed a corrupted version of the event immediately made the press.

Ignoring his squadron mates, reporters focused on Muto, attributing all four kills to him in a solo battle against a dozen Americans. His wife, Kiyoko, heard the reports shortly after delivering their daughter, thrilled to know her flier was not only safe, but famous. The press dubbed Muto "the Miyamoto Musashi of the air," after the legendary swordsman best known as author of *The Book of Five Rings*.

Elsewhere, airborne Japanese were scarce. Lieutenant Commander Fritz Wolf, the former Flying Tiger, took eight *Yorktown* Hellcats in low, just beneath the overcast, and pressed on to Konoike

Airfield east of Osaka. Recalled one pilot, "The apron was packed with neatly parked aircraft which went up in flames as we pumped our .50s and rockets into the sitting ducks. Only one machine gun was firing at us, so we made three passes." After the last run the York-towners counted nine destroyed and twenty-one damaged.

The fifth fighter sweep launched from Rear Admiral Frederick C. Sherman's Task Group 58.3, the same "Ted" Sherman who had the old *Lexington* (CV-2) sunk from under him at Coral Sea nearly three years before. His pilots were assigned targets to the west, resulting in the first Navy planes over Tokyo. Better weather farther inland permitted strike leaders to hit targets in the forenoon period, notably in the capital's northwest industrial area. The Ota aircraft plant was hit successively, following up B-29 attacks.

That afternoon *Bunker Hill's* Avengers and Helldivers finished off the Nakajima aircraft factory at Ota. But Japanese army fighters took a toll; in its first day at war *Bunker Hill's* Air Group 84 lost four planes: two bombers and two fighters with eight fliers.

Other units took even heavier losses. Since November, *Wasp's* Hellcats had logged half a dozen small battles over the Philippines and Formosa, but Tokyo was the big league. Fighting Squadron 81 lost five pilots in its first major operation, as much the victim of their own overeagerness as the skill of Japanese pilots. The *Wasp* fliers claimed fifteen kills but it was a poor exchange. "The old lesson was learned the hard way again," said Commander Frederick J. Brush, who noted young pilots' tendency to break formation.

Despite widespread combats that ranged from the clouds down to street level, some pilots found no action at all. The new *Hornet's* Ensign Willis Hardy spoke for disappointed fighter pilots when he said, "We, being high cover over the Yoko end of town, didn't see any of Tokyo and not even a peek at Fuji san."

On the last strike of the day a mixed bag of Japanese army fighters caught up with egressing Americans between the Ota engine factory and the coast, initiating a half-hour running battle. *San Jacinto's* Commander Gordon E. Schecter led his Hellcats in protecting the bombers. Previously a floatplane pilot, he had learned the fighter trade well. Schecter gunned down four planes that morning and then, in the evening shootout, he destroyed a Tojo and probably an Oscar. Turning to meet each attack, his fighter pilots claimed nine more. But some Japanese got through the U.S. escorts. Backseaters in Helldiver dive bombers manhandled their twin .30 caliber mounts while Avenger torpedo plane gunners drew a bead in their power-operated turrets. *San Jacinto* and *Lexington* bombers claimed three kills and several damaged before reaching the coast.

On the biggest day of air combat since the Marianas Turkey Shoot, carrier aviators believed they shot down 291 enemy planes. Six Hellcat pilots gained the status of ace in a day. But it appears that the actual toll was forty-four Imperial aircraft. The sixfold error was due to several factors, including inexperience: well over half the Americans were new to combat, and only experience could teach a pilot what a genuine kill looked like, as opposed to nonlethal damage on a bandit.

American losses were fifty-two carrier planes. Hardest hit was *Bennington's* new Air Group 82, with a dozen aircraft missing. Meanwhile, the six Marine squadrons got an especially rough initiation to combat: eleven Corsairs were lost from *Bennington, Bunker Hill,* and *Wasp.*

Though Task Force 58 lost somewhat more planes in dogfights than the Japanese, the hard fact was that the U.S. Navy could afford such attrition whereas Tokyo could not—especially in trained aircrews. By establishing control of enemy airspace in one day, the carrier fliers were set to press their advantage as Mitscher's staff prepared target lists for the morrow.

Moreover, the fleet was inviolate. That afternoon, as the last strikers returned to their flat-roofed roosts, Rear Admiral Matt Gardner's *Enterprise* and *Saratoga* night fliers took wing. Both air groups "capped" major Japanese airfields, preventing the enemy from harassing the task force during the night.

February 17

Predawn launches on the 17th had two goals: establishing combat air patrols to protect the force, and dispatching searchers to snoop along the coast for Japanese shipping. During the two days there were meager pickings for ship hunters, as only one large merchant vessel was sunk plus several smaller ones.

Although deteriorating weather chilled the task force's effort, literally and figuratively, missions were flown against industrial targets. Carrier bombers sought out the engine plants at Tachikawa and Musashino—the latter well known to B-29 crews as Target 357.

The aviators launched at dawn, organized themselves by divisions and squadrons, and headed inland. Said one bomber pilot, "We appeared to be floating above a pure white carpet stretching as far as the eye could see, ultimately blending away into a grayish haze. . . . The reflection of the bright sun created the illusion of being studded with 10 million diamonds. I could not escape the feeling of being in a fairy tale world of castles and fantasy."

Leading *San Jacinto*'s Avengers was Lieutenant Donald Pattie, the veteran of Morocco. His target was the Tachikawa engine factory in Tokyo's western suburbs, and the Japanese scenery offered a vivid contrast with his Atlantic cruises. "Looming out of the carpet directly in front of us was a massive tapered tower, solid white across its jagged top with white sides that blended into streaks of brown near the base. . . . The tower was, of course, the sacred mountain of the Japanese, Fujiyama. I had no time to dwell further on its beauty as we had to start the letdown toward our objective."

Mount Fuji lay sixty miles west of downtown Tokyo but the mountain's splendor was crowded aside by other concerns. The thrill of seeing Japan's most recognizable feature was tempered by tactical matters: monitoring engine gauges; keeping formation; and especially remaining vigilant. Flying northwest over Yokohama, Don Pattie glanced to port, and saw his leader attacked.

From high and behind, an elegantly flown fighter swiftly dived onto the air group commander's tail, rolled inverted, and shot down Lieutenant Commander Donald White. He bailed out, parachuting onto the parade ground of an army pilot school, and survived six months in captivity.

White's wingman, Ensign Karl Smith, reacted quickly, nosing into a diving spiral, but the attacker pursued, firing a quick shot that raked the top of Smith's Hellcat. Already inverted, the Japanese merely pulled through into a split-S and briefly chased Smith. Pattie was simultaneously stunned and impressed: "It was not a show of flamboyance but a highly professional maneuver, executed with superb airmanship."

Smith headed for the coast, found another blue airplane, and proceeded seaward. But his shot-up engine failed over the task group's destroyer screen and he splashed into a water landing, fetched back to *Langley* by a destroyer.

Despite the losses, Air Group 23 continued to the target. Off his starboard wingtip Pattie took in the memorable sight of the Imperial Palace, an excellent landmark with its huge cream-colored structure. From there the target lay twenty miles due west.

Upon sighting the Tachikawa factory Pattie waggled his wings, sending his Avengers into combat spread. He had several potential targets in the complex but selected the main assembly building.

Slanting into their glide bombing runs, the big Grummans opened their bomb bay doors. Pattie wrote, "We bore down with vengeance. To insure an effective attack I held my release till the last moment, pulling out right at the treetops." He glanced over his shoulder, pleased that his four 500-pounders had punched through the building's roof. The squadron's other bombs also seemed to impact within the factory.

Meanwhile, another Atlantic Fleet veteran made his presence known. *Essex's* Lieutenant Dean Laird already had two Germans to his credit and had dropped a Sally bomber the day before. Now he scored a Tony and a Tojo during a strike on the Nakajima Tama engine factory. Thus, "Diz" Laird became the only Navy ace with kills against Germany and Japan.

*   *   *   *   *

In the early afternoon the marginal weather only worsened. Mitscher canceled scheduled strikes and, recovering his airborne planes, reversed helm for Iwo Jima.

The recovery posed a major challenge to pilots and landing signal officers (LSOs). Landing a high-performance aircraft on a moving ship is probably the most demanding task that humans have ever routinely performed. In heavy seas even the big-deck carriers bucked and rolled, requiring exquisite timing from the LSOs, who had to judge the "cut the throttle" signal to the second. Too early and the aircraft could smash down in a "ramp strike," hitting the aft edge of the flight deck with disastrous consequences. Too late and the landing plane might sail over the arresting wires, resulting in an aborted pass at best or a crash into one of the woven-steel cable barriers. As one veteran aviator said, "On straight-deck carriers you either had a major accident or an arrested landing."

Landings were especially tough on pilots who flew from Independence class light carriers. Their decks were only seventy-three feet across—twenty-three feet less than the Essexes.

The LSOs stood on a small platform portside aft, facing astern. Some ships rigged a framework for a canvas barrier against the wind, but the "wavers" still had to balance themselves against the ship's motion while pantomiming the standard set of signals with bright-colored paddles. They coached each pilot into "the groove" representing the optimum glide slope to snag an arresting wire with the plane's extended tailhook. It was more art than science. The best LSOs developed an intuitive feel for the visual and audio cues: airspeed, attitude, engine sound. And each airplane was different: Hellcat, Corsair, Helldiver, and Avenger all had their quirks.

At the exact moment that experience and judgment told him was right, the LSO slashed his paddles down from the "Roger" position (extended outright from the shoulders). The right paddle went to the throat and the left arm dropped across the body in the cut signal—chop the throttle, drop the nose, check the movement, and land the aircraft. Usually it resulted in a "trap."

Otherwise, the LSO gave a wave-off, ordering the pilot to go around and try again. A wave-off carried force of law: to ignore it was carrier aviation's gravest sin. A landing pilot might not see a fouled deck beneath his plane's nose, so he had to rely upon "Paddles" to think for him and fly the plane by remote control.

In all, during two days the tailhookers claimed 341 Japanese planes in the air and 190 on the ground. On the debit side of the ledger, Mitscher lost more than eighty planes to all causes. But high among the U.S. Navy's strengths was the fact that it could absorb such losses and continue operating. That month American factories produced more than 300 new Corsairs and nearly 600 Hellcats.

Actual Japanese aerial losses remain uncertain. Imperial Headquarters admitted seventy-eight but was less specific about those bombed or strafed on their fields. In turn, Japanese fliers claimed at least 134 kills versus the sixty carrier planes actually lost to flak and fighters.

Whatever the score, something remarkable had occurred. For two days a major American fleet had plied Japanese waters, established air superiority over Tokyo itself, and got away clean. Only a handful of enemy aircraft even approached the task force. The operation totally refuted one of the central tenets of naval airpower's severest critic, Alexander Seversky. His Airpower Lesson Number Five held that land-based aviation must be superior to shipborne aviation. But Mitscher's sixteen carriers lofted 2,761 sorties in two days: more than a match for Imperial Japan's naval and army air forces.

Next the fast carriers steamed 750 miles south to pound Iwo Jima for three days, supporting the Marines, before returning to Japan. However, Saratoga remained off Iwo, where she was tagged by suiciders and bombs on the 21st, ending her round-the-clock support of the landings. She steamed home to the West Coast for repairs and never returned to combat.

Carrier operations against the home islands resumed on February 25 well offshore—190 miles southeast of Tokyo. The tailhookers launched into bad weather and found it miserable over land. The Japanese barely bothered to contest the effort, and sporadic combats over airfields and the capital resulted in U.S. claims of forty-six shoot-downs against sixteen losses.

Fleet aerologists predicted worsening weather so Mitscher canceled further operations at noon. He hoped to strike Nagoya the next day but roughening seas prevented the force from reaching the intended launch point. Instead, Mitscher aimed for Okinawa, striking opportune targets and conducting photoreconnaissance there on March 1.

If any Japanese had questioned who owned the Pacific Ocean, Task Force 58 operations in the thirty days after February 10 removed all doubt. Mitscher's sortie spanned the North Pacific: from Ulithi up to Honshu waters, south to Iwo Jima, westward to Okinawa, and back again—a track of some 5,000 miles without serious opposition.

March 18

The fast carriers were not long absent from Empire waters. Following a ten-day respite in Ulithi, Task Force 58 sortied on March 14, Tokyo-bound once more. The mission was to keep the pressure on the home islands, and to start paring the remaining strength of the Imperial Navy.

With fifteen flight decks deployed in four task groups, Mitscher had nearly as much airpower to throw at the homeland as he possessed a month before. The main difference was that *Enterprise* was the only remaining night carrier.

On March 18, the Navy pilots targeted forty-five airfields, as it had been impossible to shut down those briefly attacked in February. With their bases largely undisturbed, Japanese fighters rose in strength to oppose the Americans' latest effort at winning air superiority.

Most heavily engaged was *Hornet*'s Fighting 17. The skipper, Lieutenant Commander Marshall Beebe, led his Hellcats into a half-hour brawl around Kanoya, personally claiming five of the twenty-five victories. It was sweet revenge for Marsh Beebe, who had swum away from the escort carrier *Liscombe Bay*, sunk in 1943. He offered a vivid contrast to one of his division leaders, Lieutenant Robert Coats, who also earned ace in a day status, but who could not swim, had the need arisen.

Bennington's marines had a full day. Twenty Corsairs of VMF-112 flew a sweep to Kanoya East, encountering some twenty Zekes at 19,000 feet. With an altitude advantage Major Herman Hansen's pilots knocked down five in their initial pass, almost immediately splashing four more.

By late afternoon the carrier aviators had claimed 126 on the wing, a figure unusually close to the admitted Japanese losses of 110, including thirty-two kamikazes. With the initial goal of establishing air superiority largely accomplished, the next day Mitscher sent his air groups after his prime target: the Imperial Japanese navy.

March 19

Japanese bombers and kamikazes rose with the dawn. Taking advantage of a layer of haze, many eluded the American combat air patrols long enough to inflict serious harm upon Task Force 58.

Early that morning a lone bomber emerged from the overhead blind zone in the group's radar coverage and nosed down, drawing a bead on *Wasp*. The bomb exploded belowdecks, killing 101 sailors. Serious fires erupted where aviation fuel lines were severed, but Captain Oscar "Tex" Weller's well-drilled crew was recovering aircraft less than an hour after being hit.

Far worse damage was inflicted upon *Franklin*. "Big Ben" took two 550-pound bombs from another unobserved attacker descending from the clouds. The results were catastrophic: gushing smoke like a nautical volcano, *Franklin* lay immobile barely fifty miles off Kyushu. In a day-long battle the crew saved the ship, though some 800 men were killed—one in four. She limped to the East Coast to be rebuilt, but never rejoined the fleet.

Previous recon flights to Kure Harbor south of Hiroshima had located the crown jewel in the emperor's naval tiara: battleship *Yamato*, the biggest thing afloat. Therefore, on the 19th, air strikes targeted warships at Kure, Kobe, and the Inland Sea. But first the carriers launched fighters to clear the air over greater Kyushu.

Major Thomas Mobley took sixteen of *Bennington's* marines on a dawn sweep ahead of full-deckload strikes inbound to Kure anchorage, southeast of Hiroshima. The Corsairs had easy pickings the day before, but now they faced the Imperial Navy's elite.

Two of Mobley's pilots noted about twenty fighters above and behind, flying neat four-plane formations. With so many carrier planes airborne, it was impossible to know who was who. The skipper reckoned they were probably friendly but kept an eye on them. Hearing combat on the radio, Mobley turned toward Kure Harbor. The stalkers then saw their chance and they took it.

About twenty bandits hit the marines from port, then maneuvered to box them in. Two Corsairs went down in the first rush and the rest fought to survive.

Probably Japan's most professional aviation unit was the 343rd Naval Air Group, commanded by the legendary Captain Minoru Genda. Best known for his role in planning the Pearl Harbor attack, in December 1944 he had formed the group at Matsuyama on Shikoku with three fighter squadrons and a reconnaissance unit. He recruited a high proportion of veterans, and by March 1945, 20 percent of his fliers were rated as Class A combat pilots.

The "squadron of aces" flew a promising new fighter: Kawanishi's big, robust N1K, called George by the Allies. It was the Zero's antithesis: boxy rather than elegant, strong rather than nimble. With a powerful radial engine, the George was a potent weapon. Fast and rugged, it was capable of nearly 370 mph, bearing four 20mm cannon.

In its combat debut the 343rd had scrambled from its Shikoku base, bordering the Inland Sea. Fifty Georges took off in three squadrons.

Amid the confusion the Americans reported four enemy aircraft types but they were all Georges. They were led by Lieutenant Naoshi Kanno, a squadron commander and recklessly aggressive ace.

Contrary to the bunch that Major Hansen's squadron had shot up previously, the newcomers were aggressive and capable. They maintained section integrity and, unlike many Japanese, these could shoot. Mobley limped out of the fight with 20mm hits in his cockpit. The next senior pilot was Captain William A. Cantrel, an excellent aviator who had seen only one Japanese plane during his Guadalcanal tour. Now he had a skyful. In a two-minute dogfight the Oregonian shot two Georges but the Japanese scored, too. Cantrel's Corsair was hit and he sustained a painful foot wound. Yet he regrouped eight of his pilots, mostly flying damaged aircraft, and shepherded them seaward. In the running battle he engaged two more bandits and hit both, driving them off his cripples. One Corsair succumbed to battle damage near the destroyer screen, where the pilot bailed out. The others limped back to *Bennington* but three were jettisoned, too badly damaged to repair. Cantrell climbed out of his plane and collapsed from loss of blood, eventually receiving a well-deserved Navy Cross.

The marines were credited with nine kills but lost six F4Us and two pilots. It was a poor bargain: actually Kanno's "Elite Guard" squadron lost three planes on the mission to other causes. Mobley concluded that Kanno's men were "the cream of the Jap air forces."

After beating up on *Bennington*'s Corsairs, Kanno turned for Matsuyama, nursing a damaged aircraft. But he clashed with some *Yorktown* Hellcats intending to strafe his field. Though missing part of one aileron, the ever-aggressive Kanno bent his throttle toward the Americans. He fired at the lead F6F, missed and overshot. Lieutenant Bert Eckard jockeyed stick and rudder and pressed the trigger. He did not miss.

Kanno's George erupted in flames. He steered away from land and went over the side, barely in time to pull his ripcord. He landed injured but safe.

Meanwhile, twenty Japanese fighters from Ozuki and other army fields scrambled to join the growing melee. It was a come-as-you-are event with mixed units and aircraft types, including a fast Nakajima Frank flown by one-eyed transport pilot Sergeant Yukio Shimokawa.

They tangled with a like number of *Hornet* Hellcats, and from there it turned to hash. The Oscars and Franks overlapped the combat area with some of Genda's Georges, resulting in a widespread, even more confusing, dogfight.

Lieutenant Yoshishige Hayashi's 407th "Heavenly Punishment" squadron clashed with *Essex*'s new fighter outfit. VF-83 shot up Matsuyama, firing rockets into decoy targets—wrecked aircraft staked out to soak up American ordnance. The Hellcats did well against the defenders, claiming six and probably downing as many.

Additionally, elements of the 407th and 701st "Imperial Restoration Unit" engaged in a grueling twenty-five-minute fight with *Hornet*'s fighter-bombers. Six Hellcats never returned; one ditched and another was jettisoned with severe damage. Three VBF-17 pilots died and three were captured. Conversely, four of Genda's fliers were killed, including Lieutenant (jg) Yukihiro Watanabe, who had forecast his death three days earlier.

The Japanese survivors returned to Matsuyama by mid-afternoon, some having flown twice. When Captain Genda tallied the squadron reports he announced a day's bag of fifty-two Americans. The star was Kanno's section leader, Chief Petty Officer Katsue Kato. He laid claim to nine kills, all accredited by headquarters. Actual American losses in air combat were fourteen, including those damaged beyond repair.

In turn, the carrier pilots reported sixty-three kills during the multifaceted Kure mission. Genda's wing lost fifteen Georges and a recon plane while other units lost nine more. Thus, the air battle was resolved twenty-five to fourteen in favor of the attackers, but the margin was nowhere as lopsided as either side believed.

Attacks on Kure Harbor

While the air battles wound down to their violent conclusions, Task Force 58 lofted 158 Helldivers and Avengers at Kure Harbor, escorted by 163 Hellcats and Corsairs. It was a massive enterprise: 321 planes, or nearly as many as the Imperial Navy had put over Pearl Harbor.

Bunker Hill's Commander George M. Ottinger was strike coordinator for the main attack, which offered a variety of targets. The mission was briefed to hit Kure's fuel storage tanks and other installations, but Ottinger had authority to redirect squadrons to more lucrative targets.

Task force intelligence officers had warned of 160 heavy-caliber AA guns in the target area and hundreds of smaller weapons. It was no exaggeration. As *Bunker Hill's* fliers approached Kure, the sky erupted in a mottled kaleidoscope of flak bursts: the usual black amid red, yellow, green, and even purple. The variety represented different batteries using specific colors to spot their bursts.

Flying ahead of the other Americans, Ottinger surveyed the sprawling harbor. When he saw warships anchored, he radioed new instructions: half of the bombers were to attack the men-o'-war. But moments later, when he discerned the full picture, he ordered all Helldivers and Avengers to hit the biggest ships. It was a Navy bomber's paradise: seventeen combatants, including three battleships and four carriers.

"Bunky" Ottinger's crews took pride of place as the first strikers over the target, picking the juiciest ships for themselves. Skipper of Bombing Squadron 84 was Lieutenant Commander John P. Conn, who identified a Kongo class battleship, undoubtedly the well-traveled *Haruna*. But a flak hit damaged his electrical system, preventing him from releasing his bombs. He pulled off, seeking another target.

Conn's place was taken by Lieutenant (jg) John D. Welsh, who dropped a half-tonner and two 250-pounders. But somewhere in the churning cauldron of flak bursts his SB2C Helldiver sustained a crippling hit. He survived as a prisoner but his gunner drowned. Another Bombing 84 plane ditched with battle damage.

The Corsairs packed a significant ordnance load including aerial rockets. Major Herbert Long was a veteran of the Solomons campaign and had notched his seventh kill the day before. Now he intended to put the Corsair's offensive potential to good use against a ship steaming in Kure Bay. He recalled, "I was armed with only five HVARs [high-velocity aerial rockets] and fired them at what I thought to be a small freighter." Only after his combat film was analyzed did he learn that he had attacked the light carrier *Ryuho*, which had been damaged in the Doolittle Raid. The chagrined marine said, "Needless to say, I paid closer attention during subsequent ship recognition classes."

"Trigger" Long's aim was good. In concert with other pilots, he inflicted two rocket and three bomb hits on the carrier. The flight deck bulged upward and a boiler room flooded, causing the ship to settle partway on the bottom. Twenty of the crew were killed, and *Ryuho* never left port again.

Other air groups piled in, eagerly choosing prestigious targets. For instance, *Hornet*'s Avenger squadron launched twelve planes and reported fourteen bomb hits on eight ships.

The World War I battleships *Ise* and *Hyuga*, twin sisters of 35,000 tons, had been modified with stern aircraft decks in 1943 but now lacked fuel, aircraft, and aircrews. Orbiting Kure Harbor, *Wasp*'s Air Group 86 selected *Hyuga*. Now immobilized and painted shades of gray and green, the hermaphrodite warship was rocked by several near misses but only hit once: a bomb exploded port-side above a boiler room, killing about forty crewmen. Her sister, *Ise*, bore a garish scheme of two shades of green with yellow, gray, and rusty splotches. Her exotic colors failed to hide her; she was hit by two bombs.

The third battlewagon, *Haruna*, was anchored in the roadstead. She merely suffered a grazing hit to starboard.

Predictably, the few remaining carriers attracted considerable attention. Launched only five months before, the 17,000-ton *Katsuragi* took a hit in the starboard bow that blew a five-foot hole in the plating and upper deck. Even worse, a near miss opened the hull, flooding one compartment and a fuel tank. Her older sister, *Amagi*, had been commissioned in August 1944 but never left home waters. A bomb struck the flight deck edge aft while her gunners cheerfully claimed a dozen planes downed.

The escort carrier *Kaiyo* spent much of her career in the periscopes of American submarines, surviving at least seven encounters while escorting convoys in 1944. At Kure U.S. aircraft made up the deficit, striking her port-side engine room and starting a fire. The carrier listed to port, and when the flooding reached the dangerous stage she was towed to shallow water to prevent capsizing.

Among the heaviest hit was light cruiser *Oyodo*, which absorbed three bombs. She sustained flooding and was towed to Eta Jima, where she was beached. Subsequently she spent three weeks in dry dock.

Meanwhile, fliers gawked at the 64,000-ton battleship *Yamato*. Underway in the Inland Sea, she drew the attention of *Intrepid*'s air group. She sustained damage from a hit on the bridge by a Bombing 10 Helldiver, likely flown by Lieutenant (jg) James B. Davidson. Though his SB2C was hit early in his dive, he pushed through bursting flak from ships and shore to score an observed hit by one of his three bombs.

While the Americans only inflicted moderate damage, Kure's flak took a toll of the attackers: eleven Helldivers and two Avengers. But it was far less than most U.S. Navy officers had expected.

Bunky Ottinger was among three dozen aviators awarded Navy Crosses for March 19 actions but he never pinned it on. Five days later he was killed off Okinawa, one of thirty-one members of the Annapolis class of '32 who died in the war.

While disengaging from the home islands the carriers cast their patented aerial net overland to keep the enemy on the defensive. In the wake of the *Franklin* disaster, "The Big Blue Blanket" largely did its job, as only one destroyer sustained a bomb hit.

Two days' claims of 223 enemies downed contrasted with forty-four acknowledged by the Imperial Navy and an unknown number of Japanese army planes. Moreover, the U.S. figure of some 250 aircraft destroyed on the ground was clearly optimistic, but that was beside the point. The aviators had driven home their message, not only to Tokyo but to cynics in navies and air forces around the globe. Powerful, extremely competent carrier groups had completely dominated Japan's coastal waters and begun the process of clearing the enemy's skies of meaningful defense.

However, there was room for criticism. Despite the claims for hits on major warships, the carrier pilots had done poorly. Though enjoying air superiority, they inflicted minimal damage on the major combatants: merely five hits on four battleships, three of which were immobile. A carrier and a light cruiser were badly damaged. In contrast, at Pearl Harbor the Imperial Navy's elite airmen had destroyed two battleships and a target vessel, and severely damaged six more warships. In any case, Mitscher's aircrews knew two things: they could do better, and they would be back.

The Fifth Fleet withdrew from home waters to begin pre-invasion strikes against Okinawa on March 23. But despite the obligation to support the amphibious forces, the fast carriers returned to the Japanese homeland as opportunity permitted. Brief visits on March 28–29 put more tailhookers over southern Kyushu, meeting almost no opposition.

Action shifted seaward on April 7, about 100 miles offshore. The aviators could hardly believe their good fortune when the Imperial Navy made its last sortie, sending the super-battleship *Yamato* on a one-way trip to Okinawa, hoping to disrupt the U.S. landings. Swarmed by Mitscher's squadrons, she was destroyed in a huge explosion resembling a small nuclear mushroom cloud. Her escorting light cruiser and four of eight destroyers also sank beneath the weight of American bombs and torpedoes.

The fast carriers continued dominating Japanese airspace but could not prevent some kamikazes from getting airborne. Shuttling task groups between Okinawa and Japan, Mitscher kept his fliers occupied in both arenas, and one day's respite could lead to the next day's deluge. On April 15, Hellcats tallied just twenty-seven shootdowns over southern Kyushu, but on the 16th the kamikazes came out in force. Task force fighters claimed 157 kills and still could not prevent the suiciders from mauling *Intrepid* so severely that she could not be repaired for nearly four months.

Increasingly, Task Force 58 realized that it needed to sit on the kamikaze nests around the clock to prevent the lethal eggs from hatching. Therefore, beginning May 12, Rear Admiral Ted Sherman's and Rear Admiral J. J. "Jocko" Clark's task groups put the home islands of Kyushu and Shikoku in their sights. Two days and nights of counter–air operations began with *Enterprise*'s Air Group 90 launching nocturnal patrols to keep Japanese night fliers grounded. Big, gregarious Commander William I. Martin was the Navy's senior night-flying aviator and an innovative torpedo squadron skipper. Now, with a dedicated night fighter and bomber squadron in his experienced hands, he set out to show what his fliers could accomplish in dominating Japan's nocturnal skies.

In the predawn hours of the 12th, a flock of Japanese recon planes was mauled by Martin's radar-equipped Hellcats, which destroyed eight without loss. Less than twenty-four hours later *Essex*'s detachment of night fighters preceded the daylight launch and dropped three more, keeping the pressure on Japanese fliers, who paid an increasing cost for probing the seams of American radar coverage. Nevertheless, some willingly paid the price. That month the kamikazes knocked *Enterprise* and *Bunker Hill* out of the war but they were the last fast carriers removed from the lineup.

On May 27, the Third Fleet leadership team of William Halsey and John McCain relieved Fifth Fleet's Spruance and Mitscher. Okinawa was declared secure three weeks later, clearing the fast carriers for more work in the home islands, but by then Japan had nearly ceded its homeland airspace. Carrier pilots claimed 267 shootdowns in May, then merely twenty in June. Some second- and third-cruise aviators had fine-tuned their risk-benefit assessments. Said one double ace, "You began to realize that the war wasn't going to end any sooner if you chased some Jap inland."

Nevertheless, America owned Japanese skies that summer, as the B-29s and carrier-based airpower heralded America as an invincible creature of the sea and the sky. But U.S. air supremacy boded ill for the future. Tokyo's plan was obvious: Japan was hoarding its strength for the coming invasion.

CHAPTER FIVE

Firestorm

T HE CLOCK WAS running in February 1945, and Curtis LeMay counted each hour.

Hap Arnold had ordered XXI Bomber Command to support the Navy's invasion of Okinawa, slated for April 1. That meant the B-29s would be diverted from their primary mission of destroying Japanese industry in order to beat down the Kyushu airfields within range of American ships off Okinawa. Admiral Nimitz's immense naval forces would draw kamikazes like suicidal bees to nautical honey, and with the invasion beaches barely 400 miles from southern Japan, the threat was obvious.

LeMay was not enthused about the interruption of strategic operations but he saw the practical necessity of the interdiction mission. Therefore, he accelerated his plan to burn Japan to the ground. He could pursue that goal until the end of March.

Meanwhile, the U.S. Marine Corps presented the Army Air Forces with a precious gift that saved lives and aircraft. It was the sulfurous island of Iwo Jima, midway between Guam and Tokyo.

For many bomber crews, Iwo was a godsend. The first B-29 had landed there in early March, low on fuel. A small AAF support unit arrived soon thereafter, anticipating heavy use of the newly won field by homeward-bound bombers. The servicing and repair crews could hardly have known the task they set themselves. On one day in June more than 100 Superfortresses set down on Iwo, and at war's end the original detachment had grown to nearly 2,000 men.

Correspondent Robert Sherrod interviewed some B-29 crews and found that the Army fliers expressed heartfelt gratitude to the marines. Eventually one pilot landed on Iwo Jima five times in eleven missions. Another said, "Whenever I land on this island, I thank God and the men who fought for it."

Back in the Marianas, preparations continued for the upcoming blitz against Japanese cities. As with every LeMay enterprise, the bedrock was training. He huddled with his wing commanders and directed them to get their groups proficient in night bombing from unusually low altitudes—as low as 5,000 feet. The tactic ran contrary to AAF doctrine, but Curt LeMay was already known for professional heresy. He had proven that in Europe, where he demonstrated that evasive action in the bomb run only spoiled accuracy and required repeat missions to destroy a target.

LeMay would have preferred to have his four China groups available for the upcoming maximum effort, but the 58th Wing would not arrive until April and May. Therefore, the command's existing twelve groups practiced forming up and concentrating over a target in minimum time to overwhelm the defenders. LeMay called it "compressibility." Analyzing the tactical problems, he told his commanders, "We must seek maximum compressibility to confuse and saturate Japanese defenses." That meant putting as many bombers across the target as possible, not only to inflict maximum damage but to reduce exposure of aircrews to flak and fighters.

LeMay went even further than adopting unorthodox tactics. Except for the tail guns, most .50 calibers were removed from B-29s to save weight. Similarly, without having to climb to 25,000 or 30,000 feet, less fuel was required, with less strain (and therefore less maintenance) on the finicky R-3350 engines. All those factors translated into extra ordnance.

Flying in the face of airpower orthodoxy, the bomber chief impressed his subordinates with his almost eerie outward calm. But despite LeMay's stoicism, others entertained serious doubts. Recalled a 73rd Bomb Wing officer, "For almost a week most of us wondered if we were planning the greatest disaster in aviation history."

The planning behind major bombing missions involved multiple factors, often interdependent. Timing was a major challenge, especially given the geographic distribution of the bomber bases (Guam to Tinian to Saipan was 140 miles). Furthermore, barely one B-29 could take off per minute from each runway. That translated to a 300-plane bomber stream some 400 miles long, nose to tail.

Rising from their far-flung roosts, the silvery bombers spread an aerial net over the Central Pacific. Forming up by squadrons, groups, and wings, they droned through the humid atmosphere, striving to arrive at a point in time and space where each B-29 was properly positioned for its 1,500-mile-run to Japan. In order to provide the maximum concentration of force over the target, every Superfortress needed precise navigation and skilled flying for optimum results.

Between scheduled missions to Japan, the 73rd, 313th, and newly arrived 314th Wing worked hard in February, learning more about joining up, flying, and bombing at night. The building blocks of success were formed at the most basic level: eleven men per bomber, each having mastered his own specialty and fitting into the larger entity of the crew.

The 20th Air Force planned a ten-day fire blitz, using every incendiary in the Marianas and all that the Navy could deliver in that time. In early March LeMay would start with Tokyo and work his way down the list: Kobe, Nagoya, and Osaka. The logisticians told him that no replacement incendiaries would be available before the second week in April.

The effort leading up to the Tokyo raid was immense. Orchestrating the work of as many men as a light armored division was LeMay's operations officer, Colonel John Montgomery. In the day and a half before takeoff, some 13,000 men on three Pacific islands toiled almost without stop. Mechanics brought each plane's four engines to the best possible condition. By hand or by truck, ordnancemen hauled bomb bodies from storage dumps to the hardstands where "bomb builders" attached tail fins, hoisted the weapons into the cavernous bomb bays, and inserted fuses. Fuel trucks drove from plane to plane, filling their tanks with 100/130-octane gasoline. According to Montgomery, preparing a combat wing for a maximum effort was "a helluva lot worse than planning a maintenance schedule for an airline."

That was an understatement. Maintenance was the axle upon which operations turned because it dictated the number of planes airworthy for each mission. Typically, XXI Bomber Command's in-commission rate hovered around 60 percent, meaning two in five Superfortresses were unavailable. But for the Tokyo strike Montgomery drove and inspired his "wrench benders" to a superlative effort, finally preparing 83 percent of the command's B-29s for the forthcoming fire raid. In such numbers lay the secret of America's success in the Pacific air war. They also reflected the ethos of industry that would drive the country forward into the booming postwar era.

Finally the preparations were complete after thirty-six hours of nonstop toil. Blitz Week began with a green flare arcing into the moist Marianas air on Friday afternoon, March 9. LeMay and his chief of staff, Brigadier General August Kissner, watched Brigadier General Tommy Power lead the new 314th Wing off Guam's North Field. The first bombers rolled down the Guam runways at 5:36, followed by scores of others at fifty-second intervals.

Then, as the rain-wet vegetation slowly dried in the tropic air, Curtis LeMay settled down for his longest night of the war.

Playing with Fire

What is the best way to incinerate a city?

That question absorbed Allied military and scientific planners throughout the Second World War.

When the Royal Air Force discovered in 1939–40 that daylight bombing incurred crippling losses, RAF Bomber Command switched to night attacks. But finding a blacked-out city posed serious navigation problems; bombing accurately with explosive ordnance was equally difficult. Eventually the British settled on massive "area attacks"—a euphemism for carpet bombing—that produced spectacular results if a firestorm could be created. Though often condemned as terror bombing, in truth area attacks represented what could be reliably achieved with 1940s technology.

At first the Americans did hardly better, even in daylight. In 1942 then Colonel Curtis LeMay examined post-strike photographs and, counting bomb craters, found that the 8th Air Force could not account for half the ordnance it dropped. He did much to improve AAF bombing performance but Germany was one thing—Japan quite another. Incendiary raids on European cities and factories often produced marginal results owing to steel and concrete construction. Japanese cities, however, were mainly built of wood. American planners began seeking efficient means of setting Japan afire.

Probably the most innovative concept for incinerating Japan was the bat bomb. Lytle Adams, a Pennsylvania dentist, had been impressed with bats he saw in New Mexico caverns and wrote President Roosevelt in January 1942. Since bats can carry more than their own weight, Dr. Adams opined that small incendiary devices could be attached to hordes of the flying rodents, which, when released in cluster bombs over Japanese cities, would roost in rafters until the weapons ignited. Though promising, the project was canceled when some armed bats escaped at an Army airfield in New Mexico and burned the test facility to the ground.

In order to determine the best way to destroy Japanese cities, the AAF constructed buildings to Japanese standards, then tested various methods against them. A vast facility with four such ranges— "Little Tokyos"—was established at Eglin Field, Florida. Subjected to different combinations of bombs, the results were studied by ordnance experts. The fruit of the exercise was a number of terrible but important revelations. Though the standard 500-pound demolition bomb could level a house, most of the damage was inflicted by blast, leaving the surrounding area relatively untouched. But incendiaries not only destroyed what they hit—they "kept on giving" as fires increased and spread. The most effective incendiary weapon was called napalm.

Napalm was developed by Harvard chemists working under Dr. Louis Fieser, who had produced blood-clotting agents and the first synthesis of vitamin K. In 1943 his team beat industrial experts from DuPont and Standard Oil to produce an effective firebomb. The Ivy Leaguers used aluminum salts of naphthenic and palmitic acids to produce a thickening agent for gasoline. In the proper ratio, it had the consistency of applesauce and clung to whatever it touched, burning with hellish intensity. Produced by Dow Chemical, napalm was used in flamethrowers and bombs, especially in the Pacific Theater where heavy foliage concealed Japanese positions.

The chief means of raining fire upon Japan was the M69 lightweight incendiary bomb, which released napalm on impact. However, when dropped from 30,000 feet in loose packets, the six-pound weapons were strewn over miles of terrain, far from the intended target. But an "aimable cluster" (with superior ballistics), usually containing thirty-eight M69s in a finned casing, provided reasonable accuracy. Typically the cluster broke apart at 2,000 feet, spewing its submunitions over a desirable area. The ultimate M69 was the X model, which combined blast and fragmentation effects in addition to flame, either killing or deterring firemen in the immediate area.

Ordnance engineers also produced a heavier firebomb. Using the same casing as the M69, the M74 dispensed with tail fins or streamers. Its "three-way" fuses detonated whether the bomb landed on its nose, tail, or side. Upon igniting, the incendiary bombs spewed a burning stream of jellied gasoline at least 180 feet with enough momentum to penetrate typical Japanese structures.

The third incendiary weapon loaded into B-29 bomb bays was the M76, evolved from the M47 that Doolittle's Raiders had used. Weighing 500 pounds, the '76 was called the "block burner" because it delivered a much larger amount of napalm and ignited bigger, more visible, fires. Therefore, M76s frequently were dropped by pathfinders who marked target areas for nocturnal B-29s.

Among those urging wider use of incendiaries against Japan were both military leaders and civilian advisers. None was so forthcoming as Arnold's deputy, Lieutenant General Ira Eaker, when he said, "It made a lot of sense to kill skilled workers by burning whole areas."

However, some airmen were reluctant to endorse incendiaries, though apparently more for practical than ethical reasons. After all, until 1943 the U.S. military had almost no experience with such weapons. Among the most insistent advocates of fire raids was Horatio Bond, chief engineer of the National Fire Protection Association and a military adviser. After the war he recalled, "it was necessary for those of us familiar with fire destruction to keep a constant pressure on the air force and their scientific advisors to get on with the business of exploiting fire attack to bring about the end of the war."

Another influence was William M. McGovern, a member of the Office of Strategic Services intelligence agency. Having observed Japanese at home and in China, he declared, "The panic side of the Japanese is amazing," alluding to what he called "internal panic." Nothing so incited that panic as fire, "one of the great things they are terrified at from childhood."

Certainly McGovern made a strong case, and not only for Japan. The primal dread of rampant flames arose from deep within the human psyche, sowing something far beyond fear: widespread panic rooted in atavistic terror. The result could become the headlong rush of a city's population to escape the inescapable, only compounding the death toll as people were trampled in the hundreds or even thousands.

In the twenty-first century, when any violence inflicted against civilians by a nation-state is widely condemned as immoral, the norms of 1940s warfare may appear horrifically callous at best. Certainly the military engineers who designed firebombs did not consider themselves immoral, nor did the civilians who manufactured them. Rather, they were driven by wartime patriotism melded with resignation to the immediate task at hand.

Perhaps lost in the argument is the contemporary certainty that the Second World War could not be ended without destroying the enemy's ability (versus his will) to sustain the violence. As noted in Chapter One, bombing has never broken the morale of an entire nation, but in the 1940s the concept was too new to be evident.

The first firestorm had been inflicted upon Coventry during the German Blitz against England in November 1940. An industrial-munitions center, the medieval city was targeted by nearly 450 Luftwaffe bombers that rained fifty-six tons of incendiaries (30,000 firebombs) and more than 500 tons of explosives in an all-night deluge. As many as 200 small fires grew into one huge, raging inferno that destroyed or damaged about three-quarters of the city's factories, leaving some 550 people dead. It was reckoned a success by the Luftwaffe, but a modest one compared to the firestorms that followed.

Owing to doctrinal and technical concerns, British retaliation was two and a half years in the making. But in July 1943, the Royal Air Force delivered many Britons' heartfelt sentiment: "Give it them back." More than 720 bombers set Hamburg ablaze, killing an estimated 45,000 people. In war's ghastly ledger, the mere numbers told the progress of aerial destruction. Using Coventry as a baseline, the Germans killed barely one Briton per bomber, whereas at Hamburg the RAF killed sixty-two Germans per sortie. Subsequently Kassel, Darmstadt, Braunschweig, and Heilbronn were scoured in fire raids through the end of 1944.

Then came Dresden. In three days of February 1945, the city was savaged in an Anglo-American night-and-day strike intended to destroy German transport and support a Soviet offensive, but critics saw the operation as terror bombing. Some 1,300 8th Air Force and RAF bombers hammered the city with almost 4,000 tons of ordnance, igniting a firestorm that left at least 25,000 dead.

Ten nights later 700 British bombers burned down 83 percent of Pforzheim, killing one-quarter of the population, some 17,000 people. The result became a matter of pride among some bombardment professionals who appreciated the extremely high ratio of area burned and the depopulation of most of the city.

It is uncertain to what extent XXI Bomber Command in the Marianas knew of the recent fire raids in Germany. As a close student of his craft, LeMay was unlikely to have lacked some preliminary information on the events half a world away. Certainly the mechanics of generating a man-made firestorm were well understood in 20th Air Force, especially given the volatile nature of Japanese cities. The challenge to air commanders was timing: placing a maximum number of aircraft over the target, compressed as closely as possible to overwhelm the defenses. Simultaneously, optimum atmospheric conditions were needed: a dry season with high winds to fan the flames and spread burning embers beyond the bomb zone.

Those conditions were met over Tokyo on the night of March 9–10, 1945.

Civil Defense

Humans are supreme procrastinators, and no better example exists than in the near universal indifference to the threat of bombing. Despite months, years, or even decades of awareness, no capital city was prepared for enemy air attack in the Second World War. London, within easy range of France, waited until the last minute to begin adding more firemen, standardizing equipment, and refining procedures. Britain only consolidated the national auxiliary fire service with local organizations in 1941. That same year the Berlin Feuerschutzpolizei had fewer than 2,000 firemen, apparently owing to Hermann Göring's boast that Reich airspace would remain inviolate.

Despite the European examples, Japan failed to heed the obvious lessons. Once cities began burning, the nation's near total lack of civil defense would have generated a political firestorm in most other nations. Instead, Japan's population had no option but to

Admirals Chester W. Nimitz (left) and
William F. Halsey, key players in the
Doolittle Raid against Japan. Nimitz
approved the joint Army-Navy operation,
and Halsey commanded the two-carrier
task force that carried it out.

Lieutenant Colonel James H. Doolittle (center left) and USS *Hornet*'s Captain
Marc A. Mitscher with other Raiders prior to bombing Japan, April 1942.

A B-25 takes off from the *Hornet*, headed for Tokyo and environs, April 18,
1942. All sixteen bombers safely got off the deck, but fifteen were lost to fuel
exhaustion over the China coast. The other landed in Russia.

4

General Henry H. Arnold (left) of the Army Air Forces and Admiral Chester W. Nimitz, commanding the U.S. Pacific Fleet. They oversaw grand strategy in the air campaign against Japan, not always in full accord but with unmistakable results.

5

Army engineers and Navy Seabees literally reshaped the earth to provide level ground for airfields in China and the Mariana Islands. Heavy equipment was used to remove huge boulders and clear enough space for runways to accommodate B-29s.

6

Rock crushers were used by aviation engineers to provide the base material for runways that would support heavy bombers. The engineers often set up their equipment within days of initial landings on Japanese-occupied islands.

Two of the leading players in the strategic bombing of Japan. Major General Curtis E. LeMay (left) consults with Brigadier General Haywood Hansell on Guam in early 1945. LeMay relieved Hansell, who had conducted initial B-29 operations from the Marianas.

Three B-29s in formation over Kure Arsenal, a major target complex on the Inland Sea. One of the largest naval shipyards in Japan, it was repeatedly attacked by U.S. aircraft in 1945.

The bomb bay view of the war as ordnance falls toward its target, Osaka's port facilities and warehouses. The city was attacked numerous times, resulting in 35 percent of the urban-industrial area being destroyed.

The cockpit view of the war. Superfortresses approach a target at Kobe that has already been struck, sending a cloud of smoke thousands of feet into the air. More than half the city was razed during B-29 missions.

Air-sea rescue received a high priority in the Marianas bomber command. A crew from a downed B-29 is rescued from the ocean and transported from a destroyer to a seaplane tender.

Lieutenant Isamu Kashiide examines the wreckage of a Superfortress he shot down over Tokyo. He claimed seven B-29s to become recognized as one of the leading B-29 slayers.

12

13

Eight of twelve men in Major Sam Bakshas's crew perished in this crash on March 10, 1945; the others died in captivity. Hidesaburo Kusame, a child at the time, later erected a large monument at the site.

14

A Japanese cameraman caught the last moments of this Superfortress descending on fire, one of some 400 lost on combat missions in 1944–45.

Admiral William F. Halsey (left) and Vice Admiral John S. McCain, who led the fast carriers. Halsey's Third Fleet included McCain's Task Force 38, which conducted most of the U.S. Navy air operations over Japan from May through August 1945.

16

Namesake of the ship that launched the Doolittle Raiders in 1942, the new *Hornet* steamed to Japan's shores three years later, part of the mightiest carrier fleet of all time—Task Force 38/58 under Vice Admirals Mitscher and McCain.

17

The Fast Carrier Task Force at Ulithi Atoll, 1,300 miles south of Japan. The flattops are anchored in what sailors called "Murderers' Row," awaiting departure for the initial series of U.S. Navy attacks on the home islands.

Hellcat fighters prepare to launch from USS *Randolph*, one of sixteen flat-tops engaged in the first carrier raids against the Japanese home islands in February 1945.

Kure's large harbor shielded most of the remaining Japanese fleet in July 1945. Carrier aircraft struck the facility repeatedly that month, sinking or neutralizing several warships but sustaining heavy losses in the process.

The new aircraft carrier HMS *Indefatigable* transiting the Suez Canal en route to joining the British Pacific Fleet in late 1944. She operated with the Royal Navy's task force with the U.S. 5th and 3rd Fleets from March to August 1945.

The Royal Navy relied heavily upon American aircraft such as the Grumman Hellcat, as sailors relax aboard a Pacific Fleet carrier in 1945. Note the nonstandard roundel with white center, rather than Britain's usual red center, to avoid confusion with Japanese markings.

"Two navies separated by a common language" explained the differing terminologies of the U.S. and Royal Navies. This Fleet Air Arm "batsman" served the same purpose as American landing signal officers, but during joint operations off Japan, each service mostly continued using its own signals and terms.

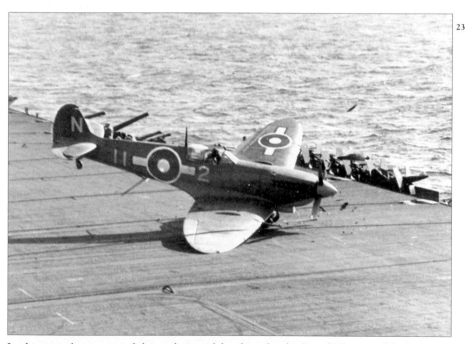

Lacking modern carrier fighters designed for the role, the Royal Navy modified RAF aircraft such as the Supermarine Spitfire, resulting in "navalised" seagoing versions. The Seafire possessed excellent performance but, as shown aboard HMS *Implacable*, often lacked the ruggedness to withstand the rigors typical of flight-deck operations.

Iwo Jima from the south. Five miles long and less than three wide, the island was conquered at the expense of 6,000 American lives. Few of the 20,000 Japanese defenders survived. Halfway between the Marianas and Japan, Iwo was the only possible base for U.S. fighters to escort B-29s.

The 46th Fighter Squadron's blue-nosed Mustangs warming up for a mission to Japan. The pierced steel planking was necessary because of Iwo Jima's ashy surface.

A silent testament to courage. The driver of this grader drove into a burning fighter on Iwo Jima to clear the wreckage off the runway so that airborne pilots could land.

A crashed Superfortress burns on Iwo Jima, narrowly missing a squadron of Mustangs parked alongside the runway.

Brig. Gen. Mickey Moore (center) hears from two P-51 pilots just returned from Iwo Jima's first escort mission to Japan. Captains Harry Crim and DeWitt Spain were flight leaders on the mission of April 7, 1945.

On August 9, 1945, Okinawa-based B-25s attacked the Japanese aircraft carrier *Kaiyo* moored in Beppu Bay, Kyushu. The lead bomber was shot down with loss of the entire crew. This sequence shows the B-25 crash, with the camouflaged carrier in the upper left background.

29

33

Dr. Robert Oppenheimer, director of the atomic research and development program at Los Alamos, New Mexico, 1943–1945. His team of physicists and scientists produced the world's first nuclear weapons in barely two years.

34

Members of the Los Alamos brain trust. Left to right: Ernest O. Lawrence (1939 Nobel for the cyclotron); Italian Enrico Fermi (1938 Nobel for research on radioactivity); and Austrian-born Isidor I. Rabi (1944 Nobel for Physics).

The B-29 *Enola Gay* preparing to load "Little Boy," the uranium bomb dropped on Hiroshima on August 6, 1945. The aircraft is being backed over the loading pit where the weapon will be raised into the bomb bay.

Destined for Nagasaki, the plutonium bomb called "Fat Man" on its cart prior to loading in the B-29 *Bocks Car*. The 10,200-pound weapon yielded about 20 kilotons of explosive power, considerably more than the Hiroshima bomb.

Nagasaki on August 9, 1945. The distinctive mushroom cloud obscures much of the city, largely destroyed in the second atomic attack ever undertaken. Faced with such massive destruction, Japan capitulated six days later.

The gateway of a Shinto shrine is one of the few structures left standing after the B-29 *Bocks Car* delivered a plutonium bomb on Nagasaki.

endure the genuine conflagrations that winged their way north from the Marianas.

As was often the case in Japan, civil defense lacked central command. Control was split between a national organization in Tokyo and those nominally at the prefecture level but actually run by community associations. The result was inefficiency and duplication of effort.

It needn't have been so, as the national government knew a great deal about catastrophe. In 1923 an 8.3-magnitude earthquake—"the Great Kanto"—destroyed 60 percent of Tokyo and 80 percent of Yokohama, killing as many as 140,000 people. Whipped by winds, widespread fires consumed vast areas, including much of the region's industrial facilities, causing long-term economic effects. Rebuilding took a decade, with lesser but still significant quakes striking the main island of Honshu in 1927 and 1933 that killed 6,000 or more.

Incredibly, twenty-two years after the Great Kanto Earthquake, merely six Japanese cities maintained full-time fire departments; the others relied on volunteers. However, even Tokyo's measures were inadequate. As one historian has written, the Tokyo fire department was driven "by ritual more than science." Dating from the 1880s, the department's formal uniform included a sword, evidence of its founding by an order of medieval knights. While the agency never lacked for Bushido élan—frequently a company's flag-bearer was the first into a burning building—the firemen desperately needed modern equipment.

Tokyo had begun occasional air raid drills circa 1930 but held relatively few until July 1941. However, the latter were likely morale-building efforts to inure the population to prospects for war. In any case, the Ministry of Home Affairs slowly increased the size of existing fire departments and created new ones in selected industrial areas, although still relying upon amateur forces.

But the expansion of civil defense created its own problems. A postwar assessment concluded, "Men were recruited so rapidly that proper training was not possible. Peacetime fire departments were increased from three to five times their normal size. Tokyo's department was enlarged from 2,000 firemen to 8,100 men, including 2,700 junior firemen in 287 stations. An effort was made to increase personnel to 12,500, but the manpower shortage in Japan made it prohibitive."

By contrast, in 1945 the Fire Department of New York was composed of more than 9,000 men. Organized into 365 companies (225 engine, 126 hook-and-ladder, and several rescue, specialist, and support companies), they could access more than 91,000 hydrants throughout the city.

Japanese administrative policy only complicated the situation. As in Germany, in major metropolitan areas the police oversaw fire protection, but the Japanese variant lacked the Nazi advantage of competence. Consequently, Allied analysts deemed Japanese efforts unprofessional because local police were incompetent in firefighting. The situation was compounded by vastly different missions and mind-sets: the police focused on controlling a large population rather than protecting it from external threats of biblical proportions.

While Japan's actual firefighting structure made sense—cities were divided into divisions, battalions, and stations—equipment proved wholly insufficient. Not even the Tokyo department's considerable expansion was adequate. From 280 trucks, carts, and portable pumps in 1943 the capital's inventory grew to 1,117 two years later, as Tokyo received nearly all the wartime production. Excepting a few American-made rigs dating from the 1920s, the 559 domestically produced 450 gallon-per-minute pumps were among the largest in Japan—a fraction of what American rigs could produce. The deficit was taken up by commandeering lesser equipment from outlying towns.

The "large equipment" was laughable, even in high-priority areas. A fire company's typical inventory included a four-pound axe, two twelve-foot ladders, two pike poles, two four-foot crowbars, an eighteen-foot length of one-inch rope, a fifty-foot length of one-and-a-half-inch rope, two smoke masks, three spare nozzles, forty sections of two-and-a-half-inch single-jacketed linen hose, and two hose carts.

Almost any American fireman visiting Japan would have been astonished at the absence of basic gear. One survey noted, "The common
portable fire extinguisher of the CO_2, carbon tetrachloride, foam,
and water pump can types were not used by Japanese firemen."

In one of the most urbanized nations on earth there were four
aerial ladders: three in Tokyo and one in Kyoto. But in 1945 only
one of Tokyo's trucks was operational, a German-built eighty-five-
foot extension. Their 500-gpm pumps were therefore largely useless.

As an island nation, Japan should have led the world in marine
fire protection. But in 1942, Tokyo had merely three small pumper
boats to cover perhaps 100 miles of waterfront, canals, and rivers. By
1945, eight "navy-type patrol boats" had been obtained, featuring
500-gpm pumps. The boats produced the largest water streams in the
country, but still barely one inch wide. In vivid contrast, at the same
time New York City operated ten boats, most capable of 7,000 gpm
and two producing 18,000 and 20,000 gpm.

Even where fire trucks were available, many were idle. A shortage
of mechanics and spare parts rendered approximately 20 percent inoperable during 1944–45. Kyoto may have been the only city with fully
powered equipment, the others relying wholly or largely upon manually operated gear. Moreover, backup equipment was seldom available.

Before the March fire raids, every department save Tokyo's was
limited to two hours of gasoline per engine. It was a penurious policy:
during the March 14 attack on Osaka, forty-eight pieces of equipment burned where they stood, out of fuel. Thereafter a five-hour
supply was approved for the remaining pumpers. Even then, fuel
drums were seldom delivered where needed in the smoke and confusion of a major conflagration.

No Shelter

Given Japan's inability to defend its airspace, and the universal inef-
fectiveness of fire protection, the last resort was air raid shelters. But

there, too, the government failed on a colossal scale. In 1940 an American military attaché in Tokyo noted that the few bomb shelters were "totally inadequate." His report demonstrated how little the Japanese had learned from the hard experience of earthquake-induced fires.

Some official explanations for poor preparations sound disingenuous. Home Affairs Minister Genki Abe reflected, "The reason we had no definite policy of air raid shelter protection . . . is that we did not unduly wish to alarm our citizens concerning the necessity for underground shelters, as we feared it would interfere with normal routine life and have some effect on war production." He conceded that after the late May raids on Tokyo, most residents considered civilian defense "a futile effort." Lacking sufficient steel and concrete for major shelters, a poor substitute was tunnels bored into the sides of large hills.

Meanwhile, in the summer of 1944 Japan began cutting block-wide firebreaks through some urban areas. Tokyo reported 615,000 buildings razed to clear areas for firebreaks, though four times that number were destroyed by bombing. The one advantage was that the wide swaths provided relatively uncluttered escape routes for people who otherwise would have been trapped in congested streets.

There was one notable exception. In late 1942 an air raid shelter was constructed inside the Imperial Palace, and the royal couple spent increasing time there from December 1944, after XXI Bomber Command began operations. However, rather than publicly conceding the need for the all-highest to seek refuge in a bunker, the facility was designated "the library *Obunko.*"

Thus did the subjects of the reclusive *Showa tenno* hope to survive the destruction of their cities and their nation.

Tokyo Aflame

Mission 40 from the Marianas was code-named Meetinghouse. It set such a standard of success that each subsequent fire raid was called "a Meetinghouse."

Of 325 B-29s airborne on March 9, 279 unloaded 1,665 tons on the Tokyo urban area while twenty planes diverted to alternates. LeMay's weight-saving measures worked dramatically well. The fuel saved by stripping guns from most B-29s and cruising at lower altitudes had doubled the February ordnance average to nearly six tons per bomber.

Approaching the Japanese coast beneath a quarter-moon, B-29 crews tugged on flak vests—heavy, cumbersome garments with steel plates that could stop a shell splinter. Some also donned helmets that interfered with earphones, but the airmen were flying into the enemy's most cherished piece of sky at a frighteningly low altitude.

The primary target was a section of downtown Tokyo measuring three by four miles, recalled by historian John Toland as "once the gayest, liveliest area in the Orient." Though wartime shortages had closed most businesses, the area teemed with life: an estimated 750,000 workers crammed into twelve square miles of low-income housing and family-operated factories. It was probably the most densely populated place on earth.

The sirens blared at midnight but evidently few Japanese were concerned. They were accustomed to repeated alerts, mostly annoying false alarms. Furthermore, radio reports only mentioned American aircraft orbiting at Choshi, a port city fifty miles northeast—no immediate threat to the capital.

Choshi was one of the coast-in points for XXI Bomber Command.

The first bombers were pathfinders, sweeping in low and fast over Tokyo, doing nearly 300 miles per hour at 5,000 feet. Their navigators had worked to perfection with an identical time over target of 12:15 A.M. Approaching at right angles to each other, the B-29s' bomb bay doors snapped open and the bombardiers toggled their loads. Bundles of M47 incendiaries spewed into the slipstream, cascading onto the urban congestion that was Tokyo. As the napalm sticks ignited they formed a fiery cross on the ground.

The pathfinders did their work well, marking targets for the following bombardiers. Among the best work was the load that marked the Tokyo Electric Power Company. The firebombs seared the buildings, which were engulfed in flames, providing an almost unmissable aim point.

For trailing bombers, X literally marked the spot. Each group and wing had designated target areas, as mission planners had divided the sprawling city into fire zones to avoid excessive concentration in one locale. Attacking between 4,900 and 9,200 feet, 93 percent of the B-29s struck the briefed urban-industrial area. As LeMay foretold, the defenses were wholly saturated. Searchlights swept their pale white arcs skyward, occasionally illuminating a passing bomber, but seldom long enough for flak gunners to draw a bead.

It was Major Arthur Ray Brashear's tenth mission. The 499th Bomb Group's target was the First Fire Zone between the Ara and Sumida Rivers. His navigator's notes summed up most fliers' reactions to the defenses: "Night incendiary at 5,000 ft. KEE RISTE! Caught in lights for a short time. All kinds of flak, mostly inaccurate. No hits but this one had us scared! No fighters."

Almost half a million M69s cascaded down from the night sky, and wherever they hit they spurted their napalm-filled cheesecloth bags. In a matter of minutes thousands of small fires from the little "fiery pancakes" were swallowing everything they touched, coalescing and swelling into a roaring conflagration unlike anything man had previously inflicted upon man, anywhere on earth, Dresden included.

A Vichy French journalist reported the scene, writing in the present tense common in Europe, "Bright flashes illuminate the sky's shadows, Christmas trees blossoming with flame in the depths of the night, then hurtling downward in zigzagging bouquets of flame, whistling as they fall. Barely 15 minutes after the beginning of the attack, the fire whipped up by the wind starts to rake through the depths of the wooden city."

As the sky over the city became superheated, huge amounts of air were sucked upward through multistory buildings in the "stack effect," draining the cool air from ground level to feed the insatiable stack. As more and more ground air was drawn into the conflagration from further afield, the storm naturally spread of its own predatory accord.

A fully developed firestorm is a horrifically mesmerizing sight. It seems a living, malicious creature that feeds upon itself, generating ever higher winds that whirl cyclonically, breeding updrafts that suck the oxygen out of the atmosphere even while the flames consume the fuel—buildings—that feed the monster's ravenous appetite. Most firestorm victims do not burn to death. Rather, as carbon monoxide quickly reaches lethal levels, people suffocate from lack of oxygen and excessive smoke inhalation.

In Tokyo that night some citizens felt that hell had slipped its nether bounds and raised itself through the earth's crust to feed on the surface. People fled panic-stricken from searing heat amid the demonic roar of flames, the crash of collapsing buildings, and the milling congestion of terrified human beings. Some survivors found themselves suddenly naked, the clothes burned off their bodies, leaving the skin largely intact.

In those frightful hours humans watched things happen on a scale that probably had never been seen. The superheated ambient air boiled the water out of ponds and canals while rains of liquid glass flew, propelled by cyclonic winds. Temperatures reached 1,800 degrees Fahrenheit, melting the frames of emergency vehicles and causing some people to erupt in spontaneous combustion.

With barely 8,000 firemen to cover an area of 213 square miles, decades of Japanese unpreparedness and complacency took their terrible toll. There were insufficient shelters and, perhaps worst of all, too few fire lanes to provide buffers that might prevent one conflagration from spreading into another. But even adequate firebreaks might not have helped, not on that night. The bombers possessed an invincible ally in the form of stiff southeasterly winds that whipped and whirled burning embers from one neighborhood to another. Wherever the fiery brands alit, they spread the flames uncontrollably.

Tokyo's fire department fought a losing battle from the first few minutes. The fire chief spent a horrible night dashing from one area to another, trying to coordinate his insufficient resources. His sedan caught fire twice.

The firemen were gallantly ineffective with their towed water carts and hand pumps—poor substitutes for gasoline-driven trucks, many of which were stalled in the human congestion and, immobilized, melted into the street. Nearly 100 fire trucks were incinerated with 128 firemen and perhaps 500 auxiliaries assigned to help them. Those numbers, pitifully small within the greater catastrophe, further emphasize Tokyo's woeful unpreparedness over the previous three years.

Extension ladders that could have helped suppress fires in multistory buildings were almost nonexistent, and of limited use where power and phone lines formed a barrier that prevented such equipment from extending beyond the overhead latticework.

It was no better in residential areas, where the burden fell upon thousands of pitifully prepared neighborhood associations. Small groups of families swore to uphold government dictates to swat at fires with dampened cloths or sandbags, and vainly doused blazing napalm with buckets of water. Historian Richard Frank attributed much of the massive death toll to the no-retreat policy. He concluded, "The key to survival was to grasp quickly that the situation was hopeless and flee."

Everywhere people were thrown upon their own meager resources. Hidezo Tsuchikura saved his family and himself by climbing into a water tank on a school roof. Though a factory worker, Tsuchikura made a Dantesque comparison. "The whole spectacle with its blinding lights and thundering noise reminded me of the paintings of purgatory—a real inferno out of the depths of hell itself."

Susumu Takahashi, a teenage medical student, watched the spectacle from a neighborhood overlooking the primary target area. His studies had been interrupted by the sirens but he shunned his family's rudimentary shelter to cram for an upcoming test. When the house ignited he gamely tried to beat out the flames but soon realized the futility. Grabbing his texts, he dashed outside. One end of the street appeared a roaring wall of flame so Takahashi ran to his left, passing an immobilized fire engine with limp hoses. Firemen directed people to cross the bridge over the Kanda River, but the path was blocked by more flames. The seventeen-year-old student took responsibility beyond his age, leading a line of stragglers through a gap in the fire-choked street. He leapt charred, fallen trees and phone poles, strewn around "like match sticks." Gasping for breath in the cloying smoke, Susumu Takahashi reached the safety of the concrete bridge—the only structure in sight that had not burned.

Not even the Imperial Bunker was immune. When the firestorm's high winds dropped burning embers onto the emperor's *Obunko*, shrubs and camouflage material were ignited, and palace guards and staff were reduced to subduing the flames with water pails and even tree branches.

Safely underground, Emperor Hirohito and Empress Kojun sat out the attack in their bunker. The empress had observed her forty-second birthday three days previously, and now they had planned on celebrating their grandson's first. Instead, they tasted the acrid outside air that slipped through the filters and vents.

General Tom Power's B-29 had fuel to spare and circled the spreading inferno for ninety minutes, radioing a play-by-play of the growing catastrophe. Because post-strike photos would not be available for a day or more, he had some cartographers onboard to plot the extent of the fires for immediate assessment back at Guam. He noted that it took just thirty minutes for the first bombs to spread into a fully developed conflagration. Actually, it was half that time. On the ground, some witnesses reported that from the moment the first firebombs struck, only fourteen minutes passed before "the hell-fire began."

A firestorm also could threaten the airmen who created it. Bomber crews over urban areas had to contend with wind shear as well as incredibly powerful thermals. With temperatures exceeding 1,500 degrees Fahrenheit, firestorms created incredibly violent cyclones and vertical winds that could toss fifty-ton bombers onto their backs.

Captain Gordon B. Robertson and his 29th Group crew flew their first mission that night, receiving a terrifying combat initiation. Caught by searchlights at 5,600 feet, nearly blinded by the glare, Robertson and his copilot fought to keep the wings level until "bombs away." By then the attack was well developed, with incredible updrafts that lifted some B-29s 5,000 feet. It felt "like a cork on water in a hurricane."

Abruptly Robertson's plane rolled, its wings tilted at an angle alarmingly past the vertical. Pilots and crew were conscious of a rain of debris inside the bomber: everything from sand and cigarette butts to oxygen masks falling from the floor. The fliers realized they were upside down. It was a chilling sensation to see the fiery world "below" suddenly appear through the top of the cockpit.

Previously a flight instructor, Robertson oriented himself to the ground. In a maneuver more suited to a fighter, he allowed the huge bomber to fall nose-first through the bottom half of a loop, completing a split-S maneuver that compressed the crew into the seats under the onerous foot of gravity's elephant. The B-29 accelerated rapidly, clocking 400 mph at the bottom—about as fast as a Superfort ever went. Fighting the heavy aerodynamic loads on the controls, Robertson expended much of the momentum to regain precious altitude. Then he called for a course for home, immensely grateful to be alive.

About ninety fliers died that night and at least six more later perished in captivity. Aircraft losses among the 299 effective sorties totaled fourteen planes downed, ditched, or demolished by enemy action or accident. That equaled 4.6 percent, right in line with LeMay's eerily accurate prediction of 5 percent. That included two crews lost in bad weather, three bombers ditched in the sea, and one plane crash-landed on Iwo Jima.

The surviving B-29s turned southward with ashes streaked on their glass noses and appalling odors sucked inside the fuselages. Though well below the standard 10,000 feet for oxygen masks, some men strapped on their masks to escape the stench of burning flesh.

* * * * *

Tokyo's survivors struggled to deal with the massive calamity and found no standard of comparison. Medical services were reduced to insignificance: the only military rescue unit in the capital numbered nine doctors and eleven nurses. Not even the capital's combined civil and military emergency services could ease human suffering on an industrial scale.

One resident, Fusako Sasaki, recalled, "Stacked up corpses were being hauled away on lorries. Everywhere there was the stench of the dead and of smoke. I saw the places on the pavement where people had been roasted to death. At last I comprehended first-hand what an air raid meant."

American intelligence monitored a Japanese radio report that said, "Red fire clouds kept creeping high and the tower of the Parliament Building stuck out black against the background of the red sky. During the night we thought the whole of Tokyo had been reduced to ashes."

Spread by panic-driven rumor, exaggerated Japanese accounts of the disaster had as much as 40 percent of the city destroyed. In truth, 7 percent of metropolitan Tokyo had been razed that night—sixteen square miles. But with that level of destruction inflicted in less than three hours, the capital could well be completely razed in two weeks of continuous operations.

The grimmest measure of Meetinghouse's meaning was found in a single astonishing number. In ten previous attacks since November, Tokyo had sustained fewer than 1,300 deaths. Then, literally overnight, some 84,000 were killed and 40,000 injured. More than a quarter-million buildings were destroyed, leaving 1.1 million people homeless.

Damage to Japan's industry was considerable. The sixteen facilities destroyed or badly damaged included steel production, petroleum storage, and public services. Probably no one could calculate the number of small feeder factories and family shops that were incinerated in the residential areas.

One of the most illuminating comments on Meetinghouse came from Major General Haruo Onuma of the Army General Staff: "The effect of incendiary bombing on the capital's organization and the disposition of factories of Japan was very great, and, accompanying this, the main productive power was stopped. It [also] decreased the will of the people to continue the war."

A matching civilian perspective came from Tokuji Takeuchi of the Ministry of Interior. "It was the great incendiary attacks on 10 March 1945 on Tokyo which definitely made me realize the defeat."

The irony of the March 10 attack could not have been lost on General Onuma's colleagues—it was Army Day, observing Japan's victory over the Russians at Mukden forty years before.

Blitz Week

On the night of the 12th it was Nagoya's turn.

The industrial center of Nagoya lay between Tokyo and Osaka. Home to 1.3 million people and numerous aircraft and engine plants, the city had been attacked seven times since December but effective sorties totaled only 340 B-29s. Given the size of the city (nearly forty square miles) LeMay's planners hoped to deliver a crippling blow with 310 bombers in one night.

However, post-strike reconnaissance on the 12th showed barely two square miles destroyed. The operations order calling for a wider bomb pattern had started innumerable small fires, but they lacked the concentration to merge into a full Meetinghouse conflagration. On the other hand, interceptors were poorly equipped to handle a massed night raid and only one bomber was claimed shot down.

On Tuesday night, March 13, the B-29s went after Osaka, Japan's third-largest city with a population estimated at 3.2 million. The mission plan returned to the close bomb intervals so effective at Tokyo: tight patterns and maximum compression of the attacking force. For the first hour, two planes crossed the target each minute, mostly attacking below 9,000 feet.

Although concentration was achieved, once again weather affected results. An undercast forced most planes to drop by radar, and the previous Friday's high winds were absent. Nevertheless, more than eight square miles of industrial area and port facilities were razed—about 13 percent of the built-up area.

Once again incredible vertical winds pummeled the Superforts. One tail gunner was battered so violently that he received a Purple Heart. A 9th Group aircraft was flipped inverted but Captain Stanley Black coolly righted the bomber by completing a high-speed barrel roll. The maneuver cost several thousand feet, and the B-29 flew back to Tinian with warped wings, but it got its crew home. Black received a well-deserved Distinguished Flying Cross only to perish with his crew in May.

At 7,000 feet Major Ray Brashear's 499th Group crew gaped at the spectacle below. One crewman wrote, "Looked as though the whole city was burning." Their plane was illuminated by searchlights for an agonizing three minutes but the B-29 sustained no hits. In fact, only one of the 285 attacking bombers failed to return in exchange for more than 4,000 shops and factories destroyed.

After a record 330 Superfortresses congregated for a Meetinghouse over Kobe on March 16–17, Blitz Week ended on Sunday the 19th with Nagoya II. Attacking below 10,000 feet, nearly 300 planes centered their loads on the area called Incendiary Zone One, north of the harbor. Flying through searchlight cones, some B-29s were spotlighted for as long as fifteen minutes, but none was downed. Despite heavy flak, the bombers destroyed or damaged the freight yard, arsenal, Aichi aircraft factory, and the Yamada engineering works, though incomplete coverage permitted the Mitsubishi plant to escape serious harm.

The cost to the Americans for scorching three square miles was one bomber that splashed at sea. The crew was rescued the next day.

*　　*　　*　　*　　*

Although the four missions after March 10 each destroyed two to eight square miles of urban area, they were disappointing by Tokyo standards. But operations analysts recognized that the first strike had been a rarity: seldom would the same factors combine to raze sixteen square miles in one mission. Compressing the bomber stream, proper bomb release interval, and strong surface winds all were necessary to produce a major firestorm.

Overall, in five missions 1,434 sorties burned or damaged thirty square miles in four cities. In return, the blitz exacted a toll of twenty-one Superforts.

Hap Arnold sent a congratulatory message to XXI Bomber Command, concluding, "This is a significant sample of what the Jap can expect in the future. Good luck and good bombing."

LeMay celebrated by indulging in a box of Havana cigars cadged from the Navy post exchange. His stash of pipe tobacco had mildewed in the tropic climate and he did not favor the American cigars stocked by the Army PX.

Meanwhile, XXI Bomber Command staff well knew that the blitz could not be sustained, nor was it expected to. Five maximum efforts in ten days left the maintenance crews slumped in exhaustion. Additionally, the command had depleted its stock of incendiaries, and the Navy would not deliver the next two shiploads until April 9.

The View from Tokyo

Japanese officials reeled with the implication of Blitz Week. They had seen that America's vast resources could be massed in homeland airspace almost without limit, inflicting appalling damage while sustaining small loss. The Americans' sudden shift to low-level attack with incendiary weapons had changed the nature of the air campaign, literally overnight. Freed of the doctrinal tether of high-altitude precision bombing, the B-29s now could sweep away factories by the dozens, rather than trying to hit them singly from 30,000 feet.

A reasoned assessment was made by Lieutenant General Noboru Tazoe, commanding the 5th Air Division. After the war he stated, "It became apparent in March 1945 that Japan could not win the war when the B-29s wrought extensive damage, especially in the case of small factories scattered throughout the cities."

Apart from the enormous damage inflicted on Japan's industrial infrastructure, another factor quickly emerged: absenteeism. The Swiss Red Cross reported from Nagoya, "After the first B-29 raid with fire bombs, fear became so great that workers began remaining at home merely because they were afraid to be caught in war plants when another raid might strike."

Physically and psychologically, Japanese industry was being dismantled. But Tokyo fought on.

Meanwhile, Emperor Hirohito insisted on seeing the carnage for himself. His retainers were concerned that an Imperial motorcade would draw the Americans' attention, so a small convoy was arranged with minimal security and no advance notice. Palace staffers had ventured far enough afield to acquaint themselves with the situation. They were appalled, returning with ghastly tales of mounded bodies melted together in barriers over two meters high. Nevertheless, on the 18th—eight days after the Tokyo calamity and the same day as Nagoya II—the emperor ventured forth.

As crown prince, the twenty-two-year-old Hirohito had ridden a horse through much of Tokyo's rubble following the catastrophic earthquake and fire of 1923, but that sad memory faded in comparison to 1945's appalling reality. Riding in his suitably appointed and armored limousine, Hirohito realized that relatively few of his dazed, surviving subjects noted the gold chrysanthemum pennant on his Mercedes-Benz 770, and some were too numbed to bow.

The big, two-tone auto made its way through the rubble-strewn streets at 20 mph, the emperor occasionally stopping to speak with local officials. In one ward alone, fifty houses remained of nearly 13,000, and more than 10,000 people were known dead or injured. Everywhere the heart-wrenching sights and reeking smells lingered:

blackened wreckage, eviscerated buildings, broken water mains, some spewing sewage. Ultimately, four weeks would be required to dispose of at least 84,000 corpses.

On days that might have been resplendent with cherry blossoms, logjams of blackened, bloated corpses clotted Tokyo's Sumida River. One resident remembered, "I felt nauseated and even more scared than before."

The emperor's thoughts must have been varied: from the incredible loss of life to irreparable damage to the city to reduction of manufacturing capacity. Apparently the last thing that occurred to him was to end the war.

Suppressing the Kamikazes

Japan's aerial suicide threat was well established by March 1945, and it was not going away. Kamikaze squadrons had debuted in the Philippines five months before, with spectacular effect. Between late October 1944 and the end of January 1945, about 375 kamikazes sank sixteen American ships and damaged eighty-seven. The *Tokkotai* (suicide troops) would certainly appear at Okinawa to contest the upcoming April landings.

Complying with the Joint Chiefs directive, the 20th Air Force attacked kamikaze bases from March 27 to May 11. In those six weeks three-quarters of the Marianas B-29 missions hammered nineteen Kyushu and Shikoku airfields with nearly 2,000 sorties.

The airfield campaign resembled nothing so much as a contraceptive directed against the kamikaze hatcheries. Rather than trying to smash every potentially lethal egg, the B-29s sought to ravage each nest by destroying the bases or rendering them impotent.

Most of the attacks were conducted in squadron strength, typically with eight to twelve bombers dropping fifty tons of bombs on each field. Though hangars and workshops were targeted, the major damage was done to runways. However, the industrious Japanese proved efficient in conducting repairs, leading to frequent repeat B-29 strikes. Therefore, on some missions more than half the bombs were delayed-action—from one to thirty-six hours—to dissuade repair crews.

LeMay ran the airfield campaign in three phases, beginning slowly. Phase One involved just three operations over thirteen days, totaling 265 effective sorties against seven primary targets. The missions had little to show for their efforts. In fact, Vice Admiral Matome Ugaki, the kamikaze warlord, reckoned the effort "pinpricks." He noted that one of the early attacks missed the target entirely and killed a lone farmer in a field.

Phase Two represented a serious effort. Between April 17 and 29 the Marianas command operated on eight of thirteen days, averaging 133 bombers each. LeMay firmly believed in a "restrike" policy, targeting some fields six or seven times to keep the bases beaten down. Kokubu, Kanoya, and Kanoya East on southern Kyushu especially drew repeated visits.

The heaviest bomber losses of the campaign occurred on April 28 when five B-29s went down. But that figure represented 4 percent of the 122 planes that attacked six bases.

Even with small losses, every statistic concealed a heartache. Outbound from Japan that day, the 39th Group's *Black Sheep* saw another B-29 in extremis. Ganged by "a swarm of interceptors," and with one engine afire, Lieutenant Alexander Orionchek's bomber had no chance by itself. But Captain John H. Pulley, Jr., never wavered. He maneuvered *Black Sheep* into position to defend his squadron mate, remaining with him until ninety miles offshore.

Pulley's crew watched the crippled aircraft execute a water landing and counted all twelve fliers in the water. Though running low on fuel, *Black Sheep* remained overhead, dropping life rafts, radios, and supplies to the downed crew while summoning a B-29 "super Dumbo" with more rescue equipment. Then *Black Sheep* lightened its load by jettisoning guns and other gear, milking every pint of fuel. It was just enough: Pulley landed at Iwo Jima, probably with insufficient gasoline for another circuit of the landing pattern.

The next day three Superfortresses were dispatched to relocate Orionchek's men. Hours later word came that a full crew had been rescued—from another group. Nothing more was ever heard of Alexander Orionchek or his eleven crewmen.

In the third anti-kamikaze phase XXI Bomber Command scaled back the effort. Though flying on eight days between April 30 to May 11, only 390 B-29s attacked their primary targets: fewer than fifty per day.

The Japanese could do nothing to stop the airfield strikes, but they still tried, and twenty-one B-29s were lost on the ninety-one missions from March to May. On April 29, the 498th Group lost a plane and crew to air-to-air bombing—a tactic frequently tried but seldom successful. However, Lieutenant Greer's unnamed airplane was forced out of formation by conventional fighter attacks, leaving it vulnerable. Other crews from the 873rd Squadron saw a bomb strike the center of the fuselage. "Shortly afterwards the plane was seen to go into a steep dive, then a violent spin. The aircraft crashed on land and was mercilessly strafed by Jap fighters."

Whether the serious U.S. naval losses off Okinawa would have been worse without the B-29 effort is uncertain. The three major kamikaze attacks from April 6 to 16 involved some 700 suicide sorties. The next three *kikusui*, or large-scale "floating chrysanthemum" kamikaze operations launched during the B-29 airfield attacks totaled 490, or one-third less. By that measure the Army Air Forces effort was somewhat successful.

However, in the forty-six days of 20th Air Force attacks on suicide bases, twenty American ships were sunk by air attack and forty damaged so severely that they never returned to action. Therefore, the naval hemorrhaging averaged 1.3 ships a day in that period, three times the rate before and after the B-29 missions. How much worse the Navy might have suffered without the Superforts at the height of the Japanese effort can only be surmised, though LeMay's skepticism about bombing airfields apparently was borne out.

Whatever the pros or cons of diverting B-29s from the strategic mission, there was room for reflection. One Superfortress crewman summed up the AAF attitude when he said, "These airfields are certainly not a strategic target but the Navy must be hurting to divert our attention to them."

Strategic Attacks Resume

In striking contrast to Japan's declining industrial output that spring, America's was still accelerating. Female workers personified as "Rosie the Riveter" represented only about one war worker in ten, but her robust, can-do image spoke for all Americans engaged in the headlong rush of production. Men and women, young and old, wielded rivet guns and bucking bars, torque wrenches and welders. Factories expended unprecedented efforts at reducing absenteeism, from pay bonuses to providing day-care centers. Coming off a decade-long economic depression, employees earned more money than some had seen in all their lives, and many worked as much overtime as they could manage.

But behind the enormous energy and dedication lay something stronger if subtler. Virtually every war worker had relatives in uniform: eventually nearly 400,000 families were entitled to display the gold star pennant denoting a loved one who died in their nation's service. To thousands of workers, every bomber rolling off the production line meant the war drew incrementally closer to its end.

Unlike Japan's factories, which were increasingly blasted into rubble or starved of essential materials, America's remained unmolested Vulcan's forges, churning out ever greater numbers of aircraft. Renton, Omaha, Wichita, and Marietta outproduced not only Tokyo, Yokohama, Nagoya, and Osaka, but the rest of Japan combined. No statistics better state the vast disparity between the two nations than the fact that from 1942 to 1945 America produced nearly 4,000 very heavy bombers while Japan built none. Counting all multi-engine bombers (B-17s, '24s, '29s, and '32s), the score was 34,000 to ten.

*   *   *   *   *

After the March fire blitz and the kamikaze diversion there still remained much to do. The Army-Navy Joint Target Group had marked thirty-three urban areas for destruction, but Japan's aviation industry remained the top priority. LeMay decided that with a growing force he could have it both ways. He would continue the daylight "precision" attacks against aircraft factories when sorties could be scheduled within the wider bombing campaign against other target sets.

A later generation would call LeMay's philosophy a "force multiplier." Not only was XXI Bomber Command going to conduct a two-phase campaign, it would do so with greater efficiency than before. As already demonstrated, the low-level missions against urban-industrial areas permitted double the bomb loads with less wear and tear on often overstressed engines. Thus, more sorties could be launched to destroy the dispersed factories that eluded precision attacks. Increasing emphasis was placed upon heavy industries producing machine tools, electrical systems, and ground-combat equipment such as artillery.

In order to continue a sustained effort, the 20th Air Force required increased logistic support, especially more bombs and fuel. LeMay needed to convince Admiral Chester Nimitz that the results would justify the logistic effort, and while the Pacific Theater commander was leery of the airman's claim that crews could fly 120 hours per month—about eight missions—he saw the potential. Despite their cool relationship, LeMay was impressed with how Nimitz and the Navy delivered. Later he conceded, "How they got the ships and the supplies out there in six weeks I don't know."

Nor was that all. As reports of the devastation wrought upon Japan reached the Marianas, a surging spirit grew at pierside and spread inland. The attitude was contagious: not only Army Air Forces personnel but Army engineers, Navy Seabees, and even off-duty marines pitched in hauling ordnance from the docks. With so many willing hands, the airmen began bypassing the ordnance dumps, delivering bombs straight from cargo ships to the aircraft hardstands. There the weapons were loaded directly into waiting bomb bays, fitted with fuses, and made ready for the next mission.

If simplistic, the mood was clear: the more bombs on Japan, the sooner every GI, sailor, and marine could plan on going home.

While the constant arrivals and departures of supply ships in the Marianas represented a major endeavor, it was only one part of a massive whole. Nearly every bomb, bullet, and gallon of gasoline loaded into B-29s came by sea, but Chester Nimitz also oversaw other huge undertakings. That April, newly secured Iwo Jima required continual support, while the Okinawa campaign—the largest land battle of the Pacific War—was well underway amid the heightened kamikaze crisis.

Of necessity, Pacific Theater logistics was a joint-service operation. Nimitz's J4 chief was an Army two-star general coordinating overall logistical planning, transportation priorities, fuel allotments, even medical facilities and general construction. Even so, there were interservice hitches. LeMay's own supply officer, a colonel, had to find ways around the turf-protecting tendencies of the Army's Central Pacific commander, a three-star with claims on shipping allotments. Ever the pragmatist, LeMay handled a potential clash by deciding not to ask too many questions of his subordinate.

That spring the Americans sought not merely air superiority—it had already been achieved—but outright air supremacy. Japanese airframe, engine, and propeller factories were targeted in an all-out effort to ensure control of the sky over the invasion beaches of Kyushu (Operation Olympic) and Honshu (Coronet) scheduled for November 1945 and March 1946, respectively. The overall campaign, code-named Downfall, would involve perhaps 1.7 million Allied troops ashore supported by millions more afloat and serving on island bases. With 1,300 seagoing amphibious assault ships committed to Olympic alone, suppressing the kamikazes was vital.

However, even with air superiority, B-29 losses were unavoidable. For instance, April 1 was a bad day for the 498th Group, committed to a 120-plane mission against Tokyo's Nakajima engine plant. Possum Hansell's original *Joltin' Josie the Pacific Pioneer* was lost with its crew in a ditching shortly after takeoff; two were shot down, another made a successful water landing, and a fifth was written off after returning to Saipan. Six other B-29s also were lost, three on mining sorties.

Three days later thirteen B-29s went down on two missions to Kawasaki and Tokyo. Among the 9th Bomb Group's missing was the crew of Captain, then Lieutenant, Raymond F. Malo, who had made the first emergency landing on Iwo Jima five weeks before. Only one of Malo's men survived the war.

On April 7, an almost cloudless day, LeMay made the most of the opportunity by sending two wings to Nagoya and one to Tokyo. More than 150 bombers left the Mitsubishi engine plant a blackened, mangled ruin, approximately 90 percent destroyed. Simultaneously 101 planes of the 73rd Wing put Nakajima Aircraft's Musashino factory in the crosshairs, and though the facility survived, Rosie O'Donnell's one-ton bombs inflicted heavy damage on the machine shops.

That same day B-29s enjoyed fighter escort for the first time. Two groups of P-51 Mustangs from Iwo Jima tangled with Japanese interceptors, downing twenty-six for the loss of two Mustangs. Bomber gunners eagerly claimed 100 kills versus seven Superforts destroyed, including one that crashed after takeoff.

One crew was lost to ramming as Lieutenant Takahashi Kawano of the veteran 244th Regiment got past the Mustangs and penetrated the 500th Group's defensive gunfire. The Kawasaki Tony pilot smashed into Lieutenant Robert King's bomber, which broke up in flight. Nearby, Kawano's family watched spellbound as a Japanese fighter collided with a B-29, clearly visible in the spring sky. The witnesses had no way of knowing that their son and brother had just perished. The bomber's remains smashed into a primary school in the Kumagaya district, killing a civilian and destroying two houses as well. But Kawano received a posthumous double promotion and, in an exceptional honor, the emperor heard his name.

Across the International Date Line on April 12, Franklin D. Roosevelt died of a cerebral hemorrhage. The reaction of Robert Sanders, a 40th Group pilot on Tinian, was typical. "One morning in mid-April word filtered down the ranks that President Roosevelt was dead. F.D.R. had been the country's leader since I was 10 years old. We were so accustomed to his presence in Washington that we never thought about anybody taking his place."

But someone had to. Roosevelt was succeeded by Vice President Harry S. Truman, a plainspoken Missourian who in 1943 had headed a Senate investigation of the inordinate delays in production of the R-3350 engine.

On that same date in the Pacific, more than 250 Superfortresses in three task forces attacked aircraft and industrial targets. One of 130 bombers aiming for the Koriyama chemical complex was the 29th Group's *City of Los Angeles* flown by Captain George Simeral. His crew was a well-drilled team, having flown together since June 1944, including ten previous missions.

Nearing the coast, Simeral as lead pilot ordered a flare dropped to mark the assembly point for his squadron. Sergeant Henry "Red" Erwin, a redheaded Alabaman, picked up a phosphorus flare and placed it in the chute. He pulled the arming pin prior to dropping it—and his world burst into flames.

Prematurely ignited, the pyrotechnic flew backward into Red Erwin's face. Searing 1,300-degree heat blinded him, burning off his nose and one ear. The compartment filled with white smoke, almost immediately obscuring the pilots' view of their instruments.

A devout Christian, Erwin thought of his friends. If the phosphorus were not disposed of, it could burn through the cockpit floor into the bomb bay and detonate the ordnance. Groping blindly for the fiendish device, somehow Erwin found it and picked it up.

The twenty-two-year-old radioman walked forward, intending to throw the flare out the copilot's window. His path was blocked by the navigator's table, which hinged downward. But the navigator was in the astrodome taking a sighting. Erwin had the presence of mind to tuck the burning flare under one arm, raise the table by feel, and continue forward.

Though he was blind, Erwin sensed that he neared the open window and, in a providential toss, flung the device into the slipstream. Then he collapsed over the throttle console.

In a hellish few minutes the B-29 had lost nearly all its altitude. The pilots only recovered control at about 300 feet, having opened their windows to vent the aircraft. The rest of the crew did what little it could to ease Erwin's agony, marveling that he only spoke to ask about everyone else. Meanwhile, Simeral set course for Iwo Jima.

Doctors could do little for Erwin on Iwo so he was flown to Guam with its fleet hospital. LeMay was quickly informed of the situation and, being advised that Erwin probably would die, determined to get the Alabaman the Medal of Honor, and damn the regulations.

First LeMay dispatched an airplane to Hawaii with orders not to return without a medal. The crew took its responsibility seriously and procured the only one available by breaking into a display case and taking the decoration.

Most Medals of Honor required months to be processed. But LeMay got on the wire, insisting that Sergeant Erwin's award be approved immediately. Hap Arnold concurred and the citation was placed on Harry Truman's desk. In one of his first acts as president, he signed the document and 20th Air Force was notified.

In an impromptu bedside ceremony, LeMay presented the nation's highest decoration to the suffering airman merely six days after the mission. The general order formally issuing the award was not published for nearly three months.

Red Erwin astonished everyone not only by surviving, but recovering. In the next two and a half years he endured reconstructive surgery, regained his vision and the use of one arm. Discharged in 1947, he devoted nearly four decades to helping other veterans in the Birmingham VA hospital. He married, raised a family, and died in 2002, age eighty. He believed to the end that he wore the Medal of Honor for all who served.

Meanwhile, in April, Roger Ramey's 58th Wing moved from India to Tinian and the 315th alit on Guam, fresh from the States under Frank Armstrong. By the end of the month, XXI Bomber Command was complete with one notable exception, which would arrive in July. The five B-29 wings (twenty groups with sixty squadrons) now constituted the most powerful striking force on the planet, despite larger Allied formations with less capable equipment still blasting Germany.

Almost lost amid the unrelenting pace of operations was awareness of events in Europe. The world learned at the end of April that Adolf Hitler had died in his Berlin bunker, and a week later the Third Reich surrendered. Said B-29 pilot Gordon B. Robertson, "We received the news quite calmly and without celebration. While we were certainly glad and relieved, we realized that our Pacific War was far from over."

May Climax

By the first of May, XXI Bomber Command had made serious inroads against Japan's aircraft industry. AAF intelligence reckoned that 70 percent of the known aero engine plants had been hit hard enough to interrupt or seriously reduce output, and assessed that Japan's factory dispersion program would further interfere with production. Consequently, eight remaining engine or propeller plants became the priority precision targets.

Five notable missions were flown in May, including only the second daytime incendiary strike, on the 14th. It was also the first time that four wings were committed to action, with the China veterans of the 58th Wing joining the lineup. And what a lineup it was: 480 Superforts ranging over the home islands, nearly all attacking northern Nagoya. Bombing below 20,000 feet, they scorched more than three square miles.

Nagoya was home of the Tokai Army District, headquartered in the historic castle, which was destroyed in the raid. Apparently the area commander was so enraged that he had eleven captured fliers tried for "undiscriminating bombing" and executed by decapitation on July 12. Three more were retrieved from the water by the Imperial Navy and sent to prison camp where one perished.

A second mission pounded Nagoya the night of the 16th with 450 effective sorties more than doubling the damage from the previous mission for seven square miles torched. Two aircraft factories, an arsenal, and a vehicle plant were among the identified targets in the southern part of town. As the bombers winged southward, one-fourth of Nagoya's forty square miles had been destroyed or seriously damaged.

The previous four fire raids had gutted Nagoya and destroyed some thirty-four square miles of Tokyo, but the capital's western area, which included the Imperial Palace, remained largely intact. On May 23, LeMay dispatched a new record of 550 Superfortresses to Tokyo, bearing 3,600 tons of fire bombs and high explosives.

Crews had been briefed to spare the Imperial Palace since Hirohito was deemed, in the sterile words of command, "not at present a liability and may later become an asset." Therefore, the pathfinders put their markers south of the palace and west of the harbor, and the heavy haulers burned out five more square miles.

The bombers reported occasional fighter attacks among 150 or more searchlights but the interceptors were largely ineffectual, accounting for only one of the seventeen missing Superfortresses.

The trailing formations found "swell fires" producing thick smoke clouds topping 7,000 feet, forcing some bombers to swerve dangerously near their companions. The aerial traffic was further complicated by the compressed schedule: more than four aircraft crossing the target every minute. As often occurred in firestorms, aircraft were jarred and thrown about by surging heat waves. Meanwhile, the orange-red glow from the burning city merged with the pale whiteness of searchlights to render the night bright as day.

Even fliers nearing the end of their thirty-five-mission tours were shaken by what they had experienced. A bombardier later wrote, "When crews returned to their bases they handed in their reports with hands that shook, with shock and horror still reflected in their eyes from what they had witnessed just a few hours before."

Only thirty-six hours later, on May 25, the bombers were back. Some 460 Superforts razed more than seventeen square miles of the nation's capital: the commercial-financial district and government buildings, including the Foreign Ministry, the Navy Department, headquarters of the Greater East Asia Co-Prosperity Sphere, and even the prime minister's residence. Quipped one flier, "Tokyo just isn't what it used to be."

The firestorm swirled around ordinary citizens like Fusako Sasaki, who had survived the March 10 debacle. "As I ran I kept my eyes on the sky. It was like a fireworks display as the incendiaries exploded. People were aflame, rolling and writhing in agony, screaming piteously for help, but beyond all mortal assistance."

The flames swept inexorably toward the Imperial Palace. Previous damage to homes of royal family members was limited to an area outside the palace walls, but this time the emperor's residence felt the heat, all too literally. Wind-borne embers were blown over the moat, producing uncontrollable brush fires that ignited buildings within the compound. While the emperor and empress waited out the conflagration in their underground bunker, twenty-eight palace denizens perished in flames that consumed several buildings.

Sergeant Kevin Herbert, a literate tail gunner, witnessed a bedlam of violence that night: "a netherworld scene worthy of the imagination of a Virgil, a Dante, or a Milton: roiling columns of smoke thrust up from lurid red and yellow lakes of fire; murk and haze swept along amid the darkness; random bolts of light piercing the gloom in search of victims; tracer lines, flak bursts, thermal buffetings; the pandemonium of weaponry, tornadic noise, and urgent calls to comrades; and epiphanies and vanishings of other craft, friendly and hostile, from the dim shores of this molten sea."

By the time the raiders returned to their island roosts, half the capital's built-up area had been reduced to a burning, smoking, stinking ash heap—the accumulated toll of all missions since November. No further fire raids were inflicted upon Tokyo. The city was no longer worth the effort.

In exchange, on May 25 the previous record B-29 loss was eclipsed when twenty-six Superfortresses were written off—the worst toll ever. It amounted to 5.6 percent of the 464 attacking aircraft, but only four or five were known lost to flak or fighters. About 100 sustained battle damage, four being lost when their crews bailed out rather than buck worsening weather over Iwo Jima.

Prior to the 23rd, the May missions had cost thirty-two bombers; now forty-three had been destroyed in just two nights, though apparently no more than ten to enemy action.

The worst American losses were sustained on the enemy's ground.

Prisoners

Every Allied airman who parachuted into captivity knew what he faced. Before the March 9 Tokyo fire raid, XXI Bomber Command had instructed aircrews: "If you are shot down, try and get picked up by the Japanese military as quickly as possible. The civilians will kill you outright." The instructions proved accurate, occasionally in reverse fashion. In February an Imperial Navy pilot had bailed out of his stricken fighter. Badly burned, he was mistaken for an American and beaten to death by a civilian mob. Thereafter Japanese aviators usually wore a rising sun patch on their flight suits.

Nearly 550 Allied fliers were captured in operations over the home islands, excluding the Kurils. However, twenty-nine were captured in the barest sense, being killed almost immediately upon reaching the ground. Another 132 were murdered in prison and ninety-four more died in captivity, notably in a Tokyo fire raid the night of May 25–26, when sixty-two airmen perished in a western suburb. The firestorm engulfed the area, burning the wooden jail and incinerating most of the POWs while 300 civilian prisoners were moved to safety. The few Americans who escaped the building were caught and beheaded by the Kempei Tai, the military police. Concluded navigator Hap Halloran, who had been confined with some of the casualties elsewhere, "May 25 was a very sad day. All B-29ers gave their best, always. Some gave their all."

Most POWs were tortured; all were abused and some were rendered insane. Those held more than a few months emerged from prison as emaciated as some concentration camp survivors.

Dying in a flaming aircraft—or building—was perhaps not the worst fate possible. A scratch-built crew from the 29th Group was downed on May 5, and met horrid ends. Apparently all bailed out but one was murdered in midair when a Japanese fighter shredded his parachute canopy. Two were killed on the ground and another shot it out with enraged Japanese, literally saving the last bullet for himself. The pilot was captured and sent to Tokyo where he was tortured and interrogated but survived the ordeal. At least six others were moved to Kyushu Imperial University in Fukuoka, between Hiroshima and Nagasaki. There they were subjected to vivisection by the anatomy department. Reportedly some of the Japanese acquired a taste for human liver but no witnesses would so testify after the war. Eventually twenty-three Fukuoka military and medical personnel were found guilty of various charges; five received death sentences and four life terms. However, none were executed and all were freed by 1958.

Relatively few war crime perpetrators against Americans were punished owing to postwar big-picture concerns in Washington and Tokyo. Nor was anything like full justice possible, given thousands of incidents throughout Asia from 1937 to 1945. But even in the limited context of Allied personnel in Japan, accountability usually went begging. In one June 1945 incident an injured P-51 pilot being treated in an infirmary was delivered to a mob that lynched the American. Though some of those involved were known, none was punished.

The most egregious sanctioned murders occurred at Western Military District headquarters in Fukuoka on August 15, immediately after the emperor's radio speech announcing the end of hostilities. Seventeen B-29 crewmen were dragged from their filthy cells, made to kneel outside, and their heads were severed from their bodies. Some perpetrators were imprisoned but no death sentences were carried out.

That left 283 Americans and seven Britons alive after the surrender, a survival rate of barely 50 percent versus about 99 percent in German hands. Concluded more than one survivor, "The time to get captured by the Japs was when they were winning."

Return Visits

Unprecedented losses on the two previous missions convinced LeMay to shift tactics again. Ignoring Tokyo, which was already 51 percent destroyed, he sent his air fleet to Yokohama in daylight on May 29. Escorted by 100 Mustangs, 475 bombers wiped out nearly seven square miles of the business district and waterfront containing twenty specific targets. Most of the firebombs were dropped above 20,000 feet, and left a pall of smoke nearly reaching that height.

Some of the fifty-plus airborne interceptors got through the P-51 pickets and hacked down five B-29s, one by ramming. But in a sixty-five-minute brawl the Mustang Jockeys gunned down twenty-eight defenders, and the bombers staked a claim to six more. Though three more B-29s were lost in accidents, attrition had been conquered; from June onward it averaged less than one percent.

In a very short time—from late February through May—XXI Bomber Command had inflicted catastrophic damage upon the Japanese homeland. In May alone one-seventh of the nation's built-up urban area had been devastated, raising the overall total to 36 percent. That amounted to a staggering ninety-four square miles, including more than 100 priority targets.

Despite the appalling evidence, many Japanese officials and citizens insisted that the misery befalling themselves and their nation was somehow illusory. In some cases reality kicked in only after the May fire blitz, when Home Affairs Minister Iwao Yamazaki conceded that civil defense was "considered to be futile." About that time a police liaison officer with the Japanese Army Air Force admitted that the public increasingly regarded Dai Nippon's defenses as "useless."

Nevertheless, Tokyo's cabinet insisted that the war would continue.

CHAPTER SIX

Pacific Ponies

The 1,500-Mile War

From B-29 bases on Guam, a glance at the map showed the next stepping-stone to Japan: the Bonin Islands, midway between the Marianas and Honshu, some 750 miles south of Tokyo. In early 1945 they also presented an excellent emergency field for stricken Superfortresses and put the home islands within range of the long-legged North American P-51D Mustang. With the Bonins in American hands, B-29s could have fighter escorts anywhere over southern Japan.

In February, Iwo Jima, the largest of the Bonins with three Japanese airfields, was taken by three Marine Corps divisions at enormous cost: 6,821 Americans killed and some 19,000 wounded. It ranked among the highest casualty rates sustained by U.S. forces in the twentieth century.

On March 4—two weeks before Iwo was declared secure—a B-29 named *Dinah Might* landed nearly out of gasoline on Motoyama Number 1, the southernmost field. The 9th Bomb Group's Lieutenant Raymond Malo made the first of some 2,400 emergency stops that Superforts would log over the next five months. Most of the landings were precautionary, but if 10 percent of the crews were saved, that represented about 2,600 airmen.

Seventh Air Force fighters were ready to move to Iwo as soon as facilities were readied. Planning for very long range (VLR) escort missions had begun the previous summer, as Brigadier General Ernest M. Moore alerted his VII Fighter Command "Sunsetters" for the challenging mission.

"Mickey" Moore was typical of the young flying generals in the Army Air Forces. A thirty-seven-year-old West Pointer (class of '31), he was an experienced fighter pilot who had been in the Pacific since 1939. Having assumed command in August 1944, he led from the front and landed the first Mustang on Iwo on March 6. Behind him were the three squadrons of the 15th Fighter Group. Eleven days later the first element of Colonel Kenneth Powell's 21st Fighter Group arrived at Airfield Number 2. Many of his pilots were new, averaging about 300 hours flight time with perhaps twenty in P-51s. Though the group had recently transitioned from P-38 Lightnings, the pilots and the Mustangs were equal to the task.

Iwo Jima was crammed with airplanes: two Army night fighter squadrons, Navy and Marine strike aircraft, and air-sea rescue planes. But the P-51s were the most numerous and strategically the most important. They broke in slowly by flying local patrols, but Japanese aerial intrusions were rare—only two during May and June.

Other than flying, pilots on Iwo had precious little diversion, but some didn't mind, preferring to focus on the job. Captain Harry Crim said, "Iwo was perhaps the most hostile ground environment an airman could find himself in. Nature provided an active volcano [Mount Suribachi], and man provided the war."

There was literally no place to go, not much to do, and precious little to see. The Army fliers did, however, find ways to spend their off-duty time—primarily in commerce with the eminently "negotiable" Navy Seabees. Busily engaged in expanding Airfields 1 and 2 (Number 3 was never completed), the sailors' motto was, "We'll do anything for whiskey." When it was discovered that the Seabees had an ice machine but no booze, the law of supply and demand took over. The 21st Fighter Group traded fifteen bottles of whiskey for the ice machine, installation included.

The next priority was an officers club, which was constructed with the same interservice negotiations that attended procurement of the ice machine. Said one pilot, "When the war ended, we had enough supplies to last us another year and all the material and equipment to build a swimming pool—including a concrete mixer." Eventually there was even a spa—the brainchild of the 21st Group's flight surgeon, who suggested converting a bomb shelter into a sauna with piped-in hot water from Iwo's sulfur springs. Harry Crim observed, "It really took out the kinks and probably added to our embellishment of mission accomplishments."

Crim, an aggressive twenty-six-year-old Floridian, was one of the Sunsetters' most experienced pilots with 2,200 flight hours. He had flown fifty P-38 missions in North Africa, Sicily, and Italy, enduring sand, flies, and disease while losing fifty pounds. Consequently, he became "an Iwo booster." He believed that being able to concentrate 100 percent on combat training, without serious diversions, was one of the island's strong points. He helped his pilots devote their attention to flying and fighting and thus prevented their going "rock happy."

Before the first VLR mission, something entirely unexpected literally brought the war to the pilots' front door. The 21st Group had been ashore barely a week when, at 4:00 A.M. on March 27, eight dawn patrol pilots were walking to the field. They were suddenly overcome by 350 to 400 Japanese who poured out of underground caves and tunnels. Instantly the Mustang pilots were embroiled in a vicious infantry war.

Responding to the attack, Harry Crim and others established a skirmish line, moved the wounded to the rear, and shot it out with .45 pistols, .30 caliber carbines, and even Browning Automatic Rifles. After five hours of intermittent fighting, the marines ended the affair: some 330 Japanese were dead and eighteen captured. But VII Fighter Command had suffered heavily, with forty-four killed and nearly 100 wounded. Crim replaced the wounded commander of the 531st Squadron, and the next day the group flew its first mission, strafing the Bonins. After that debut, the next step was Tokyo itself.

The View from Tokyo

Whatever the challenges facing Mustang pilots, the latter-day samurai defending Japanese airspace had their own serious problems. By early 1945 more than three years of attrition had reversed Japan's initial advantage in aircrew quality. Beginning with a pool of well-trained, often combat-experienced airmen, Japanese army and navy squadrons enjoyed a period of pilot superiority over their Allied opponents in the Philippines, Java, Burma, and elsewhere. But the edge of that aerial blade had been dulled in the sanguinary battles of 1942. Like every military elite, Japanese aviation lacked depth, and losses could not be replaced in kind. The varsity had to play almost every inning, while increasing numbers of Americans came off the bench, fresh and ready.

Consequently, when American aircraft began appearing in homeland skies in 1944, the emperor's aviators were poorly prepared or equipped to counter them. Late that year even front-line combat units were showing a precipitous decline in flight hours. Taking one navy fighter squadron as an example, of thirty-three pilots only four were rated Class A—fully combat-ready—and just five had flown more than 500 hours (the median was 315 hours, while nearly half logged fewer than 200). Nevertheless, while fuel lasted most pilots flew thirty to fifty-five hours per month, trying to build badly needed experience.

In contrast, in 1945 many American fighter pilots entering combat had 600 hours in the cockpit, and some boasted over 1,000. The Japanese retained some star performers but the Yanks possessed immense depth across the entire roster.

Still, some Japanese aviators were dangerous by any measure. Arguably the most spectacular of Japan's airmen was a naval aviator, Lieutenant (jg) Sadaaki Akamatsu. In a thirteen-year flying career he logged more than 6,000 hours, flying from land bases and from carriers. He had entered combat as a veteran fighter pilot, claiming four kills in his first dogfight over China in 1938.

It says much that so rebelliously unconventional a character as "Temei" Akamatsu could thrive in the rigid hierarchy of the Imperial Navy. A functional alcoholic, erratic and often personally violent, he carved a wide swath through the Pacific, from the Philippines to the Dutch Indies and Burma. Along the way he claimed downing squadrons of Allied aircraft, brashly proclaiming himself "King of the Aces." To the amazement of his colleagues, he was commissioned in 1943.

Returning to Japan, Akamatsu joined the 302nd Naval Air Group at Atsugi. Under close scrutiny at home, he could not indulge himself to the extent he had abroad, but his drinking continued largely unabated. According to legend, when B-29 raids began in 1944, he lounged in a geisha house until informed by phone of inbound bombers. At that point reputedly he drove to the flight line, climbed in his fighter, and, roaring drunk, took off to engage the enemy. Regardless of his wild reputation, everyone acknowledged Akamatsu's value in the air. Devoid of fear, the thirty-five-year-old ace readily tackled any odds.

On April 19, 1945, flying a Jack, Akamatsu waded into a group of Mustangs. "We spotted the enemy planes over the southern end of Tokyo Bay," Akamatsu recalled. "Five Raidens raced into the fight. The enemy always kept their tail covered. . . . I hid behind a P-51, there was a blind spot. After following awhile I had the advantage to attack. I fired my guns from very close range and hit its fuel tank. Suddenly it fell on fire."

The other Mustangs immediately responded, attacking Akamatsu head-on. Unperturbed—he had been in that situation repeatedly—he ignored the tracers swirling around him and responded with his four cannon. He claimed another kill before the P-51s broke off, probably short of fuel.

By skill or fortune, Akamatsu survived the war, making extravagant claims to anyone who listened. Quipped historian Henry Sakaida, Akamatsu claimed 260 victories when sober; 350 when drunk. But whatever the numbers, he met and matched every plane and pilot the Americans threw at him.

Despite the exceptional records of a few super-aces like Aka-matsu, not even Japan's finest squadrons could dent the American onslaught. Arguably the most professional air defense unit in Japan was Captain Minoru Genda's 343rd Naval Air Group, boasting a high proportion of combat-experienced pilots with long victory records. In some twenty encounters between March and August 1945, Genda's pilots boasted 170 victories. But close examination of U.S. records shows barely thirty successes against ninety Japanese losses. That's instructive—by 1945 Japan's finest fighter wing claimed a two-to-one kill-loss ratio but in fact finished on the short end of one-to-three.

In truth, Japanese aviators were triple-damned. They often faced superior numbers of better aircraft flown by generally more competent pilots. In the end, facing a losing battle like their Luftwaffe allies, the emperor's fliers fought for their comrades and their own self-respect.

Riding a Mustang

For American fighter pilots, Iwo Jima was the start of a long-range war. In 1945 a P-51 pilot based near London knew that his Mustang's 750-mile radius could take him well beyond Germany: Berlin was "only" 590 miles away. But the Mustang could fly to Poznan or Vienna, down to Trieste at the head of the Adriatic, or to Firenze, Italy. Discounting that Spain was neutral, he could fly beyond Barcelona and back without landing. The difference was that, excepting the English Channel, the Britain-based pilot flew over land. For the fliers of VII Fighter Command, the distance was entirely over water.

The lurking dread faced by fighter pilots flying very long range escorts from Iwo Jima cannot be understood by anyone who has never taken a single-engine airplane beyond sight of land. Flying 1,500 miles round-trip, a pilot developed enhanced hearing. Over water he might hear—or imagine—little hiccups in the satin-smooth purr of his Rolls-Royce Merlin engine. Maybe it was just the spark plugs fouling on the return trip. Nursing its remaining fuel, the Mustang would lope along at 210 mph.

Returning southbound from Japan, the flier would wriggle on his seat cushion. He was "butt sprung," the parachute pack feeling more uncomfortable than ever. There was no way to adjust his buttocks so they didn't hurt. Five and a half hours into a seven-hour mission, the glamour of flying "the Cadillac of the skies" diminished in proportion to the ache of his sciatic nerve. He squirmed in the confined cockpit, stomped his feet on the floor, and tried to ignore the Pacific sun beating down through the canopy. He was tired and hot and bored.

Two hours before, the youngster had reveled in the firepower at his fingertips and the raw thrill of flying at fifty feet, shooting anything that moved. Now he stifled a yawn. That, too, was war.

Thirty years later General Mickey Moore wrote, "I don't believe there is any question about the P-51 being the best prop fighter of World War II. It was a top air fighter and, hence, best for escort missions and equal to the P-47 as an attacker against ground targets." Squadron and group commanders were just as enthusiastic and described the sleek North American as "perfect for these missions."

With their heavy fuel loads, the Mustangs needed a long takeoff run, even at sea level. Originally the Iwo Jima strips were barely 2,000 feet long, and that was often inadequate for B-29 emergencies, when Superfortresses could run off the end. After a typical mission, fifty or more Superfortresses might land on Iwo rather than risk the extra 700 miles to the Marianas. The hazards also extended to the locals: the 531st Fighter Squadron's flight line coffee tent was wiped out three times before it was moved to the upwind side of the runway, away from landing aircraft.

When Colonel Bryan B. Harper's 506th Fighter Group arrived in mid-May, it lifted some of the burden on the first two groups. The 506th alternated with the others in escorting bombers to the home islands, so one group usually could ease pilot strain and catch up on maintenance.

Like Harper, some 506th pilots were self-confessed "escapees from Training Command" who had languished in the States most of the war. Many possessed more experience than their 15th and 21st colleagues, as Lieutenant Neil Smith, Jr., recalled. "I had about 500 hours of fighter time in P-39s, '40s, and P-47s, and another 150 in '51s before arriving at Iwo. Probably a third of the pilots in our outfit had that much '51 time."

Pilots received nearly all the publicity, but they got nowhere without flyable aircraft.

The universal comment from Sunsetter pilots was, "Maintenance on Iwo was tops." If a flier wanted a new carburetor, he needed only mention it. Many crew chiefs kept their planes waxed for extra speed, though some joked that there was nothing better to do. The mechanics conscientiously changed spark plugs after every VLR mission to avoid fouling, as prolonged low-RPM cruising could burn up the plugs. Lieutenant Harve Phipps of the 72nd Squadron recalled, "We had practically no aborts because of bad maintenance." Pilots deeply appreciated such diligence: the last thing they wanted to worry about was engine failure 600 saltwater miles from home.

A far greater concern than mechanical failure was the North Pacific weather. Three to five fronts usually moved south daily from the Japanese coast, and that made mission planning difficult. High, dense cloud formations were often a factor.

The Mustangs seldom penetrated a front but tried to fly between the thunderheads. When possible, they remained in the clear to avoid major turbulence, as the eighty-five-gallon tank behind the pilot became a critical factor. In rough weather "the '51 with the fuselage tank full didn't fly like anything resembling an airplane," Harry Crim said. Before entering weather, standard procedure was to run the tank down to forty gallons to put the center of gravity on the near side of controllability. Even then it was no fun flying a P-51 in turbulence. When the under-wing drop tanks were partially empty, the gas sloshed from front to back, creating a roller-coaster sensation. It was almost impossible to fly straight and level visually; far less so on instruments.

On one occasion, escorting bombers, Crim took his squadron into a light spot in a full thunderstorm. With his canopy cracked three inches for ventilation, he was guiding on a bomber when abruptly it disappeared and his lap was covered in snow. There was only one option: he called for a 180-degree turn, descending at 500 feet per minute. "After what seemed like 20 minutes, we were back in the clear. My whole squadron of 16 planes was tucked into the tightest formation I've ever seen. I looked back a couple of times and couldn't even see my wingman, so I don't know how they flew formation."

Such events were not unusual. From late April to late June, 832 P-51 strike sorties were dispatched but fewer than half (374) reached their targets. Four missions were completely spoiled by heavy clouds, and the Mustangs were grounded for ten days in early May.

The worst weather problem occurred on June 1 when the command launched 148 Mustangs only to encounter a solid front from sea level to 23,000 feet. B-29 weather recon planes that preceded each strike had reported the front thin enough to penetrate. But the Mustangs hit a severe thunderhead and had no option but to make an immediate turn out of "the soup."

Flying completely blind in extreme turbulence, several P-51s collided and others fell prey to violent winds. Twenty-seven fighters were lost with all but three pilots. The 506th Group, operational for only two weeks, lost fifteen planes and twelve pilots. Eventually twenty-seven Mustangs broke through to escort the bombers over Osaka. On another mission, a 21st Group pilot stuck it out through the weather to find himself the sole escort for about 400 B-29s.

The pilots insisted that if there was a cloud in the Pacific, it sat on Iwo Jima. Ground heat and the presence of sulfur in the salt air made Iwo even more prone to cloud formation than other islands, often producing a ceiling of fifty feet. Consequently, Iwo received one of the early ground control approach (GCA) radars. It was established on the main runway of Airfield Number 1, presenting an instrument approach within 100 feet of Mount Suribachi's northwest slope. "It takes a lot of good-weather practice approaches before you'll trust the thing," observed more than one pilot.

Flying single-engine fighters on 1,500-mile round-trips over a vast ocean with minimal navigation aids required a confidence born of experience. It was a task few pilots were experienced enough to attempt on their own. The standard P-51D had a magnetic and gyro compass plus a radio compass—the latter of limited range. Voice communication was available on one VHF four-channel radio, and that was all. "You lose your radio or dynamotor and you have to dead-reckon 600 nautical miles to a spot in the ocean less than four miles in diameter," said Harry Crim. "Coming back, if your radio worked you could get a steer for the last hundred miles from radar, if it was working. That's why you didn't want to be alone."

Fortunately, help was available. Six B-29 navigation planes in three pairs led about 100 Mustangs on each mission to a designated point off the Japanese coast, circling while the fighters flew inland. When the Mustangs began to return to the rendezvous point, the first pair of B-29s waited until about half had arrived, then set course for Iwo. The other two pair of bombers departed the coast at ten-minute intervals to allow latecomers to latch on to one navigation group or another. The last B-29 to depart transmitted Morse Code letters permitting stragglers to get their bearings. When on the correct heading the fighter pilot heard the letters U (..–) and D (–..) overlapping into a steady hum.

The bare statistics of what was involved in one VLR mission do not begin to tell the story. In round numbers, nearly 100 Mustangs, whose combined 1945 value was a little under $6 million, took off with 57,000 gallons of high-octane fuel and some 230,000 rounds of .50 caliber ammunition. The round-trip distance was equal to halfway across North America, from Los Angeles to Little Rock. Except for the time spent over Japan, the entire mission was flown above water. Seven-hour sorties were routine; eight hours were not unknown.

Unlike the procedure in Europe, VII Fighter Command Mustangs did not escort specific bomber formations but guarded a stream of B-29s as much as 200 miles long. One fighter group was assigned target cover near the bomb release point while another provided withdrawal support. Usually flying 2,000 feet above the bombers, the three covering squadrons flew two on one side of the bomber stream and one on the other, with four-plane flights about half a mile apart. The three squadrons were staggered line astern, flying in the same direction as the Superforts that were approaching the drop point. The most likely point of interception was near the beginning of the bomb run, so the escort concentrated there, ready to pounce.

Flak was the most frequently encountered resistance, but 90-degree course changes with slight altitude variation allowed the fighters to remain under antiaircraft fire for nearly an hour with little damage.

Enemy fighter opposition could be fierce and determined, but generally the Sunsetters had little respect for their opponents. The biggest problem was locating Japanese in the air, and actual engagements were rarer. In more than four months of combat the Mustangs clashed with Japanese only fifteen times. "Finding enemy aircraft was difficult," Crim recalled. "They weren't interested in tangling with us, and the only aggression I saw was when they thought they had us at a great disadvantage. Some of the pilots were skillful, but there weren't enough of them to make much difference."

The first VLR escort, a Tokyo mission on April 7, was an exceptional occasion. It featured beautiful weather and plenty of bandits. The 15th and 21st Groups escorted 107 B-29s, and during the fifteen minutes over the target encountered stiff opposition. Pilots estimated seventy-five to 100 Japanese fighters were seen and claimed twenty-one downed for the loss of two Mustangs.

The 15th Group saw the most combat that day, returning with claims of seventeen destroyed. Major James B. Tapp was belle of the brawl, tangling with four aircraft types and bagging three. First he damaged a twin-engine fighter, then he downed a Kawasaki Tony, a Nakajima Oscar, and a Nakajima Tojo. Harry Crim headed the

21st's score column with two of the group's four kills. Tapp and Crim became two of Iwo's four aces, Tapp being first to achieve that distinction when he bagged a Mitsubishi Jack on April 19.

Nothing else over Japan had the Mustang's speed, and nothing could match its acceleration or high-altitude performance. The Mitsubishi Zero ("Zeke") was some 80 miles per hour slower, and could only hope to out-turn or out-climb the P-51 at low to medium altitudes. Among the fastest enemy fighters, the Nakajima Frank gave away 40 miles per hour to the '51, but it climbed and turned better. Still, a Mustang using maneuvering flaps could stay with a Frank long enough for a kill if the '51's speed was not excessive.

Nevertheless, Mustang jockeys could not always take the opposition for granted. During sweeps of Yokohama and Atsugi on May 29, the Sunsetters claimed twenty-eight victories, but not without loss. A twenty-three-year-old Kentuckian, Captain R. Todd Moore, Iwo's leading ace, shot down three planes but was more impressed with one enemy pilot. A lone Zero waded into the 15th Fighter Group, shot down a Mustang, and got away clean. It was Temei Akamatsu, the boozing, brawling rogue of Atsugi. Moore declared that an American duplicating the feat would have received the Medal of Honor.

Few pilots fired their guns at airborne bandits on more than five missions; top gun Todd Moore got eleven kills in eight engagements over the home islands. A handful of others added to previous records, most notably Colonel John W. Mitchell, who took over the 15th Group that summer. Highly experienced, he had led the 1943 interception resulting in the death of Admiral Isoroku Yamamoto, who directed the Pearl Harbor attack. Mitchell downed four planes over Japan to run his total to eleven, and would down four MiGs in the Korean War.

Despite the fame accorded top scorers, "ace fever" was relatively rare in World War II. Most pilots simply wanted to do as much as duty and honor required, and return to their civilian lives. But a few were like First Lieutenant Robert Scamara. The husky Californian had grown up reading the exploits of Great War aces, and he wanted to earn that title for himself. Assigned to the 15th Fighter Group, he notched his first kill on June 1 and was 20 percent toward his goal. Then he launched on a fighter strike near Tokyo on the 23rd.

Two dozen Mustangs were inbound to Shimodate Airfield northeast of the capital when the roof fell in. Attacked by seventeen defending fighters, the Americans were immediately forced on the defensive. The first Scamara knew of his peril was when the radio became a babble of shouts and warnings. Then tracer bullets snapped past him, from astern.

After the initial tussle, Scamara and wingman John V. Scanlan broke free and headed for the rendezvous point. Passing over a lake, they drew the notice of several Imperial Navy pilots who pounced on the vulnerable P-51s. Scamara watched, appalled, as Scanlan ignored his screams to turn away. Apparently suffering radio failure, Jack Scanlan flew straight and level as the Japanese opened fire, scoring repeated hits. Bob Scamara fought to protect his wingman but the odds were entirely lopsided: Scanlan abandoned his stricken fighter and parachuted near the beach.

Heartsick, Scamara turned south for Iwo. He had just experienced the best day of his combat career, and the worst. His gun camera film showed three kills and seven enemy planes damaged, but Jack Scanlan was never seen again. After the war, U.S. investigators determined that he had suffered multiple injuries and, after surviving a severe beating, was briefly held at an army headquarters. Then that afternoon he was thrown to a civilian mob that beat him to death.

Time over Japan

Always fuel-conscious, the Mustang pilots crossed the coast at a fairly high power setting to keep their spark plugs clean and their aircraft in fighting trim. They wanted the fuselage tank to contain less than forty gallons because in a steep turn, shifting fuel weight could cause the aircraft to roll violently.

To some pilots, the twenty to sixty minutes over Japan were just the thing to shake off the lethargy of the long northward flight. Harve Phipps recalled, "I think the combat break midway in the missions served to stimulate you enough that you didn't get bored. The main problem was the cramped cockpit space for the time involved."

For the return flight, Harry Crim explained, "We dropped our external tanks, shot up all our ammo, and tested the relief tube." Then it was a matter of managing fuel for the 750-mile flight home. Cruising at forty gallons per hour could burn up a set of plugs but the hardy Merlin engines did not seem to mind.

In addition to bomber escort, the Mustangs flew an increasing proportion of strike missions. Their primary targets were Japanese airfields or industrial facilities, and P-51s were often loaded with five-inch high-velocity aerial rockets. Six HVARs added about 700 pounds to takeoff weight but they packed a tremendous punch—equal to a destroyer's broadside—and proved effective against shipping and reinforced buildings.

Two coast-in points normally were used for sweep-strike missions. One was Inubo-Saki, a spit of land eighty miles east of Tokyo (Jimmy Doolittle's crews had used it as a checkpoint). The other, more circuitous, route was fifty miles north of there at Kawagaro. The latter allowed P-51s to enter the Tokyo area from the northeast—an unexpected direction.

The first strafing mission was intended for April 16 against Atsugi, Japan's largest airfield, but the P-51s were diverted to the Kanoya base, and in the confusion and poor visibility only fifty-seven of the 108 that took off actually attacked. Later missions were more successful, and from April 7 to June 30, VII Fighter Command claimed 666 enemy planes destroyed or damaged, mostly on the ground.

The standard strafing technique involved a squadron in close line astern flying at 1,500 feet and 200 mph. When the last flight leader was abreast of the field, he called for a 90-degree turn inbound. Each pilot then flew low across the field, shooting anything in front of him. At 200 mph there was time for careful aiming, and the sheer volume of fire from sixteen Mustangs' ninety-six guns was often enough to suppress flak. "You could really put a lot of ammunition into a place" Crim remarked.

After the first pass, a smart fighter pilot kept going. Returning to an alerted, angry target did not enhance longevity, and nobody relished the thought of becoming a prisoner of the Japanese.

The Sunsetters' last aerial combat occurred near Tokyo on August 10, when the 15th and 506th Groups claimed seven victories. In all, Iwo's Mustangs were credited with 236 Japanese planes shot down between April and August 1945—80 percent of all Pacific Theater P-51 aerial victories.

Search and Rescue

In some crucial ways the Japanese represented the lesser enemy for American airmen in the Marianas and Iwo Jima. Flying vast distances over the North Pacific meant that losses at sea were unavoidable. In that immense expanse, the task of finding the minuscule yellow dot of a life raft approached the nearly impossible. Yet it was done.

Air-sea rescue began almost as an impromptu enterprise but grew into a thoroughly professional, joint-service operation. Before March 1, 1945, forty-eight Marianas Superfortresses ditched with 528 crewmen. All of the 164 located were retrieved, but that represented fewer than one in three. The first commander of the Marianas bombers, Haywood Hansell, had noted divided responsibilities between finding downed fliers and rescuing them—generally along Army-Navy lines, respectively. He was working toward integrating the operation when LeMay took over, and the situation improved thereafter. By the end of May, eight fliers in ten were being saved from the sea.

Three means of rescue were available to downed fliers: seaplanes, submarines, and destroyers. Destroyers were generally stationed at 100-mile intervals from Iwo to Japan, while submarines and amphibious aircraft worked in enemy coastal waters.

From start to finish an airman's chances of rescue from the Pacific were just about even. Overall, 654 of 1,310 Army fliers known down at sea were saved. Of those, half were aboard bombers that ditched, demonstrating that water landings afforded greater survival prospects than the risk of drowning under a waterlogged parachute.

The Mustang pilots faced an additional problem. The P-51 handbook warned that the aircraft would float for perhaps two seconds after hitting the water, so standard procedure was to bail out rather than ditch.

Fear of capture prompted some crews to exercise excess caution, to the point of shunning use of radios or even flares. But gradually the situation improved. The AAF and Navy achieved fully joint operations with B-29 men riding submarines from Guam, and naval rescue personnel flying in Superfortresses. Thus, each side of the team learned firsthand about their opposite numbers.

Once a man was down in Empire waters, at least one flight "capped" him, orbiting overhead to guide submarines or "dumbo" seaplanes and to disrupt Japanese attempts to capture him. In extreme cases, Mustang pilots spent ten hours in the air on such a mission, abandoning their briefed targets and circling a squadron mate for four hours before heading home. On one occasion pilots saw an American submarine within a half-mile of shore trying to pick up a flier. Later a submarine skipper tired of the game, went in close to shore, sank a harassing patrol craft, scooped up the airman, and departed. At one time the 21st Fighter Group had ten rescued pilots on the duty submarine.

Some B-17s and B-29s were employed as rescue planes, specially modified to drop large motorboats to downed bomber crews or even to a single pilot. Based on Iwo Jima, the "super-dumbos" circled fifty to 100 miles off Japan until called in, with as many as eight assigned at a time.

Despite all the rescue efforts, nothing was certain. The 531st Fighter Squadron watched while one of its pilots climbed into one of the air-dropped boats only five miles offshore, expecting him to crank up the motor and head out to sea. But the pilot could not get the outboard started, and when the Mustangs had to leave, the Japanese came out and took him. Quite naturally, that caused a sensation back on Iwo where all available boats were checked. "Sure enough, none of them would start," Harry Crim recalled. "Needless to say, boat maintenance picked up after that."

One of VII Fighter Command's lingering concerns was that many new pilots had little or no idea of how to survive in the water. After watching one of its men drown because he couldn't get out of his parachute harness, the 21st Group urged a weekly training program that included tossing pilots out of a boat while instructors stood by to demonstrate or lend a hand.

It was said that some pilots were so satisfied with the rescue service that they came back for more. Lieutenant Frank Ayres limped his gimpy Mustang almost 500 miles back from the first Tokyo mission before he had to bail out over a destroyer. Two and a half months later, after battling three enemy fighters, Ayres again hit the silk over a lifeguard submarine and landed so close that he didn't have time to inflate his rubber raft.

By mid-August the Pacific command had fourteen submarines, twenty-one flying boats, nine super-dumbo aircraft, and five ships deployed for air-sea rescue. In all, some 2,400 men were assigned to the effort—one-quarter of the number engaged in flying B-29 missions.

Whatever the assets, a successful rescue effort involved equal commitment between men determined to live and other men—usually strangers—determined to save them. That was proven on June 26 when B-29s attacked the Nagoya Arsenal. The only loss over the city was to flak, erratically described as "heavy, meager to moderate, inaccurate to accurate."

Leading the mission was the 39th Group's commander, thirty-nine-year-old Colonel George W. Mundy. A West Point classmate of Rosie O'Donnell, he had graduated in the same pilot class as Curt LeMay. Like most airmen of that vintage, Mundy rose fast. At the time of Pearl Harbor he was a major but he pinned on his eagles the next year and took over the group in March 1945.

The Nagoya mission was Mundy's fifteenth. He flew with Major John Miranda's crew in the daytime strike, bombing at 24,000 feet. *City of Galveston* took two crippling hits from 120mm flak that shot off six to eight feet of the right wing, jammed the bomb bay doors open, and damaged two engines. With no chance of making base, the pilots got the crippled bomber headed out to sea.

Meanwhile, radio problems prevented *City of Galveston* from transmitting normally so another B-29, *Lord's Prayer*, acted as radio relay, contacting the lifeguard submarine. The escorting bomber was flown by First Lieutenant Robert L. Spaulding, at twenty-three probably the youngest aircraft commander in the group. Miranda called, "Bob, get me to a sub." Spaulding's navigator, Lieutenant Edward S. Edmundson, immediately went to work, calculating that the *City* needed to turn from its southerly course to due west.

Precise navigation was crucial, as the stricken bomber could not maintain altitude, and an error in the course to the sub would put the crew in the water short of safety.

Nevertheless, Edmundson hit the position spot-on, with only 2,000 feet altitude to spare. There, eight miles offshore, Mundy and Miranda held the faltering bomber wings-level while the crew bailed out near the submarine *Pintado*. The pilots jumped seconds before the plane dropped into a spin.

Aboard *Pintado*, an officer recorded the scene. "We came in sight of a burning aircraft, plunging helpless into the sea. As we looked up into the sky, following the burning smoke screen, twelve men were merrily gliding down towards the sea. . . . The two sister airplanes that were giving us air cover dipped their wings in a 'well-done boys' and disappeared, homeward bound."

Miranda and Mundy got out at nearly the last moment—about 800 feet. But in forty minutes the submarine scooped up the dozen Army men, who enjoyed a mixed reception. The sailors quickly "commandeered" everything resembling a souvenir, from sunglasses to pistols, but the airmen did not object overmuch. As Mundy observed, "You don't come out with a thing except your life."

Later Miranda's crew expressed its gratitude by christening a new B-29 USS *Pintado*. It was probably the only time an airplane was named for a submarine.

Bomber crews represented nearly a dozen lives, but extraordinary efforts were made to save one American from the Japanese or from the sea, and no better example exists than Captain Edward Mikes. On August 3, as the 506th Fighter Group strafed near Atsugi, Mikes's Mustang took a lethal hit in the engine. The Merlin ran long enough to get him to the bay, where he bailed out. Once in the water he lit a flare to mark his position four miles offshore.

Capping the "splash," another P-51 pilot called Jukebox 70, the B-17 rescue aircraft standing by with a droppable boat. But the Japanese also were interested. A picket boat that ventured from Misaki was promptly sunk by Mikes's guardians, but enemy aircraft were reported inbound.

Meanwhile, Jukebox arrived, flown by Second Lieutenant Burt Klatt with an eight-man crew. On the first pass over Mikes the twenty-seven-foot boat refused to drop so Klatt banked around for another try. Finally the boat fell free on the third pass—just as bandits were reported inbound.

At the same time the submarine *Aspro* had been summoned, with Lieutenant Commander James H. Ashley, Jr., coordinating the multitiered efforts after the B-17 departed. The sub skipper had contact with the Mustangs as well as two navy Privateer patrol bombers that had just sunk a coastal transport.

About then, Japanese fighters arrived. Lieutenant Yutaka Morioka, who had lost a hand to B-29 gunners, led three other Zeros from Atsugi. He led the bounce on the top-cover Mustangs orbiting at 1,500 feet. One P-51 spun into the water on the first pass, and the fight degenerated into individual tail chases. Morioka latched on to another American but the intended victim put the spurs to his Mustang, leaving the Zero in his slipstream.

Undeterred, Morioka led his flight down to investigate the strange boat and recognized it for what it was. Making repeated runs, the Zeros fired more than 1,000 rounds of machine gun ammunition into the hardy vessel, which remained afloat though Mikes sustained minor wounds. When the Privateers turned toward the action, the Japanese departed, low on ammunition.

But the fight was not yet finished. Mikes was mere yards from *Aspro* when a Japanese floatplane clattered overhead, forcing the sub to "pull the plug" and dive. The two Privateers, led by the aggressive Lieutenant Commander Raymond Pflumb, met the intruder head-on and shot it down in flames.

Minutes later *Aspro* surfaced, as Ashley had seen the fight through the periscope. Just as Mikes prepared to hop aboard, another enemy floatplane dropped in, scoring near misses on the sub. Again Ashley took her down, still without Mikes, and again Pflumb's team dispatched the intruder.

Finally, nearly two hours after bailing out, Ed Mikes scrambled aboard *Aspro*. His first words were, "Let's get the hell out of here."

Four Japanese fliers and one American had died in the rescue of Ed Mikes. In 1991 he met his one-handed enemy, Yutaka Morioka, who said, "I'm very sorry about our first meeting." Then Morioka grinned. "You are alive today because our shooting was bad!"

In such meetings among once bitter enemies, perhaps both sides could agree that in war the greatest victory lay in survival.

CHAPTER SEVEN

The Harbor War

BLUE-EYED, WHITE-HAIRED ADMIRAL Chester Nimitz commanded the Central Pacific Theater and the U.S. Pacific Fleet from his headquarters on Guam. He had assumed the latter title on the last day of 1941 and steadily built his command from the oil-scummed waters of Pearl Harbor into the greatest naval striking force of all time.

Now, in 1945, America had carried the war to Japan's home islands, and that summer the Army Air Forces and Navy, concentrating on the enemy's vulnerable coastline, launched "the harbor war."

As an island nation Japan was vulnerable to blockade. It imported most of the essential materials for an industrial nation, including food, 80 percent of its oil, and 90 percent of its iron ore plus other strategic materials. Pacific Fleet submarines had preyed upon Japan's merchant marine with increasing success since 1943, and after two years Tokyo was feeling the strain. Nimitz intended to push the enemy over the edge. But he needed the Army's cooperation to do it.

The Committee of Operations Analysts in Washington supported Nimitz's request for a B-29 aerial mining campaign. After initial reluctance, Curtis LeMay agreed to devote part of one wing to laying mines in Japanese waterways. The operation began in late March 1945 and almost immediately proved itself. Today it remains one of the least known, most efficient, and cost-effective air campaigns in history. The airmen called it Operation Starvation.

Operation Starvation

Institutionally the AAF considered mining "the Navy's job" and saw little in the mission to enhance the airmen's goals. Strictly speaking, that was correct: mining choke points did nothing to reduce urban-industrial areas to smoking rubble, and there would be little to show for the effort. But beyond the parochial considerations of service pride, B-29 mining had both immediate and long-range benefits: it reduced Japan's already dangerously low level of strategic imports—and it helped end the war.

Having expressed his reservations about mining, once the order came down, LeMay said "Yes, sir," and raised B-29 mining from Hansell's previous group-strength effort. When the 313th Wing arrived in January 1945, LeMay immediately put Brigadier General J. H. Davies's command to work, training for low-level, over-water night flying. Three years older than LeMay, the boyish, slender Davies was well qualified for the job: he had flown bombers since 1932 and commanded two combat groups, beginning in the dismal Philippine days of 1942 when he led "maximum effort" missions of three planes. One of the few commanders truly loved by his men, Davies was highly regarded as "a motivator and organizer."

The timing was fortunate. With mining to begin around April 1, LeMay would have an extra four groups just as support of the Okinawa landings occurred. Therefore, he could have it both ways: comply with Nimitz's and Arnold's directives without diminishing either.

The prime choke point was obvious from a quick look at the map. Shimonoseki Strait between Kyushu and Honshu was the only outlet from the Inland Sea to the Sea of Japan. The Americans also monitored the eastern straits flanking Shikoku.

On the afternoon of March 27, "Skippy" Davies shoved his

throttles forward and rolled down Tinian's runway with 103 bombers behind him. In Operation Starvation's debut, ninety-two Superfortresses dropped mines in their designated areas while three never returned. From that night on, Japan's remaining large warships shunned Shimonoseki.

Three nights later eighty-five more "miners" placed their loads in the strait. Aerial reconnaissance was enthusiastically received on Guam: initial reports showed a 75 percent reduction in shipping transiting Shimonoseki. It looked as if the original minefields would be sufficient for up to two weeks, while much smaller missions mined the Kure-Hiroshima area containing Japanese fleet units.

Most mining missions required flying 3,200 miles round-trip, permitting a payload of 12,000 pounds of mines. The common types were 1,000- and 2,000-pound weapons, depending on availability. But they had to be delivered accurately, and aircrews were required to fly straight and level along predictable paths within reach of guns from shore. Though tension ran high among bomber crews, losses were blessedly low.

However, casualties were unavoidable, and all left a gap. On the night of July 9, the 6th Group lost a revered squadron commander, Lieutenant Colonel Elmer Dixon. Flight engineer Virgil Morgan recalled him as "an outstanding leader who had completed a North Africa tour before joining the Sixth." Dixon was flying with the crew of *Take It Off*, a new plane that had not received black paint on the undersurfaces. Caught by searchlights, it was hit by flak and/or fighters, then exploded. Dixon was "very popular with the enlisted men for his willingness to talk and listen to us," said Morgan.

Originally mines were fitted with magnetic or acoustic detonators, but many fell on land and, lacking self-destruct fuses, were examined by Japanese engineers. A countermeasures officer recalled, "On 27 May we recovered 30 mines and . . . we discovered the magnetic pressure type." Shortly thereafter a low-frequency acoustic detonator was introduced, further complicating Japanese defenses.

Radar worked reasonably well for delivering mines. Sharp pictures were readily displayed because land and sea contrasted best on radar scopes, though bombardiers had to use "offset bombing" from identifiable landmarks since the water provided no aim point. The greatest complication was accurately assessing wind velocity, as the parachute-retarded mines could drift considerably when dropped from 5,000 to 6,000 feet.

Starvation became a joint operation between XXI Bomber Command and the Naval Mine Modification Unit on Tinian. The "ordies" provided the "flyboys" with a variety of options ranging from delay fuses to ship counters and various settings for magnetic and acoustic detonators. Throughout the campaign, the Americans fought a seesaw war, seeking optimum balance between effectiveness in sinking ships and difficulty in sweeping mines.

The campaign progressed through five stages, each targeting specific areas while "reseeding" previous minefields. Only five additional missions were launched through April, averaging just ten bombers each. Consequently, most of the 313th Wing continued with conventional bombing attacks.

Colonel Robert A. Ping's 505th Group became LeMay's designated hitter for mining, and in the words of a postwar study "became expert in its task." From May to July Operation Starvation averaged twenty-five to thirty bombers per night as about one-fourth of the 505th's total sorties laid mines.

In July the miners achieved a near total blockade of Shimonoseki, Honshu, and Kyushu, plus some Korean ports. The campaign put the cork in Tokyo's bottle—that summer the food situation approached critical.

The results exceeded expectations as losses to mines rocketed from eighteen ships sunk in April to more than eighty each in May and June. Shimonoseki traffic fell 90 percent between March and July while tonnage entering industrial ports dropped from more than 800,000 in March to a quarter-million in July. Imports of selected commodities that ran over 20 million tons in 1941 were halved in 1944, plummeting to 2.7 million tons through June 1945.

Operation Starvation did not totally eliminate imports to Japan but it reduced them below minimum acceptable levels. Japan's inadequate road and rail networks forced increasing reliance upon coastal shipping, which was adversely affected by mining.

B-29 mines sank 293 ships from late March to mid-August, averaging two a day. Furthermore, Japanese shipyards became clogged with damaged vessels awaiting repair. Eighteen of the nation's twenty-one large repair yards were bottlenecked in the Inland Sea or on the east coast. Japan's admiralty had no option but to close its Pacific ports. That left only the west coast harbors to receive what little cargo survived the perilous voyage from China or Korea. The result was a huge dent in the emperor's remaining merchant marine, which represented about 60 percent of shipping losses from April through August.

Lacking anything like sufficient minesweepers, the Imperial Navy simply could not clear enough minefields to keep choke points open. LeMay ensured that fields were resown often, and in sufficient density to prevent more than a trickle of ships from getting through.

Perhaps 20,000 Japanese and nearly 350 vessels were engaged in minesweeping efforts, which were largely ineffective. Radar, searchlights, and underwater sound equipment were used in spotting mines but located just 30 percent of those dropped. Furthermore, sometimes two months were needed to counter a new type of mine.

After the war Captain Rokuemon Minami described Seventh Fleet problems in Shimonoseki Strait: "Due to the fact that the United States did not use mines extensively during the first years of the war, the Japanese allowed their research efforts to relax and consequently were in no way prepared for the saturation type of attack that was delivered in Japanese waters in the spring of 1945." He added that sometimes traffic in the straits became so congested that it was necessary to force ships through regardless of losses.

The 313th Bomb Wing performed one of the significant feats in air warfare, but due to the sensitive nature of its mission, it received little attention. Operation Starvation met the doctrinal concept of economy of force: maximum damage to the enemy for minimum expenditure of effort, lives, and treasure. In forty-six missions Davies's crews delivered 12,000 mines, losing 103 fliers and fifteen aircraft from 1,500 mining sorties. Even more remarkably, just nine of the B-29 losses were due to enemy action.

Accolades came from all quarters, not least from on high. In April Nimitz wrote LeMay expressing profound gratitude for Starvation, calling the results "phenomenal."

The greatest tribute came from Captain Kyzue Tamura, head of the Imperial Navy Mine Sweeping Section, who had studied physics and served as naval attaché in Rome. "About 1 April your mines changed from a nuisance to a problem. We increased the aircraft and searchlight units attached to certain areas such as Niigata and Shimonoseki at the expense of the cities. . . . The use of aircraft units against dropping of mines by B-29s was more important than protection of the cities because the life lines from the continent which furnished food and supplies were of first priority. The result of the mining . . . was so effective that it eventually starved the country. I think you probably could have shortened the war by beginning earlier."

Fast Carriers Versus Japan

The invasion of Japan began on July 1, 1945. On that Sunday, Task Force 38 steamed from its Philippine anchorage, launching Phase One of Operation Olympic, the run-up to the Kyushu invasion planned for November. A series of strikes lasting into mid-August would establish air supremacy over the home islands, setting the stage for Operation Coronet, the Honshu landings.

Admiral Bull Halsey's Third Fleet hierarchy included Vice Admiral John McCain, who had succeeded Marc Mitscher as commander of the fast carriers. Riding the new Essex class carrier *Shangri-La*, "Slew" McCain was considered "a real salty old dog" who cultivated a disheveled appearance. He affected a brimmed uniform hat with the grommets removed—strictly nonregulation—and was prone to dribble tobacco on himself when rolling a cigarette. A junior officer who had worked for him in Washington recalled "his striking resemblance to Popeye the Sailor . . . McCain looked as if he had slept in his uniform three nights running."

Hailing from the Annapolis class of '06, McCain was a JCL, a Johnny Come Lately to flying. He had received wings of gold in 1936 at age fifty-two and commanded the carrier *Ranger* but had little cockpit experience. (A subordinate said, "I don't think he could fly an airplane to save his life.") In 1942 McCain eked out an undistinguished record commanding aircraft in the South Pacific, then held administrative posts in Washington. However, he performed reasonably well commanding one of Mitscher's task groups off the Philippines during late 1944 and ascended to command of Task Force 38 the next year. Not quite sixty-one, he had nine weeks to live before his heart failed.

Despite American air and sea supremacy, there was only so much that carrier aircraft could accomplish. In June, Rear Admiral Arthur Radford, a task group commander, noted that the fast carriers' mission had changed. Previously a mobile striking arm, now TF 38 was less concerned with mobility than blockade. He conceded, "Working with the B-29s, we can do the pinpoint work on small targets, while the big bombers go after large industrial establishments."

In truth, Radford—a future chief of naval operations—was acknowledging the Navy's reduced status in the aviation hierarchy; blockade was essentially a defensive measure, whereas the greatest offensive airpower belonged to LeMay's B-29s. That situation would continue if Operation Olympic-Coronet proceeded, when the carriers' primary mission would be providing fighter screens over the invasion fleet. However, naval aviators would have a major investment in providing close air support for assault troops who crossed the high tide mark.

*   *   *   *   *

Approaching the enemy coast on July 10, Third Fleet fully expected "the kamikaze boys" to come out in force, hence the welcome cover of weather. Only one Japanese plane was felled by Hellcats, fifty miles from the task force. When the first missions were launched, McCain's aviators were astonished to find that they owned the sky over Tokyo. Not a single enemy rose to challenge them.

Tokyo ceded control of its homeland airspace for a valid reason. Expecting the invasion in October, the Japanese acknowledged the futility of engaging superior aircraft flown by more skillful pilots. Consequently, Tokyo began hoarding its airpower for massive suicide attacks against the Allied fleet.

Halsey and McCain raised their sights, planning strikes against northern Honshu and part of Hokkaido on July 13. But the weather turned sour, forcing a forty-eight-hour delay. While Japanese fighters remained grounded, carrier planes scoured the coastlines, sinking local shipping and a few minor naval vessels.

Silent Victory: Hokkaido's Ferries

A far better use of carrier squadrons was a series of attacks against strategic targets on northern Honshu and nearby Hokkaido. American intelligence understood that coal powered most of Japan's industry, especially on Honshu, which imported 83 percent of its requirement. Analysis further indicated that a significant reduction in Honshu coal would result in immobilizing the island's rail lines.

On July 14, McCain's air groups launched against northern airfields to establish air superiority before the planned strikes. But fog forced the pilots to divert from their briefed targets for better weather along the coast. Most of the 850 sorties struck several Hokkaido ports, many crowded with merchantmen sheltering from air-dropped mines. The naval aviators sank a destroyer escort, eleven naval auxiliary vessels, and twelve merchant or military cargo-transport ships.

One of *Hancock*'s youngsters recorded a spectacular success as Hellcats descended on shipping off the port city of Nemuro. Ensign C. M. Craig ripple-fired his load of rockets into a vessel estimated at 4,500 tons, "setting off an explosion which broke the ship apart." She was *Toyu Maru*, actually rated at 1,256 tons, but still the effect was impressive.

Far more importantly, the Navy destroyed seven of the dozen train ferries in the Aomori-Hakodate area. Twenty years previously Japan had produced four 3,400-ton ferries capable of carrying twenty-five railroad cars bearing a total 375 tons of freight. The vessels were powered by steam turbines—rare for the period—yielding 17 knots speed. Other ferries were launched in the late 1920s, carrying forty-three cars at 14 knots. All were crucial to Japanese industry.

Dodging through the weather, flying low to keep visual reference, the pilots found their vital, unglamorous targets. *Essex*'s air group contributed heavily to the operation: her fighters and bombers sank four ferries and hit another hard enough to force it ashore.

The next day TF 38 squadrons returned to sink a merchantman, four auxiliaries, and another invaluable ferry.

The result was astonishing. Literally overnight the amount of Hokkaido coal delivered to Honshu factories dropped more than 80 percent. Since Hokkaido typically produced one-fourth of Japan's indigenous coal, elimination of the ferries represented a crippling loss that was not replaced. Scores of much smaller vessels still carried loose cargos but those were sunk by the dozens in low-level bombing and strafing attacks.

For the admirals still obsessed with "the fighting navy," the Hokkaido strikes represented extreme ambivalence. While proving carrier aviation's contribution to the overall strategic effort, the operation also demonstrated that lowly ferries represented far greater strategic targets than Japan's remaining first-line warships.

The Saga of Oliver Rasmussen

The two-day strike against Hokkaido cost forty-four aircraft to all causes and twenty-six fliers. One of the first day's eight Helldiver losses was *Shangri-La*'s Lieutenant (jg) Howard Eagleston, who descended into the undercast and smashed into a mountain. He was killed on impact but his gunner, twenty-three-year-old radioman Oliver B. Rasmussen, survived, beginning an incredible ten-week odyssey.

With only the clothes he wore and an empty knapsack, Rasmussen had merely a general idea of his location. But he knew what the Japanese did to prisoners. Part Chippewa Indian ("second generation out of the teepee"), he preferred to take his chances in the Hokkaido wilderness.

As a sailor, Rasmussen instinctively sought the sea. He spent seventeen days reaching the coast, dodging anyone he encountered, living off the land. On July 31, his first genuine nourishment came from an unexpected source: a farmer's cow. For the next nine nights the aircrewman crept to the tethered animal, helped himself to fresh milk, and returned to his hideout. At length the owner turned the cow loose, apparently concluding she was no longer producing. As Rasmussen related, "He never got wise that I was the guy getting all the milk."

Next Rasmussen tried launching a small boat but the breakers prevented him from reaching the open sea. Disappointed, he withdrew into the mountains and established himself in a railroad shack. There he dined on raw onions, bird's eggs, and uncooked rice. On good days he added frog's legs.

On August 16, thirty-two days into his ordeal, Rasmussen was seen by a Japanese civilian. Probably neither man knew that the emperor had announced surrender the day before, but Rasmussen was wise to scamper away—many Allied airmen were murdered after the radio address.

Scouting around, Rasmussen found a spot within reach of five farms. Using scavenged lumber, he built a small hut and helped himself to the local largesse. His new arrangement was even better than the first farm, since the locals cooled their milk in nearby streams. Skimming the cream, he helped himself to generous servings—his best night was nine quarts.

Then, on the night of September 5, some dogs got the American's scent—he had not bathed in seven weeks. Their owners began searching and Rasmussen had to make a break. "Several Japs came out jabbering and some of them started to close in on me. I bowled a couple over and ran like hell."

Deprived of his commissary, Rasmussen kept moving. When he noted more American planes flying low every day, drawing no gunfire, his hopes soared.

Unable to attract a passing aircraft, Rasmussen opted for a direct approach. On September 19 he walked into the port of Tomakomai. The police chief gave the unexpected guest a cigarette and confirmed that Japan had surrendered. Then, concerned with recent events in his jurisdiction, the chief asked about disappearing milk over the previous month. Rasmussen blandly declined any knowledge of the thefts and enjoyed his first real meal and a bath in sixty-eight days.

Upon return to the *Shangri-La*, Oliver Rasmussen related his exceptional adventure to a rapt crew, then caught an aircraft for the States, traveling Priority Two. He spent a full career in the Navy but died of cancer in 1980, only age fifty-seven.

Allies

In mid-July, Task Force 38 received reinforcements. The Royal Navy task group, built around four fast carriers, represented the striking arm of the British Pacific Fleet (BPF), which had participated in the Okinawa campaign under Mitscher's Task Force 58.

British naval policy in the Pacific had been established at the Quebec Conference in September 1944. After discussing Allied occupation of a defeated Germany, Roosevelt and Churchill turned to the Royal Navy's role against Japan. Churchill offered the Americans a sizable Royal Navy force in the Pacific, and Roosevelt readily accepted. The details were left to the respective admiralties.

The BPF had been established in November 1944 with its main base at Sydney, Australia, and the advanced base at Manus in the Admiralties ("Scapa Flow with bloody palm trees"). Its mission was at least as much geopolitical as operational, since London insisted that British forces appear as an active if junior partner in operations against Japan's home islands. The Royal Navy regarded a front-rank role "of the utmost importance" in contrast to General Douglas MacArthur's frequent use of Australians in supporting actions.

With barely 150 ships in the world's greatest ocean, the BPF was top-heavy with braid. In overall command was Admiral Sir Bruce Fraser, who remained ashore in Australia. His seagoing commander, Vice Admiral Sir Henry Bernard Rawlings, was a battleship and cruiser officer who had seen combat in the Mediterranean. More relevantly, Vice Admiral Sir Philip Vian commanded the carriers: HMS *Formidable*, *Indefatigable*, *Indomitable*, and *Victorious*. A nonaviator, Vian had extensive experience in the North Sea and Mediterranean, and directed the Royal Navy's landings in Normandy. Though capable, he irritated many of his countrymen, some of whom described him as "a very nasty piece of work with an acid tongue, and a snobbish social climber to boot."

Halsey—always companionable—enjoyed His Majesty's admirals as social and drinking partners but kept a professional distance. In truth, few Americans wanted the British poaching on U.S. Navy turf. Third Fleet staff saw the "Brits"—correctly—as latecomers to the game, whose government might expect to share the inevitable victory. While Halsey indulged the Royal Navy as much as diplomacy required, he usually sent the BPF on lesser errands with concurrence of America's profoundly Anglophobic chief of naval operations, Ernest King.

Nevertheless, Halsey extended what courtesy he could, sailor to sailor. Given a choice of integrating into TF 38 or operating independently, Rawlings readily accepted the former. Thus united, the allies agreed upon the tasks at hand: maintain air superiority over Japan, strike worthwhile targets inland, attack remaining enemy shipping, and probe northern Honshu and Hokkaido.

Vian later wrote that Halsey seemed "fully aware of our difficulties, and from that moment onwards, by kindly word or deed, he availed himself of every possible opportunity to offer encouragement and to smooth our path."

Certainly the nautical path needed some smoothing. Britain's Fleet Air Arm was not expected to match the more experienced Americans' operating tempo, though Vian strove mightily. Halsey later wrote disingenuously that the British "were able to match us strike for strike." In truth, there was little opportunity, as RN aircrews only flew over Japan for the last four weeks of hostilities.

To paraphrase George Bernard Shaw, the Americans and British had two navies separated by a common language. That certainly applied to communications; the BPF had no choice but to adopt U.S. codebooks and procedures. Additionally, standard phraseology differed. Royal Navy catapults were "boosters" and elevators were "lifts." British landing signal officers were "deck landing control officers" or "batsmen" who used different signals. The American signal for "high" meant "You are too high" but in the Fleet Air Arm it meant "Go higher." The Brits had no signal for "too slow," and the two services used opposite signals for "lower your hook." Apparently the differences were never fully resolved.

Furthermore, Britain's aerial torpedoes were incompatible with Grumman aircraft bomb bays so RN Avengers only carried bombs. Standard "kit" such as radios and even oxygen masks also were different.

Other problems rose from the keel up. British carriers were designed to operate in the freezing Atlantic and the balmy Mediterranean, posing serious habitability problems in the sweltering Pacific. Additionally, the size and nature of the Pacific War forced unaccustomed strains upon the Royal Navy, which historically operated near bases much closer to home. Consequently, the British had too few tankers—often old, slow ships ill suited to operating with fast carriers. Additionally, the RN still used the stern-to-bow method of refueling at sea, far slower than the Americans' more efficient side-by-side method. A British correspondent who had been aboard USS *Lexington* marveled that the Yanks refueled a fleet carrier in barely two hours whereas the RN took most of a day.

Nine of the BPF's fifteen carrier squadrons flew American aircraft: Hellcats, Corsairs, and Avengers. The Seafire, a "navalised" version of the legendary Spitfire fighter, proved an excellent if short-legged performer but suffered under the severe strains of carrier landings. The two-seat Firefly fighter-bomber represented an outdated concept, designed under the assumption that a carrier pilot needed a navigator.

With armored decks, RN carriers were more resistant to bomb and kamikaze damage than their wooden U.S. counterparts. However, with smaller hangar decks the Fleet Air Arm embarked fewer planes in its largest carriers, and often was hard pressed to keep up with perennially heavy losses to all causes. In one series of strikes the BPF lost forty-one planes in just 378 sorties—a 10.8 percent loss rate that would have rocked even the casualty-numbed RAF Bomber Command. There was also a high incidence of operational losses, sometimes more than half the total.

Despite serious drawbacks, the British Commonwealth aircrews and sailors stuck to their duty. In four weeks operating over Japan, BPF aircraft sank or destroyed at least three warships, two transports, and a coastal defense vessel.

The British fliers paid a high price for their contribution, but they took pride in their work. A TF 38 staffer recalled a British Corsair pilot who landed aboard USS *Shangri-La* to refuel. "The kid was 18 or 19 years old but he handled an F4U perfectly well. I was impressed."

The Immobile Fleet

Through much of the war the Imperial Navy's striking arm was designated the Mobile Fleet. But in October 1944 the Battle of Leyte Gulf ended Japan's offensive naval capability, prompting the American taunt of the "immobile fleet."

On paper the emperor's remaining armada appeared impressive: Kure Naval Base in the Inland Sea boasted three carriers, three battleships, and three active cruisers plus nautical cats and dogs. But the ships represented no threat beyond the traditional naval "force in being." Undermanned, lacking sufficient fuel oil, deprived of meaningful air cover, they could only sulk in their mined-in harbors.

Nevertheless, Admiral Ernest King in Washington wanted the Kure armada put on the muddy bottom in July 1945. Nimitz concurred, and Halsey was delighted to comply.

The official explanation for the July attacks appears a facade to cover other agendas. Officially, the Joint Chiefs held that when the Soviets finally entered the war they would demand increased Lend-Lease supplies. With the Third Fleet overwhelmingly committed to supporting Operation Olympic from October onward, presumably early strikes to knock out the remaining Japanese warships would reduce the need for powerful forces up north.

A cogent assessment was offered four decades later by then Lieutenant Commander William N. Leonard, McCain's assistant operations officer. Leonard recounted, "Some Neanderthals back at PacFleet Headquarters wanted continuation of a navy versus navy fight and we lost many good people to no good purpose. With the Jap navy lying doggo, PacFleet began to assert itself more and more into the assignment of missions and objectives of the fast carriers."

Leonard's attitude largely mirrored that of Commander Task Force 38 (CTF-38). McCain considered the Kure strikes "a waste of time" but could only go so far in objecting. Occasionally he argued with Halsey, though seldom successfully. Instead, he talked to pilots over coffee, asking their opinions and sometimes accepted their advice.

McCain opposed targeting shipping, preferring to strike airfields and aircraft factories, though he kept his counsel for the moment. However, his priorities also were skewed: events had already shown the benefits of sinking Japanese coastal traffic such as Hokkaido's rail ferries—a task that carrier aircraft could accomplish with relative ease. But whatever their service, airmen were magnetically pulled toward the enemy's aviation industry, while steamers and merchantmen lacked the perceived glamour of aircraft factories.

Nobody would admit it—certainly not in writing—but at least some of the impetus for the July operations probably had more to do with service politics than winning the war. Both the Navy and the Army Air Forces were looking not far downrange when the inevitable Washington battle would be joined, determining whether there would be an independent air force. Almost certainly the admirals wanted to run up the score, demonstrating naval aviation's huge contribution to destroying the enemy fleet, and the fat pickings at Kure became irresistible: over 200,000 tons in major combatants.

In some ways, Kure represented the greatest flak trap in history. The big harbor contained nothing that could seriously harm the Third Fleet, as the remnants of the Imperial Navy lacked sufficient fuel and trained crews—let alone the raw naval power—to pose a major threat. But geisha-like, Kure smiled (or smirked) behind her ornamental fan, crooked a fetching finger at King, Nimitz, and Halsey, and coyly invited them in.

They rushed to accept.

The final campaign against the Imperial Navy began on July 18 when carrier squadrons swept over Yokosuka Naval Base. Just south of Tokyo, Yokosuka (pronounced Ya-*kus*-ka) harbored a small armada including the battleship *Nagato*.

Though hailed as the world's first 16-inch-gun ship, *Nagato*'s twenty-four-year career had been unremarkable. Following bomb damage off the Philippines, she had been laid up at Yokosuka since

November 1944. Nevertheless, Halsey considered her a prestige target: she had been Admiral Yamamoto's flagship.

Recon photos showed *Nagato* moored pierside beneath one of the largest cranes in Japan, providing the Americans an excellent reference point. In a vain attempt to hide her bulk, the Japanese removed the top third of her mast and funnel to lower the silhouette, but not even bow-to-stern camouflage netting concealed her 42,000 tons. With her boilers idle she had a minesweeper alongside to provide power.

Nagato's position in port, with nearby mountains, limited dive approaches, while the shallow harbor precluded torpedoes. Consequently, preliminary air strikes focused on beating down the defenses, estimated at 250 antiaircraft emplacements around the harbor.

The afternoon target coordinator was *Essex*'s Commander Harmon T. Utter. He directed his bombers onto the battlewagon while fighters strafed AA guns. Leading the Helldivers was Lieutenant Commander David R. Berry, a 1942 hero with three Navy Crosses.

Following the skipper, Ensign Ernest E. Hutto jinked his way through bursting flak, looking for the target. Ernie Hutto was a rare bird: he had dropped out of Annapolis, citing physical abuse, and applied for flight training. A year later he was flying missions over Japan.

Abruptly Berry dived, leaving Hutto with Lieutenant James T. Crawford and Lieutenant (jg) Larry Gordon. Lacking time to reduce throttle or extend his dive brakes, Hutto could only open his bomb bay before nosing over. He recalled, "I passed the other two planes in a blur."

With only seconds to line up the target, at 2,500 feet Hutto placed his sight on the bridge and pressed the red button on the stick grip, releasing his half-ton bomb. Then he pulled hard. Under heavy g-force, his Helldiver's nose came level with the horizon about 1,000 feet over the harbor. He asked his gunner, Radioman Jim Reynolds, "What did it look like?" Reynolds, groggy from the high-g pullout, had not seen the bomb strike.

Simultaneously, Crawford and other pilots dived from other directions, compounding the enemy gunners' problems.

One bomb—likely Hutto's—was precisely aimed, exploding on the bridge, wrecking the wheelhouse. It killed thirteen of the eighteen-man bridge crew, including retired Rear Admiral Miki Otsuka, who had been recalled to duty in 1939. Location of the hit was symbolic: it was where Yamamoto had issued the order for the Pearl Harbor operation.

Another heavy bomb, possibly Crawford's, exploded against the base of *Nagato's* number three turret, killing twenty-five AA gunners and destroying four 25mm mounts. In all, *Essex* aviators claimed six hits while losing two aircraft.

Amid a deluge of bombs and rockets, some were bound to fall wide of *Nagato*. One struck the minesweeper tied alongside, blowing it apart. Other strikes sank an aged cruiser (veteran of the 1905 war with Russia), an incomplete destroyer, a submarine, and five lesser vessels. In exchange, the Yokosuka attackers sustained five losses. At least twenty-one aircraft were lost in other missions. Especially hard hit was *Bennington's* Air Group 1, which left seven planes at Kure Harbor, while *Hancock* wrote off four aircraft in a landing accident.

After the attack *Nagato's* AA guns were removed for more profitable use elsewhere. She survived the war to expire radioactively in the 1946 Bikini A-bomb test.

The Kure Blitz

On July 24, McCain's aviators began a two-day blitz against Kure Naval Base. The operation included sweeps of airfields around Nagoya and Osaka, though aerial opposition generally was light.

The Americans had to shoot their way into Kure on the 24th, but the fighter sweep preceding the bombers did its job. Hellcats from *San Jacinto* and Corsairs off *Bennington* tangled with two dozen of Captain Minoru Genda's elite "flying circus," downing six Georges while losing four Hellcats or Corsairs. In a nose-to-nose shootout, rookie Corsair pilot Lieutenant (jg) Robert M. Applegate traded gunfire with Ensign Kaneyoshi Muto, hero of the dogfight over Atsugi back in February. Both fighters went down but the twenty-three-year-old Oregonian slew "the toughest dogfighter in the Imperial Navy" and lived to tell the tale.

The main events occurred in Kure Harbor, whose prime targets included the hermaphrodite battleships *Ise* and *Hyuga*, both modified with aft aircraft decks. Bull Halsey nursed a grudge against the sisters, which had eluded him at Leyte Gulf and again in the South China Sea. But on the morning of July 24, *Ise* was rocked by three bombs on the flight deck, main deck, and number three turret. More planes inflicted further damage later in the day.

Even the fighters attacked warships. In the morning, diving through flak below 3,000 feet, *Hancock's* Hellcats scored three observed hits: two on *Ise* and another on the cruiser *Aoba*. In the afternoon strike Lieutenant Robert Klinger's four-plane division dropped aluminum strips to foil Japanese radar, then attacked with bombs. They went after the new carriers *Amagi* and *Katsuragi*, claiming a 1,000-pounder on the latter's fantail. Actually it exploded in a gun tub, killing a thirteen-man antiaircraft crew.

At noon the blue airplanes were back, thirty going for the battleship *Ise*. A direct hit on the bridge killed Captain Kakuro Mutaguchi, who received the customary posthumous promotion to rear admiral. Throughout the day *Ise* took at least five direct hits, leaving fifty dead. The antiaircraft officer, Lieutenant Commander Isamu Morooka, was appointed acting CO—probably the most junior officer ever to command a battleship.

Ise settled by the bow, but damage repairmen began a long fight against the rising water. Three days later she had achieved an even keel again, and plans were made to tow her to dry dock.

In more than seven hours of air operations, battleship *Hyuga* was targeted repeatedly. The crew reckoned that as many as 200 bombs were aimed at her, with ten hits on the old veteran. Some of the heaviest blows were struck by *Ticonderoga* dive bombers.

The mission started poorly. Lieutenant Commander Franz Kanaga led a dozen Helldivers, each bearing an asymmetric load of under-wing bombs and fuel tanks. On takeoff one plane lurched into the water, the crew lost. The others proceeded as planned.

Coordinating with *Ticonderoga*'s Avengers, her bombing squadron nosed into steep dives over *Hyuga*. Amid blistering flak, Lieutenant H. Paul Brehm closed his dive brakes to reduce his exposure to AA gunners. Ahead of him Lieutenant (jg) E. L. Vaughn crashed alongside the target. Undeterred, Brehm pressed as low as he dared, toggled his bombs, and hauled the stick into his stomach. He blacked out in the high-g pullout, recovering level flight so low that he felt the explosion of his bomb on the stern.

Returning to the task force low on fuel, in poor weather, Brehm and two other pilots made water landings. They were rescued but the cost was high: twelve Helldivers took off; seven returned.

Hyuga's bridge and conning tower were demolished, killing Rear Admiral Kiyoshi Kusakawa, recalled from retirement to command the ship. The crew counted at least ten bomb hits and at least as many near misses that ripped open her seams, causing immediate flooding. Inundated with tons of water, she was run aground to prevent sinking, but the result was the same.

The carrier *Amagi* had been commissioned in August 1944 but had never left home waters. Slightly damaged in the March 19 attack, her 22,000 tons rested fifty meters from shore, bedecked with camouflage netting, trees, and imitation houses. Nevertheless, she was struck repeatedly in three attacks. The heaviest blow, apparently a one-ton weapon, went into the sweet spot: "almost exactly on the centerline, dead amidships between the elevators."

The delayed-action bomb detonated on the hangar deck. In that confined space, the blast effect was incredible: it blew out the hangar walls and both sides of the hull, flinging a 150-foot section overboard. A twenty-five-foot hole was torn in the upper hangar deck, and fragments penetrated to the lower hangar. The overpressure ruptured the flight deck over a length of 200 feet and collapsed the forward elevator into its well. Additional bomb and rocket hits on two port-side boiler rooms started flooding, further settling the carrier.

Though she was not in danger of sinking—the harbor was too shallow—the unrelenting violence unnerved *Amagi*'s senior officer. (The captain may not have been aboard.) In any case, around noon somebody yelled "Abandon ship," reinforced by a rocket sizzling past the bridge and yet another bomb that started flooding astern. Some dedicated sailors ignored the order until that afternoon. The next day *Amagi* remained afloat, listing slightly to port, though the flight deck was destroyed.

Escort carrier *Kaiyo* was moving to safer shelter when the Anglo-Americans arrived overhead. While maneuvering she struck an air-dropped mine that damaged her rudder and caused partial flooding in an engine room. Then British Avengers scored two bomb hits, causing increased flooding. Towed to Beppu Bay on Kyushu's east coast, the small flattop was grounded. Eventually the crew pumped out most of the water and began sealing the hull.

The senior combatant in the area was the heavy cruiser *Tone*. Her career read like a Pacific War roadmap: the Pearl Harbor force, Indian Ocean, Midway, Guadalcanal, Philippine Sea, Leyte Gulf. Stashed in Hiroshima Bay west of Kure, the big, handsome warship was selected by *Monterey*'s Avengers, which scored three bomb hits. Her hull was blasted open and she began settling, so was pushed ashore to facilitate salvage.

Overall, the July 24 missions cost the fast carriers twenty-nine fighters and twenty-eight bombers. In exchange, they knocked out a battleship and cruiser, sinking three lesser vessels and damaging at least thirteen warships.

The next day Task Force 38 again spread its wings over the Inland Sea, Kure, and elsewhere, sinking three tankers and a merchant ship and damaging a cruiser plus five other vessels.

The two-day total of U.S. aircraft losses came to eighty-seven, nearly identical to the initial home island strikes in mid-February. Relatively little had been accomplished other than keeping the pressure on Japan, but that pressure immediately increased. While the task force replenished, global events were underway in Europe. On July 27 the Allies issued the Potsdam Declaration, calling for Japan's unconditional surrender. The Tokyo war cabinet ignored the ultimatum, setting in motion events that no one in Japan—and few in America—could possibly envision.

July 28

The tailhookers were back on the 28th, hoping to finish off the crippled warships and perhaps turn up new targets.

At 0745, McCain's flagship, *Shangri-La*, launched thirty-six planes against the battleship *Haruna* and light cruiser *Oyodo*, both damaged on the 24th. But the two-day layoff had given Kure's gunners time to recover. Pilots reported intense flak with an Avenger shot down. Nevertheless, several direct hits left both ships burning, and *Oyodo* later capsized.

Haruna held the rare honor of being bombed more than any Japanese battleship. She had escaped with light damage in three previous attacks but now became the focus of multiple squadrons. The thirty-year-old heavyweight absorbed so many hits and near misses that Captain Matake Yoshimura could not provide a definite number; possibly eight or more. That afternoon some seventy Okinawa-based B-24s attacked ineffectively from altitude. But shortly the Navy was back, twenty-nine of "Shang's" aviators plus *Wasp's* air group. All planes concentrated on *Haruna*, which was again seriously damaged. Holed in her port side, she took on tons of water and sank next to the pier. In the two July attacks she lost sixty-five officers and men.

Nor was that all. *Ise* had been lightly damaged on March 19 and hit five times on July 24, but she was clobbered on the 28th. Pilots from at least three air groups claimed sixteen hits and likely scored fourteen. *Hancock's* Corsairs alone contributed five half-ton bombs to the total.

The carrier *Amagi* was bombed again on the 28th, though to what extent is uncertain since the crew had abandoned four days earlier. The next morning she lurched to port and capsized to about 70 degrees. At that extreme angle most of the shattered flight deck and both aircraft elevators toppled overboard. Now fully grounded, the Imperial carrier lay a ruined relic, her starboard screws exposed to the sun.

Amagi's sister, *Katsuragi*, lightly damaged on the 24th, was mauled on the afternoon of the 28th as a one-tonner struck near the carrier's island. The bomb exploded with massive force in the hangar space, blowing out twenty feet of the port hull and thirty feet of the flight deck. A blizzard of splinters swept the bridge, killing the executive officer and twelve others.

The much abused escort carrier *Kaiyo* (damaged twice previously) was found at Hiji Harbor in Beppu Bay, northeastern Kyushu. Among others, *Essex*'s Corsairs unloaded a barrage of 5-inch rockets that killed twenty men. One rocket exploded in the switchboard room, knocking out circuits and generators. Without electricity, the carrier's pumps stopped. Port-side flooding could not be contained and the ship settled to the bottom.

The next day, the 29th, a naval doctor inspected *Kaiyo*'s engine room, noting the miserable situation. Like most seaports, Hiji's salt-water contained a malodorous mixture of fuel oil, sewage, and dead fish. The doctor declared the situation unhealthy and suggested abandoning. Captain Shuichi Osuga agreed, but before departing he flooded the boilers, allowing the ship to settle firmly.

Cruiser *Aoba*, already put on the bottom on the 24th, received more attention the 28th. That morning McCain's pilots hit her four times, causing a fire in the hulk. Late that afternoon more 7th Air Force Liberators scored with four more 500-pounders. *Aoba*'s abused hull split open and the stern collapsed.

Helldivers and Hellcats also pounced on the light cruiser *Oyodo*, compounding her previous damage with four more bomb hits that killed 300 men. She rolled over and capsized to starboard, an inglorious end to her brief tenure as flagship of the Combined Fleet.

Because many ships settled on an even keel in the shallow harbor, they appeared undamaged from overhead. Consequently, AAF bombers attacked unnecessarily, though, as postwar analysis showed, the ships were "completely flooded and permanently out of commission."

Kure bloomed as a violent garden where Navy Crosses grew. A credited bomb hit on an enemy capital ship was rewarded with "a Cross," just as fighter pilots were decorated for an ace-in-a-day feat. As a result of July's three strikes, an incredible 170 aviators received Navy Crosses, five posthumously. In comparison, the four-day Battle of Midway in 1942 yielded Navy Crosses to 154 Navy men and marines including air, sea, land, and submarine personnel.

Lieutenant Commander Elmer A. Kraft was a Hellcat squadron commander on the *Randolph*. One of his junior pilots was killed shortly after the Kure strikes but Kraft, who had scored a hit on a ship there, credited the feat to the youngster. When a squadron mate questioned Kraft's generosity, the skipper said, "Don't you suppose that ensign had a mother and a father who wanted to be proud of him? What difference does it make if I don't get a medal? It means a hell of a lot to them."

Overall, Halsey's three days of strikes on Kure and environs proved costly: 126 aircraft (seventy-three fighters, fifty-three bombers) were lost with 102 pilots and aircrewmen. Eighteen of the losses occurred in "routine" operations over Shikoku.

Whether the cost of the Kure strikes was worth the result remains one of the least examined questions of the Pacific War. In his often self-serving memoir, Halsey enumerated four reasons for the strikes. He opined that America's national honor and morale required total destruction of the Japanese navy; that such destruction was necessary to prevent interdiction of future convoys to Russia; that Tokyo might use its remaining fleet for negotiating leverage as Germany had done in 1919; and ultimately that he had orders. He concluded, "If the other reasons had been invalid, that one alone would have been enough for me."

Halsey's enumerations remain transparently unconvincing. In the first place, American morale in no way turned on destruction of the rusting remnants of the Imperial Navy. The greatest morale involved was Bull Halsey's. The huge majority of Americans merely wished the war over, and the main seagoing phase had ended in October 1944.

Secondly, the U.S. Navy could easily dominate the North Pacific in the vastly unlikely event that any Japanese force escaped its mine-choked bases to deploy more than 1,000 miles from home. Furthermore, absent requests from Moscow, no such requirement pertained.

Halsey's third point was even more absurd. The Allies' preexisting demand of unconditional surrender automatically scuttled any naval bargaining that Tokyo might have attempted in such nonexistent proceedings.

The fourth point would seem the strongest, as King and Nimitz had decreed an end to the "defueled doggo fleet." But by July 1945, Halsey surely felt bulletproof. He had escaped all accountability (if not major blame) for the Leyte Gulf debacle and failing to avoid a ship-killing typhoon in December. The defenders of his position were five-star guardians: Nimitz, who allowed sentiment to trump objectivity, and the decidedly unsentimental King in Washington, who refused to hand the Air Force a political victory. But the fact remained that between Leyte Gulf in October 1944 and "Halsey's hurricane" in December, the Third Fleet commander was widely considered directly or indirectly responsible for the unnecessary loss of seven ships and some 1,450 sailors and aircrew.

Had Halsey declined to expend scores of fliers and 100 aircraft in a needless exercise, his chances of being replaced approached absolute zero. But rather than take counsel of the Task Force 38 staff, The Bull was eager to comply with orders that gratified his vanity at the expense of eighty-three young men who died at Kure attacking impotent, immobile ships.

Halsey's seeming indifference to casualties drew sharp criticism from subordinates. One aviator spoke for many when he noted,

"Halsey is going wild on publicity and we are all fed [up] to the teeth listening to all the crap he is putting out. . . . Halsey is a big disappointment to me as he is to most of us."

Typhoon weather brewed up at the end of July, and Third Fleet steamed eastward for an extended period of refueling. From August 3 to 9 the force reprovisioned at sea, conducted training, and coped with worsening weather.

Meanwhile, Nimitz directed Halsey to steer clear of southern Japan. Honoring the peculiar directive, Third Fleet remained north of the 37th parallel, striking northern Honshu. The mystery was soon made clear with word of Hiroshima and Nagasaki.

August 9

The harbor war continued on August 9. It featured significant actions by two of the U.S. Navy's allies: the British Royal Navy and the U.S. Army Air Forces.

On Okinawa Lieutenant Colonel Edwin H. Hawes commanded the veteran 38th Bomb Group. The "Sun Setters" had been in combat for three years, still flying the B-25. The first aircraft to bomb Japan also was among the last.

The 38th's specialty was shipping strikes, and Hawes declared, "If we ever find a Jap carrier in our range, we are going after it."

Reconnaissance flights had found a flattop in Beppu Bay on Kyushu, 115 miles east of Nagasaki. The Sun Setters wanted her.

She was *Kaiyo*, the 16,000-ton escort carrier damaged by naval mines and bombs two weeks previously. Inactive since July, she was painted green and strewn with camouflage netting and artificial trees, giving the appearance of a floating garden. She sat upright but mired on the bottom, useful only as an antiaircraft platform. In truth she was not worth a load of bombs but aerial photos showed her "afloat."

Ed Hawes didn't have to fly again. He had orders to return home but "he wanted to get that carrier so bad," recalled a subordinate. Hawes was thirty-four, a ten-year veteran with 4,700 flying hours, including nearly 1,000 in combat. Known for his aggressiveness (he had three Purple Hearts), he could not pass up a shot at a carrier.

Hawes led twelve B-25s away from Okinawa at 6:00 A.M. on the 9th, relying upon his lead navigator, Captain John W. Long, Jr., to plot the 530-mile flight. Organized in three-plane flights, each Mitchell carried two 1,000-pounders with delay fuses to permit trailing aircraft to escape the blast pattern.

Over Kyushu heavy clouds caused serious problems. Descending from 6,000 feet, one flight became separated and another veered slightly off course in the haze. As one pilot recalled, "The weather was lousy and the visibility was terrible."

Nevertheless, Hawes glimpsed the target and led his formation down a fairly steep slope, approaching the bay from inland. The bombers leveled off less than fifty feet above the trees.

Flying as copilot for the second flight leader was Lieutenant Chuck Crawford, who had a good view of Hawes's lead section. He saw the CO's two bombs leave the aircraft, aligned with the carrier amidships. Then the lead bomber took a fatal blow.

Crawford recalled, "It must have caught a direct hit in the right engine. His B-25 did a snap roll to the right, one and a half times around, and dove into the water, inverted and nose down. Until I saw that happen I didn't think a B-25 could roll that fast!" He knew the crew could not have survived.

Racing in about twenty seconds behind, Crawford punched off his bombs, which he believed smashed into *Kaiyo*'s hull. He had no time to watch the other Mitchells, though four of the remaining five aimed their bombs at the ship. Then they turned for home, three and a half hours southwest.

After the 38th's attack, the last of *Kaiyo*'s caretaker crew dismantled the AA guns and left the ship.

Ed Hawes, the erstwhile math teacher and tennis coach, left a widow and two sons. He received a belated Silver Star in 1990, as the paperwork had been neglected in the excitement of V-J Day.

Another airman also received a posthumous decoration for an August 9 mission as British planes attacked airfields and Onagawa Bay on Honshu's northeast coast, 170 miles north of Tokyo. Mines had bottled up half a dozen ships that lay vulnerable, though their military value was minimal. Their total tonnage barely represented a single cruiser.

Leading an eight-plane fighter strike was Lieutenant Robert Hampton Gray, a Canadian flying off HMS *Formidable*. A former art student from British Columbia, Gray had a year's fleet experience, including attacks against the German battleship *Tirpitz* in Norwegian waters. The twenty-seven-year-old flier made a specialty of Axis shipping, having helped sink an escort two weeks before. Now he deployed his Corsairs by two-plane sections, diving in from 10,000 feet.

Sweeping low over the bay, Gray went for a "destroyer" among the small craft and auxiliaries. Actually she was the 870-ton sloop *Amakusa*.

The sky erupted in flak bursts and tracers from at least four ships and the shoreline. Hit repeatedly, Gray's fighter spurted flames, and another pilot saw one of his 500-pounders shot off its rack. Nevertheless, "Hammy" pressed his run to minimum altitude, dropping his remaining bomb from perhaps fifty feet. It penetrated the hull, blowing a huge hole in the starboard side.

Gray's Corsair pulled off target, streaming smoke and flames as it swerved into the water. He perished with his victim, which sank quickly with seventy-one sailors. Other pilots sank an escort and left a minesweeper damaged.

Gray was likely the last Canadian killed in action in World War II. Admiral Sir Philip Vian lauded his "brilliant fighting spirit and inspired leadership" and nominated him for a posthumous Victoria Cross, Britain's highest honor. The presentation was made to

Gray's parents in Ottawa in February 1946. It was the sixteenth VC awarded a Canadian in World War II; only the second for a Fleet Air Arm aviator.

With the sacrifices of fliers such as Hawes and Gray, the harbor war largely ended on August 9, the same day that continued a rain of ruin upon Japan undreamt of by even airpower's most flamboyant visionaries.

CHAPTER EIGHT

"A Most Cruel Bomb"

T HE WEAPON STREAKED down through six miles of sky,
accelerating to its terminal velocity at 32 feet per second.
From the instant the 8,800-pound bomb left the belly of a
bomber with the radio call "Dimples 82," an irrevocable sequence
had begun.

Ordnance engineers had computed that the most damage would
be inflicted upon the target by an explosion 1,900 feet above ground
level. The Mark 1 weapon's fusing was designed accordingly. As
the device dropped from *Dimples 82*, an electrical plug was stripped
from an aircraft socket, beginning a timer delay of fifteen seconds,
at which point the bomb's onboard battery kicked in. The electrical circuit activated a barometric altimeter that sensed the outside
atmosphere as the blunt-nosed shape plummeted through the 6,000-
foot mark. For utmost precision, a radar-controlled detonation was
required. Therefore, at the designated height the barometer actuated
four radar altimeters, all linked to one another. When at least two
registered 1,900 feet altitude, the ignition sequence began.

The workings of the device, though requiring twentieth-century
precision, were centuries old in principle. The Mark 1 was a simple
"gun" concept built around a six-foot tube containing a gunpowder
charge that fired a six-and-a-quarter-inch diameter uranium slug at
a "target" four inches in diameter. The 85-pound projectile smashed

223

into the 56-pound target at 1,000 feet per second. Ten-thousandths of a second later, compressed between tungsten-carbide reflectors, the entire U-235 assembly reached critical mass and erupted in a chain reaction, the nuclear fuel feeding upon itself.

Almost perfectly aimed by a twenty-six-year-old bombardier, after a forty-three-second fall from 31,000 feet the bomb missed its aim point by fewer than 200 yards. There, southeast of the juncture of two rivers, it burst with the energy of approximately 15 metric tons of TNT.

First came the light—red-hued purple—then the heat, vastly searing in its intensity as the raging fireball surpassed 5,000 degrees Fahrenheit. Beneath an enormous blast wave exceeding 12 pounds per square inch, a stone and concrete building at ground zero was either vaporized or driven vertically into the earth.

The resulting firestorm measured two miles across, jumping both natural and man-made barriers. Where the rampaging blast overpressure leveled buildings, the ravenous fire consumed most of the ready-made fuel in its path. Further out, where more buildings survived than collapsed, the effects were diminished by distance. However, humans died beyond that radius, from blast, flames, and the invisible killer called radiation. The exact number of dead will never be known.

Its mission accomplished, *Dimples 82* banked away from the destroyed city of Hiroshima, having completed a process that began with a letter from a scientist to a politician six years before.

Gadgets and Firecrackers

On August 2, 1939, Albert Einstein wrote President Roosevelt, citing "recent work by E. Fermi and L. Szilard . . . [which] leads me to expect that the element uranium may be turned into a new and important source of energy."

The German-born physicist postulated a nuclear chain reaction producing enormous amounts of power. He said, "This new phenomenon would also lead to the construction of bombs," though he thought such a device would be too heavy for an aircraft to carry.

Einstein closed by noting that Germany had recently stopped selling uranium from Czech mines, and that research was being conducted in Berlin. One month later Germany attacked Poland and the Second World War began.

Nazi leader Adolf Hitler reportedly dismissed relativity theory as "the Jewish science" and thereby drove many of the world's leading physicists to America. Consequently, little came of the German program, though that was not known until war's end. But the American bomb could not have succeeded without the Jewish scientists.

The colleagues whom Einstein mentioned were the Italian Enrico Fermi and the Hungarian Leo Szilard, who, in 1942, would create the first atomic chain reaction. They became crucial members of the Manhattan Engineering District (MED), the cover name for America's atomic bomb program.

Other nations were involved, including British, Australian, and Canadian scientists and engineers. There was even a German, Hans Bethe, a leading theorist who had emigrated in 1935.

Chosen to oversee the scientific portion of the project was a first-generation American, J. Robert Oppenheimer, whose Jewish parents had moved from Germany in the 1880s. Tall and thin to the point of being gaunt, he wore himself down to 114 pounds during World War II.

When the Manhattan Project began in August 1942, the assemblage of raw brainpower was still amazingly youthful. Of the leading lights, Szilard was the eldest at forty-four. Edward Teller was probably the youngest at thirty-four; Oppenheimer was thirty-eight. Fermi, then forty-one, had begun his doctoral work at seventeen. A Czech researcher, Frederic de Hoffmann, was invited to participate at nineteen.

Commanding the Manhattan Project was Colonel Leslie R. Groves, a driven taskmaster who graduated fourth in the West Point class of '18. He had supervised construction of the Pentagon building and, considering the crucial importance of the MED and its immense budget (over $2 billion in 1945), he was surprisingly junior. He was promoted to temporary brigadier general in September 1942 and temporary major general two years later.

Groves and Oppenheimer made an odd couple: the gruff, portly general and the often eccentric, rail-thin scientist. But they made Manhattan work. At times it was difficult for Groves to support "Oppie," who made a bad situation worse by refusing to cooperate with security agents investigating his prewar Communist affiliations. (It was not known until much later that the Soviets had collaborators inside the project.) Yet Groves recognized Oppenheimer's unique ability to manage the soaring intellects and often clashing egos of so many geniuses and keep them moving toward completion of the task.

A crucial early decision was what kind of bomb to build: uranium or plutonium. Not knowing the status of the German project, America produced both types of weapons, though far more effort went into the plutonium design, which scientists called "the gadget." LeMay glibly referred to either bomb as "the firecracker."

MED had three primary facilities: Los Alamos, New Mexico; Oak Ridge, Tennessee; and Hanford, Washington. The brain center was "Los Al," in the high desert north of Santa Fe, established on a former boys ranch. From 1943 onward Oppenheimer directed the efforts of the physicists, scientists, and engineers who tackled the theoretical and practical aspects of building an atomic bomb.

The raw materials came from Oak Ridge (uranium) and Hanford (plutonium). Both places were subject of much speculation, though some "explanations" leaned toward the whimsical. Student naval aviators at Pasco, Washington, were threatened with "death or worse" for overflying Hanford. Recalled one pilot, " 'Rumor Control' had two theories as to Hanford's purpose. Republicans said it was a secret factory making Roosevelt campaign buttons. Others said, 'No, they're making the front ends of horses for shipment to D.C. and final assembly.'"

Oppenheimer the enthusiastic horseman ramrodded a scientific herd containing numerous mavericks. As Los Alamos historian Jennet Conant observed, the site "was thick with experts and know-it-alls, with more arriving every day, so Oppenheimer spent an inordinate amount of time settling disputes and preventing work from being disrupted."

Certainly there were eccentrics. Szilard, who held patents for refrigerators and microscopes, conceived the idea of a nuclear chain reaction while waiting for a London traffic light to change.

Given the professional rivalries amid some immense egos, personality clashes were inevitable. Physicist Seth Neddermeyer, who made the crucial recommendation for an implosion trigger for plutonium, could not get along with his section head, Commander William S. Parsons. The Navy ordnance officer had alienated Neddermeyer by denigrating implosion in favor of the gun assembly that would be used in the Hiroshima bomb. To keep the project moving, Oppenheimer replaced Neddermeyer with George Kistiakowsky, an imposing Harvard chemist and explosives expert. But the new arrangement worked no better—Parsons and the Ukrainian-born Ph.D. took vastly different approaches to problem solving.

However, at least "Deke" Parsons got along well with his military colleagues. Almost nobody got along with Edward Teller. His enormous talent was largely wasted during the war, as he could not be diverted from his obsession with "the super," the hydrogen bomb finally tested in 1952.

Manhattan's first two products were named "Little Boy" (uranium) and "Fat Man" (plutonium). Because the uranium bomb's gun assembly was relatively simple, it was deployed to combat without testing. The plutonium weapon, requiring exquisite symmetry in its implosion trigger, required proof of concept. That proof was delivered at the New Mexico "Trinity" site on July 16, 1945. Its yield, some 20 kilotons, proved perhaps 40 percent greater than Little Boy.

By then the Manhattan targeting committee had already selected six Japanese cities as candidates for nuclear incineration.

The Road to Total War

President Harry Truman's decision to use the atomic bombs was based upon two related principles: a desire to end the war as quickly as possible; and the demonstrated willingness of Japan's population to resist to the last man, woman, and child. The enemy's military ferocity was well known, but the scenes of Japanese mothers throwing their infants off Saipan's cliffs, and the bitter resistance at Okinawa provided additional convincing arguments.

Furthermore, by spring of 1945, U.S. intelligence knew the full extent of Tokyo's measures as the war had forced itself upon the population far beyond closed shops and rare commodities. In March, school classes were canceled above the sixth grade, presumably until victory ensued. Meanwhile, students and teachers were assigned vital tasks from growing food to moving supplies and preparing defenses. That same month the war cabinet established the Patriotic Citizens Fighting Corps, a "volunteer" mobilization involving civilian males from fifteen to sixty and females seventeen to forty.

Consequently, in July the U.S. 5th Air Force inserted a note in its *Weekly Intelligence Review*: "The entire population of Japan is a proper Military Target . . . THERE ARE NO CIVILIANS IN JAPAN. We are making War and making it in the all-out fashion which saves American lives, shortens the agony which War is and seeks to bring about an enduring Peace. We intend to seek out and destroy the enemy wherever he or she is, in the greatest possible numbers, in the shortest possible time."

Total war had come of age.

For years Japanese civilians had been force-fed an unrelenting diet of propagandistic pap as victory claims escalated from optimistic to absurd. Even faced with mounting evidence of a losing battle (naval blockade, frequent air attacks, loss of the Marianas, Philippines, Iwo Jima, and the invasion of Okinawa), some senior Japanese officials maintained a state of denial. At a POW camp in Manchuria, captives were told that the outcome would be "a matter of generations." After the war a colonel on the 18th Army Staff in New Guinea related his astonishment at the capitulation, believing the war would continue into 1948 or later. Others predicted that the climactic battle for the homeland would result in an Allied defeat or a stalemate. In February 1945—the month of the first U.S. carrier strikes, the initial B-29 firebombing, and the landings at Iwo Jima—former prime minister Hideki Tojo informed the emperor that because the Soviet nonaggression pact ran until 1946 "there was no need to be pessimistic, and Japan's cause was righteous."

Firmly gripped by the mind-set that their German allies called "cloud cuckoo land," Japan's leaders rejected the Allies' July 26 Potsdam Declaration offering either surrender or "prompt and utter destruction." In doing so Tokyo ensured an apocalyptic denouement to the saga it had initiated forty-five months before.

Hiroshima

The Manhattan Project represented only half of the equation necessary to deliver atomic bombs upon the Axis. The other half—the B-29—was already a proven factor by July 1945. Between them the two programs accounted for some $4.4 billion, with the Superfortress by far the greater share.

The unit responsible for dropping atomic bombs was unique in the world's air forces. The 509th Composite Group comprised one bomb squadron and a transport squadron; with auxiliary units the roster only totaled 1,767 men. Activated at remote, windy Wendover, Utah, in December 1944, the 509th was created to deliver "special weapons" against Germany and Japan. The commander was twenty-nine-year-old Lieutenant Colonel Paul W. Tibbets, who had flown B-17s in North Africa and Europe. He displayed a low-key earnestness; a subordinate recorded his first impression: "His manner was reserved and soft spoken, yet he projected an air of professionalism and self assurance."

The 509th received B-29s specially modified to carry atom bombs, though none of the fliers yet knew of their ordnance. Only forty-six "Silverplate" aircraft were produced during the war, and the group took fifteen to combat. Besides alterations to the bomb bays and removal of all turrets, the Silverplated B-29s had reversible propellers, permitting a shorter landing distance.

With Germany's surrender in May 1945, Tibbets's original orders to conduct a double strike in Europe and Japan were necessarily changed. His crews began landing in the Marianas in June, based on Tinian. Shrouded in secrecy—the Silverplate bombers bore markings of three other units—the group flew few missions, mostly to bypassed Japanese-occupied islands. Actually the 509th was sharpening its aim with five-ton "pumpkin bombs" of the same shape as the atomic weapons. But while other groups flew regularly and took losses, the newcomers seemed immune to routine chores. Eventually a bit of doggerel expressed the growing resentment:

> Into the air the secret arose,
> Where they're going, nobody knows.
> Tomorrow they'll return again,
> But we'll never know where they've been.
> Don't ask us about results or such,
> Unless you want to get in dutch.
> But take it from one who is sure of the score,
> The 509th is winning the war.

The weapon components completed their 6,590-mile journey from the wilds of New Mexico to the hardstand on Tinian on July 26. Meanwhile, orders were descending from Washington via General Carl Spaatz, commander of U.S. Strategic Air Forces. Having seen what the 8th and 15th Air Forces had done to Germany, he still insisted that conventional bombing could topple Japan. But it was also possible that he was squeamish about wielding a new weapon of such incredible power.

In any case, "Tooey" Spaatz tried to have it both ways and largely succeeded. Apparently protecting himself from future criticism, he required a written order to use atomic bombs against Japanese cities. On July 25 he received a directive from Army Chief of Staff George C. Marshall and Secretary of War Henry Stimson. Actually, General Marshall was attending the Potsdam Conference, and his directive was issued by his deputy. General Thomas T. Handy's message to Spaatz said in part, "The 509 Composite Group, 20th Air Force, will deliver its first special bomb as soon as weather will permit visual bombing after about 3 August 1945 on one of the targets: Hiroshima, Kokura, Niigata and Nagasaki."

The four-paragraph letter further stated that "Additional bombs will be delivered on the above targets as soon as made ready."

Suitably insulated, Spaatz passed the order to Nathan Twining and Curtis LeMay at 20th Air Force.

Thus, following thirty-eight "pumpkin" sorties over Japan, the 509th was alerted for its first special mission. On August 4, Tibbets presided over a briefing with seven combat crews, stating only that the 509th would drop a bomb "of unimaginable destructive force." Though he never alluded to atomic power, he said the weapon was expected to explode with the equivalent of perhaps 20,000 tons of TNT.

Commanding the 509th's bomb squadron was Major Charles Sweeney, just twenty-five years old. He had learned to fly in high school and joined the AAF in 1941, receiving his wings that December. He had no previous combat experience but possessed considerable background in ordnance and flight testing.

Sweeney provided a colorful comparison to his group commander. Tibbets's deadpan Midwest persona contrasted with Sweeney's Irish gregariousness. For the upcoming mission, Tibbets would fly Dimples 82, which he named *Enola Gay* for his mother. Six other B-29s launched on August 6, including three weather reconnaissance planes and a spare that landed at Iwo Jima. Sweeney and Captain George Marquardt flew the other two with observers and monitoring equipment. The target was Hiroshima on southern Honshu, home to at least 255,000 people. The secondary was Kokura on Kyushu, 100 miles east.

Hiroshima contained several military facilities, most notably headquarters of the Second General Army. The shipyard and Mitsubishi tool and die factory were primary industrial targets. Aside from the Imperial Navy's suicide boats and submarines, the port also was home to the Japanese army submarine school, which supported efforts to supply island garrisons bypassed by the Americans.

Before manning the *Enola Gay*, Tibbets's crew posed for photographs in the midnight darkness. Then the eleven men climbed aboard. They took off at 2:42, an hour behind the weather scouts.

En route, Tibbets visited each crew station. As the CO exited the tail position, Staff Sergeant Robert Caron tugged his leg. "Colonel, are we splitting atoms today?" Tibbets nodded. "That's about it." Later Caron admitted he had only seen the phrase in a science fiction text.

Meanwhile, two ordnance officers huddled in the bomb bay with the device called Little Boy. Even by wartime standards, the Mark 1 was problematic because several things could go disastrously wrong. The biggest concern was a short circuit or stray voltage. But a sudden, violent stop—as in a crash—might impel the two uranium components together. It was unlikely to cause a detonation but could release deadly amounts of radiation. Lesser threats involved fire and lightning. Therefore, the weapon was armed in flight rather than before takeoff. Commander Deke Parsons, who had clashed with the intellects and egos at Los Alamos, was assisted by an Army second lieutenant, twenty-two-year-old Morris R. Jeppson. After an eleven-step process taking twenty minutes, both officers emerged from the bomb bay. Little Boy was armed; now it belonged to bombardier Major Thomas Ferebee.

Approaching Honshu, Tibbets learned from the weather scouts that Hiroshima was clear. Thus satisfied, he approached from the east at 31,000 feet. In the seconds before bomb away, most of the crew pulled on polarized goggles to protect them from the danger of blinding light.

In the nose Ferebee hunched over his Norden sight, tracking the crosshairs onto the aim point, a distinctive T-shaped bridge. The weapon fell from the bomb bay at 8:15 local time, six and a half hours from base. The crew immediately felt two sensations: a pronounced lift as Dimples 82 was freed of nearly five tons, and a sharp bank as Tibbets rolled into his evasive right turn.

Scientists had calculated that the bomber would achieve optimum distance from the blast with 155 degrees of tangency. Therefore, Tibbets held the steep, diving right-hand turn, recovering east-northeast.

The flash lit up *Enola Gay*'s interior.

Then came the shock wave from ten miles astern. To Tibbets it felt as jolting as a near miss by a German 88mm shell. He and copilot Robert A. Lewis leveled the wings, took stock, and, confirming that the plane was performing normally, turned back to observe the results.

Hiroshima had disappeared beneath a looming, roiling mushroom-shaped cloud. Gaping at the spectacle, Bob Lewis was initially exultant. Then he jotted, "My god, what have we done?"

In the city, the explosion occurred forty-five minutes after the all-clear from a false alarm. Citizens and soldiers were going about their morning routine until the Mark 1 erupted overhead. Those structures and people not vaporized at ground zero were subjected to near supersonic winds that swept away many remaining structures. Two-thirds of the city's buildings were destroyed or left untenable.

The initial fireball measured 1,200 feet across, eventually spreading flames over two miles. Ironically, the powerful shock wave extinguished some of the initial fires.

The actual toll will never be known but perhaps 70,000 people were killed outright, roughly one-third of them military.

Parsons sent a strike report to base, describing results as "Clear cut. Successful in all respects."

On Tinian the party started early and was getting underway when Tibbets landed twelve hours after takeoff. General Spaatz pinned the Distinguished Service Cross on Tibbets, then walked off without speaking a word. The debriefing of Special Mission 13 proceeded more cordially, enhanced by beer and bourbon.

On the cruiser *Augusta*, bearing Harry Truman from the Yalta Conference in Russia, the president received word of the atomic strike. He declared, "This is the greatest thing in history."

That evening Tibbets told Sweeney to prepare for a second Silverplate mission. Sweeney doubted that it would be necessary, as he thought that Japan would now capitulate. Nearly everyone agreed that Hiroshima meant an end to the war. General Groves did not— he had always insisted it would take two bombs.

In Japan the air division responsible for Hiroshima reported in part that "a violent, large, special-type bomb, giving the appearance of magnesium, was dropped over the center of the city. . . . There was a blinding flash and a violent blast.

"The flash was instantaneous, burning objects in the immediate vicinity, burning the exposed parts of people's bodies as far as three kilometers away, and setting fire to their thin clothing.

"The blast leveled completely or partially as many as 60,000 houses within a radius of three kilometers, and smashed glass blocks, etc."

Japanese scientists who examined the incinerated city realized that the Americans had indeed used an atomic weapon.

Nagasaki

With no word from Tokyo on August 7 or 8, the next mission launched early on the 9th. It wielded the plutonium weapon nicknamed Fat Man—the type tested spectacularly at the Trinity site three weeks before. Tibbets assigned the mission to Chuck Sweeney, who thus became the only pilot on both atomic missions. Sweeney's bombardier was Captain Kermit Beahan, a former football star who had logged forty missions in Europe. His priority target was Kokura; the alternate was Nagasaki.

Sweeney's regular plane, *The Great Artiste*, was still configured to monitor bomb results so his usual crew, plus two Navy ordnance officers and a radar specialist, shifted to Captain Fred Bock's plane. However, *Bock's Car* began the mission with a serious deficiency: an inoperable fuel pump trapped 600 gallons that would be unusable. The dangerously low gasoline reserve prompted Tibbets to give Sweeney the option of canceling the mission. But the squadron commander decided to proceed: the several hours lost repairing the problem might erode the psychological effect of two A-bombs delivered close together. Additionally, a download-upload sequence to move Fat Man to another B-29 was a nontrivial function. Sweeney decided to go.

At 2:45 A.M., flying *Bock's Car*, Sweeney lifted off Tinian and set course northwest, hitting his first navigation checkpoint at Yakushima, one of the islands south of Kyushu. He circled for a frustrating forty minutes, awaiting the photo aircraft, which did not materialize. Concerned about fuel, Sweeney exclaimed, "The hell with it, we can't wait any longer." He headed almost due north to Kokura, but the target was obscured by smoke from the previous night's attack on the city of Yawata. After three aborted runs through flak, with fighters in sight, Sweeney diverted to his secondary target.

Between the delay for the photo plane and multiple runs at Kokura, *Bock's Car* was running ninety minutes late. To further complicate matters, Nagasaki was 80 percent obscured by low clouds. The crew was instructed to bomb visually but the weaponeer, Commander Fred Ashworth, could not bear to drop Fat Man in the ocean and consulted with Sweeney about attacking by radar. When the pilot assured him that the bomb would hit within 500 feet of the aim point, Ashworth consented to a radar approach.

Seconds from a radar release, Kermit Beahan—still on his sight— saw what he needed. "I've got it!" he exclaimed as the clouds broke. Later he said, "The target was there, pretty as a picture."

In Nagasaki, shortly before eleven, two aircraft were sighted "at great altitude" approaching from the east. Following a previous alert, few people headed for shelter. The streets and buildings were fully occupied when a sun-bright light burst overhead at 11:01.

In bombing terms Beahan had taken a snapshot, with merely a twenty-five-second bomb run at 31,000 feet. The aim point was the Mitsubishi Steel and Arms Works, and the weapon struck some 500 feet south of the plant. Actually, Fat Man detonated between two Mitsubishi facilities: the steel factory and an arsenal producing most of Japan's aerial torpedoes. The enormous cloud rocketed to 30,000 feet in mere seconds as the crew felt five shock waves.

Producing at least 20 kilotons, Fat Man was more powerful than Little Boy in every way. It erupted in "a superbrilliant white," producing a flash, shock wave, and mushroom cloud greater than Sweeney had seen three days before. The fliers estimated that the roiling, rising cloud crested at 45,000 feet.

The plutonium bomb destroyed about 60 percent of the city and killed perhaps 35,000 of at least 195,000 people. Fortunately for most residents, much of the blast was confined to the Urakami Valley, an urban-industrial area, rather than the docks and nearby city center.

Unable to transfer fuel from the bomb bay tank, Sweeney had no option but to head for Okinawa, over 400 miles south. His navigator calculated that they would fall at least fifty miles short, and there was no air-sea rescue plane owing to confusion in communications with Guam. Nevertheless, Fred Bock in *The Great Artiste* shepherded Sweeney, ready to provide ditching coordinates.

However, Chuck Sweeney had one last card to play. Recalling a conversation with Tibbets, he began "flying the step." Beginning at 30,000 feet, he ratcheted his bomber down by stages, gaining incremental airspeed with each small descent. Expending his precious altitude with exquisite finesse, he got back the fifty to seventy-five miles he needed. It was a brilliant piece of flying.

Still, Sweeney barely squeaked into Yontan: one engine quit on landing approach and another on the runway. He shoved the props into reverse and stood on the brakes, stopping with yards to spare. Then the third engine died. With seven usable gallons, *Bock's Car* had less than one minute of remaining flight time.

Refueled, *Bock's Car* returned to Tinian at 10:30 that night, some twenty hours after departure. Then Sweeney and company proceeded to get blissfully drunk.

That same day two B-29s were dispatched to Wendover, Utah, to stand by for the third weapon. Only a Silverplate Superfortress could transport an A-bomb by air, and it looked as if another might be needed. At least one more weapon would be available before month's end, and three or four more in September.

On the 10th, the U.S. War Department stepped up its propaganda campaign, including leaflet drops and shortwave radio broadcasts. In a nine-day paper blitz the AAF was ordered to drop 16 million leaflets on forty-seven cities, potentially reaching 40 percent of the enemy population. Half a million Japanese-language newspapers were added to the aerial cascade, with articles and photos of the A-bomb attacks. However, "only" 6 million leaflets and an unspecified number of newspapers had been delivered by V-J Day.

American psychological warfare proved effective. Speaking of the leaflets and papers dispersed over urban areas, Rear Admiral Toshitane Takata acknowledged, "The dropping of pamphlets warning of impending raids caused conditions close to panic in some cities."

Additional Airpower

Even as the first atomic bombs neared delivery to the Marianas, more American airpower was assembling closer to Japan, around Okinawa.

The Pacific air forces rendezvoused in the Ryukyu Islands that summer. The 5th came up from the Southwest Pacific; the 7th via the Central route; and the 13th—least known of all the air forces that fought Japan—from the south.

Even before Okinawa was secured, aviation engineers and Seabees went to work on the airfields required to support the invasions of Kyushu and Honshu. Sites for twenty-two runways were examined and surveyed, including improvement of two existing Japanese fields. In all, the Ryukyus would support fifty-one groups, half expected to arrive as soon as facilities could support them. In early June more than twenty fields were allotted to designated units, including three Navy and Marine groups and an air depot at Naha.

As in the Marianas, construction crews came at a premium. When Okinawa was secured on June 22, barely one-third of the 80,000 engineers were ashore, but transport of the others was accelerated. Three weeks later MacArthur's air commander marveled that new fields were "appearing like magic and construction is going on faster than I have ever seen before."

Nor was construction limited to Okinawa proper. Nearby Ie Shima's eleven square miles were crammed with airpower: at various times that summer it hosted five Army fighter groups, three bomb groups, and assorted units, plus a Marine air group. The rest of the 2nd Marine Aircraft Wing—fourteen squadrons—shoehorned itself onto Okinawa.

Meanwhile, the Navy contribution was considerable. Fleet Air Wing One based four patrol bomber squadrons ashore and seven flying boat squadrons at Kerama Retto north of Okinawa. Also within range were nine Mariner and Privateer squadrons at Iwo and the Marianas.

Seventh Air Force Thunderbolts had begun night heckler missions against Kyushu airfields in mid-May, a month before Okinawa was fully secured. Better-suited Black Widow night fighters then took up the mission, and day fighter sweeps began. During the second week of June the 318th Group encountered 244 Japanese planes, claiming forty-eight downed against three Thunderbolts lost.

Activity on Okinawa accelerated from July onward. Morale peaked that summer, best illustrated by the 43rd Bomb Group's motto of WAR: "Willing, Able, Ready." Seventh Air Force Liberators and Mitchells logged their first Okinawa missions in early July, as did the new A-26 Invaders of the 319th Bomb Group. However, Colonel Joseph Holzapple's Douglas bombers represented far more than a new aircraft in the Pacific. The 319th had flown its last mission from Italy in December 1944, returned to the United States, and in May began the long trek to Okinawa. Thus it became the first group to redeploy from Europe, earning battle honors against both Germany and Japan.

With air supremacy readily achieved, 5th Air Force fighters "quickly turned to general hell raising" by bombing and strafing rail links, bridges, shipping, and targets of opportunity. On occasion the latter included individual Japanese.

On August 5, 325 Army planes attacked Tarumizu in southern Kyushu, which intelligence had fingered as a source of rocket-powered "Baka bombs," fast suicide planes. From high, medium, and low level, 179 bombers and 146 fighters pulverized the place with high-explosive bombs and napalm. Five days later fifty-three Liberators attacked the city of Kurume and, with the aid of a stiff northeast wind, burned down 28 percent of the houses, rendering 20,000 people homeless. That same week low-flying AAF pilots reported Japanese civilians waving white cloths at the uncontested Americans.

At the end, as General Ennis C. Whitehead wrote, "The enemy could decide that enough Nips had been killed or he could commit national suicide."

Meanwhile, the Marianas got reinforcements. The last wing to join LeMay was the 315th under Brigadier General Frank Armstrong, an old flying school classmate. A founding member of the 8th Air Force, in 1942 he had led the first B-17 mission in Europe, flying with then Major Paul Tibbets.

Armstrong had assumed command of the 315th in Colorado in November 1944. Equipped with the brand-new B-29B, his wing would become the ultimate expression of conventional-bombing Superfortresses. The main distinction was the Eagle radar, optimized for precision targeting rather than navigation. It was externally mounted beneath the fuselage, resembling a small extra wing, but the minor speed loss was more than offset by exceptional accuracy.

Armstrong had put the 315th's four groups through "one of the most intensive training programs ever undertaken by an air combat unit." The wing left the States in May, arriving at Guam for the last three months of hostilities.

On the afternoon of June 26, Armstrong led the wing's first mission. He firewalled his throttles and forty-two seconds later lifted *Fluffy-Fuz III* (named for his wife and child) off Northwest Field's active runway. Thirty-seven other B-29s followed him, bound for the Utsube River oil refinery in central Honshu. The plant held the dubious distinction of a number one priority in Japan's petroleum industry, boasting an oil storage and hydrogenation plant for aviation fuel. It was a precision target—just the kind envisioned for the Eagle radar.

Thirty of the thirty-eight bombers crossed the target in less than twenty-three minutes, sustaining no losses. Post-strike photography showed 30 percent of the facility destroyed or damaged, but that was deemed insufficient. Thirteen days later, on July 9, the 313th returned to Utsube and finished what remained.

Meanwhile, Armstrong's crews maintained a standard of almost eerie efficiency. On July 6–7, two groups attacked the Maruzen oil refinery near Osaka and left it a smoldering rubble, 95 percent destroyed. LeMay, never easily impressed, was delighted: "This performance is the most successful radar bombing of this command to date."

Armstrong led the wing's first five missions, then followed doctor's orders to recuperate from persistent dysentery. (Repeated doses of "medicinal brandy" did not cure the malady, although they did improve the patient's morale.) The 315th's well-trained groups continued without him, leading to one of the most peculiar mission summaries in aviation history. After breaching the dikes surrounding a synthetic oil plant, the photo interpreters concluded, "This target destroyed and sunk."

In six weeks during July and August, Armstrong's groups were credited with shutting down what remained of Japan's oil industry.

Meanwhile, the Army asked Halsey for preventive air attacks on Misawa in northern Honshu, where the Japanese had gathered an unusual number of twin-engine bombers. The presence of parachute units at Misawa led American analysts to conclude that an aerial commando operation was being planned against Okinawa. A similar mission had been mounted in late May, when a Japanese army bomber crash-landed at Yontan Airfield, delivering troops who destroyed nine aircraft and blew up two fuel dumps.

The new Japanese plan was far more ambitious, combining airborne commandos and low-level attack bombers. Wearing American uniforms, the raiders would crash-land on Saipan, Guam, and Tinian, destroying everything in reach. Though planned for late July, Operation *Tsurgi* (Sword) was interrupted by air strikes in mid-month when Third Fleet aviators wrecked Misawa and dozens of aircraft. By the time replacement bombers were available in August, with sixty Bettys with 600 navy and army troops, it was too late.

Meanwhile, in four conventional bombing missions from August 1 to 14, LeMay launched over 2,600 B-29 sorties, losing only ten bombers. And there was more, as Lieutenant General Jimmy Doolittle's re-formed 8th Air Force began arriving in mid-July. Though none of the fabled organization's units deployed from Europe, its headquarters and Doolittle's aura were enough to garner attention. Most of a B-29 wing and a full P-47 wing were established on Okinawa before the end of August.

Japan was increasingly faced with an apocalyptic aerial armada that truly could deliver Harry Truman's promised "rain of ruin." But still Tokyo hung on.

On Tuesday, August 14, the Marianas command put up 749 Superfortresses—the second highest figure of the war—and got all of them back. The world's most destructive bombing campaign had become so routine that it operated with little more risk than most airlines. LeMay dispatched seven missions in two waves. In the first three missions, 418 Superfortresses struck urban arsenals and rail yards that afternoon.

The other four missions lifted off their island bases about the time the first wave arrived over Japan. The 315th Wing's target was the Nippon Oil Company refinery at Tsuchizaki (also Tasuchizaki), nearly 300 miles north of Tokyo. The mission had been briefed and canceled while Tokyo and the Allies engaged in peace negotiations, and combat crews grew edgy. They lived in a twilight world, suspended somewhere between war and peace, hearing rumors both dire and dear. Finally the word came down: launch the mission.

That afternoon Frank Armstrong led again in his personal B-29, *Fluffy-Fuz III*. He took 141 bombers into the air of which 132 bombed the target. It was the longest unrefueled combat mission of the piston aircraft era: 3,740 miles from Guam to Tsuchizaki and back.

Ignoring inaccurate flak between 10,000 and 12,000 feet, the wing bombed by radar through a heavy undercast. By 3:40 that morning the last B-29s were on course for Guam, seven hours away.

At sea that night, in *Shangri-La*, Corsair pilot Dick DeMott recorded, "Rumors and reports all day that Japan has broadcast and has accepted our peace treaty. We still have not accepted it or acknowledged so we don't know what the hell is going on. . . . I wish to hell we could find out if the Japs are surrendering before we go needlessly groping around over Japan again and lose more pilots needlessly. This routine is getting harder to take each time."

August 15

Sunrise over Japan came at 4:35 A.M. on August 15, revealing a cloud-pocked sky with scattered showers. Task Force 38 carriers began launching combat air patrols and assembling two strike missions. Meanwhile, 336 B-29s were still southbound from the night's missions.

Frank Armstrong later wrote, "As we returned from our strike, we listened to a stateside broadcast as an excited announcer described the victory celebration in downtown San Francisco. The war was over! Having led the first daylight bombing raid in the European Theater and the longest bombing raid the last night of the war, I had opened and closed the affair like a fan.

"Every man aboard our aircraft was outwardly jubilant, but inside each experienced mixed emotions. We wanted no more of war, but it was difficult not to think of those who had not lived to see the dawn of this day. These thoughts brought waves of sadness, irony and gratitude. Too, there was a sudden surge of awe. Some of us had been in the business of killing for nearly four years. How would we adapt to a peaceful existence, and how much would we regret the havoc we had wrought, even though it had been absolutely necessary?"

Emperor Hirohito had finally decided to override his war cabinet, but not all of his warriors received the word—or heeded it. Consequently, some Allied naval pilots paid with their lives.

The fast carriers planned two strikes on the 15th, keeping the pressure on Japanese airfields. The 103 planes of Strike Able were overland at 6:35 A.M., attacking their assigned targets. A dozen *Ticonderoga* fighter-bombers struck military and industrial facilities on the Choshi Peninsula when *Shangri-La* broadcast, "All Strike Able planes, this is Nitrate Base. All Strike Able planes return to base. Do not attack target. The war is over!"

Still in his dive, Lieutenant (jg) John McNab was the twelfth Hellcat pilot in line. He dropped his 500-pounder just as the message came through—probably the last aviator to bomb Japan.

Shangri-La pilot Dick DeMott was leading a search for downed aviators in the Tokyo area. "On our way to the target area, word was passed of the official announcement from Pearl and CinCPac of the end of the war. What a time to hear it—en route to Tokyo!" Upon return to the flagship DeMott reported to McCain, noting the admiral was "slightly burned up at the Japs for continuing to send their planes out after us. He's a funny little guy. Everyone is all smiles and happy aboard, although it's almost too hard to believe the news."

From mirthfulness, DeMott turned reflective. "Brother, I am thankful that I am alive this day and got to see the end of the war from the front seat. I hope to spend the rest of my life enjoying everything and being at peace with the world. Kick me if I don't."

Hancock pilot Lieutenant Richard L. Newhafer, a future novelist and screenwriter, said the broadcast contained "all the hope and unreasoning happiness that salvation can bring. It brought tears and laughter and a numb sense of unbelief."

Nevertheless, some of Newhafer's squadron mates had to shoot their way out of Japanese airspace. Lieutenant Herschel Pahl's four Hellcats outfought seven enemy pilots, downing three en route home to *Hancock*. But others were not so fortunate.

Lieutenant Howard M. Harrison was leading six *Yorktown* Hellcats when they were ganged by as many as seventeen Japanese fighters. The lopsided combat degenerated into a series of close-range hassles with losses on both sides. Minutes later Lieutenants (jg) Maury Proctor and Theodore Hansen were the only Americans still flying. They returned to base, mourning the last-minute deaths of four of their friends in a senseless final act.

Nor was that all. Eight of HMS *Indefatigable*'s Supermarine Seafires were escorting carrier bombers over Odaki Bay when a dozen Japanese navy fighters bounced the Royal Navy planes from above and behind. Outnumbered and caught at an altitude disadvantage, the British fought for their lives. Sub-Lieutenant Fred Hockley was shot down on the Zekes' initial pass. He bailed out but there was no time to watch him. However, in the biggest combat of its career against three Axis powers, the Seafire outdid itself. Keeping their speed up and avoiding the urge to dogfight, the Royal Navy pilots claimed eight kills, led by Sub-Lieutenant Victor S. Lowden, who, despite a jammed cannon, scored two and split another with his wingman. (Available Japanese records indicate loss of at least four planes and three pilots.)

Four Zekes got past the Seafires to attack the bombers, badly damaging one Avenger. Despite a small fire onboard, Petty Officer A. A.

Simpson remained in his turret and opened up on the closest assailant. He scored several hits and claimed a probable kill.

Lieutenant (jg) Tadahiko Honma of the 304th Naval Squadron reported downing an Avenger before his plane was flamed by a Seafire, likely by Sub-Lieutenant Randy Kay. Honma bailed out, surviving with burns.

Now unescorted, the six Grummans continued to the target and bombed accurately. However, the crippled Avenger could not make the task force, so Simpson's pilot, Lieutenant L. W. Baldwin, splashed down in a safe water landing near a destroyer.

The Seafires had scored a notable victory but their joy was deadened when the fliers learned the fate of their leader. Freddie Hockley survived the shootdown but his captors almost immediately decapitated him.

The young Briton was not the only victim of condoned murder. That same day, following the emperor's surrender speech, officers at the Western Military District headquarters took seventeen B-29 crewmen from their wretched cells and, one by one, the prisoners were murdered.

None of the killers was ever punished.

Despite the emperor's broadcast, some Japanese die-hards rejected the idea of surrender. In fact, an army faction had attempted a coup at the palace, seeking to prevent broadcast of Hirohito's announcement. Offshore, Imperial Navy fliers launched sporadic attacks upon the Allied fleet during the early afternoon, entirely without success. The thirty-fourth and last U.S. Navy shootdown of the day went to a *Belleau Wood* pilot, Ensign Clarence A. Moore. The Judy dive bomber he destroyed at 2:00 P.M. officially ended aerial combat in the Second World War.

Throughout the task force, sailors took turns blowing ships' whistles while others shot off flares and star shells. Those plugged into the intelligence network pondered the arcane verbiage of Hirohito's capitulation.

The Imperial rescript was an amazing document, containing outrageous lies ("it being far from Our thoughts . . . to infringe upon the sovereignty of other nations") and gross understatement ("The war situation has developed not necessarily to Japan's advantage"). Nevertheless, it urged the Japanese people (subjects, not citizens) to "continue as one family from generation to generation."

Aside from the war developing "not necessarily to Japan's advantage," Hirohito cited "a most cruel bomb, the power of which to do damage is indeed incalculable." Since only the B-29 could deliver the new weapon, the enemy head of state acknowledged the Superfort's pivotal role in ending the war.

After initial outbursts, surprising quiet descended upon Allied bases. On that day the victors alternately expressed joy and regret. Some of the new fliers realized that their eighteen-month journey to combat had been cut short at the last possible moment. Having worked harder than they had ever done before—and some never would again—they saw their commitment to their nation end with a whimper.

At Ie Shima off Okinawa, the veteran 348th Fighter Group had just received some new P-51 pilots. They included Lieutenant Robert Stevens, who relished the prestige of a Mustang jockey. He sported a .45 pistol in a shoulder holster, vowing, "The Japs will never take me alive." But somehow he had not gotten around to testing his weapon.

On V-J night, Stevens reckoned that he would never have a better reason to shoot his pistol. Loading the big Colt, he raised it in the Ryukyu darkness and pulled the trigger. He confided, "All I got was a very loud click." Six tries later his magazine was empty but not a shot had been fired.

The next day a chagrined Bob Stevens took his pistol to the armorer's shop for a diagnosis. The verdict: a broken firing pin. Decades later he was able to laugh at himself: "The Japs would've got me after all."

On Guam the victors cut loose in a spontaneous eruption of pure glee. For most men it meant an end to years of drudgery, the unavoidable and most common wartime experience. For the combat crews, it meant more: it meant they were young and alive and had a future.

Joyous youngsters shot rifles and pistols into the air; others ran about shouting, waving their arms, and exchanging heartfelt handshakes. A few admitted to crying.

But far sooner than anyone would have suspected, silence settled over Guam and the other islands. Engines fell silent; bombs lay inert; lights were dimmed; and, in Churchillian terms, young men slept the sleep of the saved.

Interregnum

Almost immediately General Carl Spaatz ordered a "display of air power . . . continuous and increasing between 19 August and V-J Day," slated for September 2. The intent was to demonstrate America's absolute military superiority beyond any possible doubt to Japan's bitter-enders. Toward that purpose, Marianas-based B-29s and fighters were to rotate flying show-of-force missions in the Tokyo area, armed with machine gun ammunition but no bombs. However, weather and logistics interfered until the 30th.

Though the enemy had agreed to surrender on the 15th, there ensued a tentative testing of the waters by the Japanese, coupled with the Americans' lurking dread that something might go wrong. Two days later it did.

On August 17, four brand-new B-32 Dominators from Okinawa photographed the Tokyo area and three were intercepted by Imperial Navy fighters. The Japanese were led by veterans: Ensign Saburo Sakai and Warrant Officer Sadamu Komachi, both multiple aces. In a prolonged shootout both sides scored hits but sustained no losses.

The next day, the 18th, two more unescorted B-32s again were attacked by Komachi's flight. Gunners in Lieutenant John R. Anderson's bomber claimed two definite kills but the defenders also scored.

Anderson's plane was badly damaged with an engine knocked out and three men badly wounded. On the return flight a photographer, Sergeant Anthony Marichone, bled to death. He became the last American combat fatality of World War II.

Years later Sakai described his reason for the attacks, stating, "While Japan did agree to the surrender, we were still a sovereign nation, and every nation has the right to protect itself. When the Americans sent over their B-32s, we did not know of their intentions . . . by invading our airspace they were committing a provocative and aggressive act. . . . It was most unwise for the Americans to send over their bombers only a few days after the surrender announcement! They should have waited and let things cool down."

On August 25, while Navy planes searched for POW camps, two Army pilots became the first Americans to land in defeated Japan. Lieutenant Colonel Clay Tice had fought the Japanese in 1942–43 and the Germans in 1944. Upon returning to the Pacific he led the high-scoring 49th Fighter Group from Okinawa. On the morning of the 25th, he headed six P-38s on armed reconnaissance up the Kyushu coast. After inspecting Nagasaki and other cities, Tice had been airborne more than three hours when he learned one of his pilots was critically short on fuel, which had siphoned out in flight. Flight Officer Douglass C. Hall had only about 240 gallons remaining—insufficient to make Okinawa.

Tice had to work fast. He contacted a rescue B-17 and said he would lead his wingmate to Nittagahara on Kyushu's east coast, 450 miles from their base. The Americans could only hope for a hospitable reception.

The two Lightnings landed at noon, finding the airfield largely deserted. Hall was understandably nervous, fingering his pistol, but his CO enforced calm. An hour later the B-17 landed, much to the bemusement of the Japanese army personnel who had arrived. Tice reported, "We were greeted in a friendly manner," contrary to what he may have expected. Having fought both Axis powers, he respected the Germans but held little regard for the Japanese. Nevertheless, the Nittagahara delegation began with a lone bicyclist and ended with the local mayor in top hat and tails.

With help of the B-17 crew, enough fuel was transferred to Hall's P-38 for the two-hour return flight to Okinawa. There Tice was beset by correspondents eager to relate the drama of the first Americans to land in Japan. (They were three days ahead of General MacArthur's advance team coordinating the surrender.) Tice recalled, "I started off by saying . . . it was a routine fighter mission with no highlights that made it newsworthy. I was promptly put in my place by being informed that my business was to fly airplanes, and it was their business to decide what was newsworthy. The interview continued."

Naval aviators were not to be outdone. Two days later, on the 27th, a *Yorktown* fighter pilot landed at Atsugi and, vastly exceeding his authority, ordered the Japanese to erect a banner: "Welcome to the U.S. Army from the Third Fleet." The Japanese complied, and American paratroopers saw the greeting the next day.

September 2

On September 2—six years and a day after Germany invaded Poland—Japan's formal surrender occurred aboard the battleship *Missouri* anchored in Tokyo Bay. General of the Army Douglas MacArthur headed the U.S. delegation of eighty-nine officers including thirty-nine generals and thirty-four admirals or commodores wearing a galaxy of 171 stars. That did not include forty-three other officers from eight Allied nations.

American airmen were represented by those wearing wings: at least seven with Army silver and nine with Navy gold. Regardless of rank, perhaps the most prominent were Jimmy Doolittle, who started the bombing of Japan, and Curt LeMay, who ended it.

Admiral Chester Nimitz signed for the United States, flanked by Halsey and Rear Admiral Forrest Sherman, who had contributed significantly to American Pacific strategy. Other naval aviators present were Jack Towers, Ted Sherman, and Slew McCain. Only Pete Mitscher was missing.

Present but little recognized was Rear Admiral Donald B. Duncan, who as a captain had helped plan the Doolittle raid.

No sooner had MacArthur intoned "These proceedings are closed" than the air was split with an enormous roar. Operation Airshow was underway as some 450 carrier planes and 462 B-29s thundered overhead. Leading *Yorktown*'s fighters was Lieutenant Malcolm Cagle, whose pilots had endured the last dogfight over Japan on August 15. In the crowded airspace over Tokyo Bay, the honor of participating in the historic flyover was diminished by the risk of collision. Cagle described it as "a full throttle-off throttle formation with no real order or organization."

Postwar Missions

When the shooting stopped, another campaign immediately began: locating and supplying POW camps in Japan, China, and Korea. An interim measure of large-scale air drops was quickly instituted to sustain starving Allied personnel until ground forces reached them. On August 17, Spaatz tossed the ball to 20th Air Force, which gladly assumed responsibility for feeding 154 known camps in August and September.

Massively supplied from the Philippines, XXI Bomber Command modified B-29s to carry maximum loads of provisions. A standard package was developed, containing three days of food, plus clothing and medical kits with instructions. Some 12,000 bundles were dropped by parachute in the first phase. Follow-up drops contained rations for a week, then ten days, but only about half the camps needed the latter owing to rapid advances by liberating troops. Some fliers managed to insert special touches including beer and even ice cream amid the extra food and plasma.

In three weeks following August 27, B-29s flew almost 1,000

relief sorties, dropping nearly 4,500 tons of supplies to as many as 63,500 prisoners. However, the rescue efforts exacted a toll as eight B-29s crashed with seventy-seven dead.

While B-29s conducted mercy flights, fighter pilots relished buzzing Japan, flying with impunity at low level and high speed. One was Marine Captain Jefferson DeBlanc, who had broken into combat at Guadalcanal in 1942. The exuberant Louisianan recalled the excitement of those August days: "Now with the advent of peace, a complacent attitude prevailed. I even touched my wheels on an airfield in Japan and bounced back into the air without landing as a gesture of defiance. I could not see fighting the Japanese for four years and not 'landing' on their soil. It was a weird feeling, especially as this was one of the very airfields I had strafed only days before. Maybe this was pushing my luck, but at 24 years of age, I still had a little daring left."

Thus perished the Second World War, the voracious global monster whose sulfurous breath seared three continents and consumed at least 50 million human beings. Like most wars, its immense violence was only extinguished by the massive application of greater violence: a combination of strangulation by sea, conquest by land, and ruinous rain by air. In the final extremity, beneath a heap of ashes in the chilling shadow of radioactive clouds, at length the beast was slain.

CHAPTER NINE

Legacy

THE BOMBING OF JAPAN either averted the most horrific battle of all time, or it was one of the greatest atrocities ever committed. Six decades later, advocates on both sides of the question cling fiercely to their positions even as emerging scholarship sharpens the focus.

Whatever the conflicting attitudes toward strategic bombing, some of the campaign's basic aspects apply to all students of the subject. How a vital, industrious nation-state brought itself to such ruin will still be studied long after World War II passes from living memory. Therefore, the bombing of Japan raises three questions: how the nation tried to defend itself against overwhelming air attack; why Tokyo persisted in such an obviously losing effort; and how history currently evaluates the air campaign. We shall start with the first.

Defending the Homeland

Japan's ability to repel an American bombing campaign began with very few prospects in 1942 and sharply declined thereafter. Yet an enduring question is why Tokyo squandered more than two years after the Doolittle Raid, and why so little interservice coordination was attempted once B-29s appeared in homeland skies. The answer lies in the Japanese psyche more than in its military institutions.

In defending its airspace, Japan's army and naval forces were tasked with a nearly impossible mission. Nonetheless, they failed massively in even approaching their nation's potential to ameliorate the effects of the Allied onslaught.

Japan's only prospect for staving off aerial immolation was to inflict unacceptable losses upon B-29s. Because of the Superfortress's exceptional cost—some $600,000 each—a downed B-29 represented the financial equivalent of nearly three B-17s or B-24s, plus an invaluable crew. Development of ramming units demonstrates that some Japanese understood the value of a one-for-one or even two-for-one tradeoff, but the tactic largely failed for technical and organizational reasons. Therefore, defense of the home islands reverted to conventional means: flak guns and ordinary interceptors.

The resulting failure was systemic, crossing all boundaries of government and military-naval leadership. Probably the major cause was Japan's national psychology: a collectivist culture possessing a rigid hierarchy with unusually strict protocols that inhibited break-out thinking and instilled extreme reluctance to express contrary opinions. Japan poses an intriguing puzzle for sociologists and political scientists: how an extremely well-ordered society permitted itself to make a series of disastrous decisions, each threatening its national existence. Ironically, the situation was partly explained by the atmosphere of *gekokujo* ("pressuring from below") in which strident subordinates often influenced their superiors.

If interservice rivalry constituted a "second front" in Washington, D.C., it was a full contact sport in Tokyo. The postwar United States Strategic Bombing Survey concluded, "There was no efficient pooling of the resources of the Army and Navy. Responsibility between the two services was divided in a completely impractical fashion with the Navy covering all ocean areas and naval targets . . . and the Army everything else."

In June 1944, the month of the first B-29 attack, Imperial General Headquarters combined army and navy assets in an air defense command but the navy objected to army control. A compromise was achieved with naval air groups at Atsugi, Omura, and Iwakuni assigned to the respective army district. Phone links from JAAF command centers were provided to each of the three naval units, but operational integration was seldom attempted. In fact, throughout Japan, the two air arms operated jointly in only three areas: Tsuiki on Kyushu plus Kobe and Nagoya.

A major part of the problem was astonishingly sparse allocation of fighters to air defense. As late as March 1945, Japan allotted less than one-fifth of its fighters to home defense, and the actual figure only reached 500 in July. By then very few were flying, as Tokyo hoarded its strength for the expected invasion.

In the crucial realm of radar, Japan got a jump on the world—and almost immediately lost its lead. The efficient Yagi-Uda antenna had been invented in 1926, the product of two researchers at Tohoku Imperial University. Professor Hidetsugu Yagi published the first English reference two years later, citing his nation's work in short-wave research. But such was military secrecy and interservice rivalry that even late in the war few Japanese knew the origin of the device that appeared on downed Allied aircraft.

The Allies rated Japanese radar as "very poor," and fighter direction remained rudimentary. While land-based radar could detect inbound formations perhaps 200 miles out, the data included neither altitude nor composition. Consequently, picket boats were kept 300 miles at sea to radio visual sightings—of marginal use in cloudy weather. However, what radar systems did exist were easily jammed by American radio countermeasures—aircraft dropping aluminum foil that clogged enemy screens.

Furthermore, the Japanese army and navy established separate warning systems, and seldom exchanged information. Even when unit-level pooling was attempted, navy officers generally refused orders from army officers.

Civilian observers were spread throughout Japan to report enemy aircraft, but predictably there was no unity. The army and navy established their own observer corps, and neither worked with the other.

Japanese navy doctrine contained an internal contradiction for air defense. A 1944 manual asserted, "In order to overcome the disadvantages imposed on fighter plane units when the enemy raids a friendly base—that is, getting fighter planes airborne on equal terms with the enemy airplanes—full use must be made of radar and other lookout methods. . . . These must be employed in the most effective manner." But as noted, use of radar remained rudimentary.

Some pilots dismissed the state of their nation's electronics. "Why do we need radar? Men's eyes see perfectly well."

Excluding mobile radar sets, at least sixty-four early-warning sites were built in the homeland and offshore islands: thirty-seven navy and twenty-seven army. But the rare assets often were squandered by duplicating effort: at four sites on Kyushu and seven on Honshu, army and navy radars were located almost side by side. The southern approaches to Kyushu and Shikoku were covered by some twenty installations but only two permanent radars are known on all of Shikoku.

Though the huge majority of Japanese radars provided early warning, some sets directed AA guns and searchlights. But apparently there was little integration of the two: some B-29 crews returned with harrowing tales of ten to fifteen minutes in a searchlight's probing beam with minimal or no flak damage.

Apart from inadequate radar, some of Japan's technical focus was badly misdirected. From 1940 onward, the military devoted over five years to a "death ray" intended to cause paralysis or death by very short-wave radio waves focused in a high-power beam. The nonportable unit was envisioned for antiaircraft use, but the only model tested had a range much less than firearms.

Tactically, the lack of army-navy cooperation hampered the already limited potential of Japan's interceptors. With unit commanders conducting their own localized battles, there was little opportunity to concentrate large numbers of fighters against a bomber formation as the Luftwaffe repeatedly achieved.

Overall, Japanese fighters were spectacularly ineffective against B-29s. From more than 31,300 Superfortress sorties over the homeland, only seventy-four were known lost wholly to interceptors and perhaps twenty more in concert with flak guns. Japanese pilots logged their best performances in January and April 1945, each with thirteen bombers downed. But during fifteen months of combat, losses to interceptors amounted to merely 0.24 percent of effective B-29 sorties.

The Strategic Bombing Survey concluded, "The Japanese fighter defense system was no more than fair on paper and distinctly poor in practice. One fundamental matter stands out as the principal reason for its shortcomings—the Japanese planners failed to see the danger of allied air attacks and to give the defense system the requisite priorities."

Lieutenant General Saburo Endo of Army Air Force Headquarters stated, "Those responsible for control at the beginning of the war did not recognize the true value of aviation . . . therefore one defeat led to another. Although they realized there was a need for merging the army and the navy, nothing was done about it. There were no leaders to unify the political and the war strategies, and the plans executed by the government were very inadequate. National resources were not concentrated to the best advantage."

In short, in Japan's military, parochialism trumped efficiency at every turn.

A Losing Proposition

Why Tokyo persisted with a losing war for so long remains an enduring question. The closest comparison is found in Nazi Germany, which received about 1.3 million tons of bombs in the Heimat (homeland) and slightly more throughout the greater Reich. In contrast, Japan itself was subjected to "merely" 161,000 tons of conventional ordnance plus the equivalent of some 35,000 tons in two atomic weapons. At least 330,000 Japanese died by bombing whereas Germany's toll (inflicted over five years versus fourteen months) might run almost twice as much. The salient point is that neither regime in Tokyo or Berlin ended the war out of concern for massive civilian suffering until excruciating pain and unprecedented destruction had been inflicted.

How then to explain Japan's insistence upon apocalyptic ruin?

A recurring theme in statements of military and civilian leaders is the profound belief that defeat equaled an end to Japan's national existence. In his memoir, onetime foreign minister Mamoru Shigemitsu wrote, "Day by day Japan was turned into a furnace from which the voice of the people searching for food rose in anguish. And yet the clarion call was accepted. If the emperor ordained it, they would leap into the flames."

Vice Admiral Takejiro Onishi, father of the kamikazes, provided insight to the warped perception of the Japanese high command. In March 1945, a month before the invasion of Okinawa, he issued a statement from Taiwan. He conceded that "the enemy's offensive operations are drawing ever nearer to the home islands, and air raids . . . are getting more severe by the day . . . [and] the logistical situation . . . has become dire." However, in the same paragraph he asserted, "I can guarantee absolutely that Japan will not lose . . . the war is just beginning."

Onishi further stated that the expected Allied invasion would be repelled with "acceptable" Japanese casualties of 3 to 5 million, though he allowed that eventually 20 million might perish. Nevertheless, with sufficient "Japaneseness of spirit" the struggle might be maintained for years or even decades.

Nor was Onishi a lone voice. Historian Alvin Coox quoted a staff officer who served at Imperial General Headquarters in 1945: "we must fight in order to glorify our national and military traditions; that it was an engagement which transcended victory or defeat."

Against an enemy who seemed bent upon extinction, there was precious little middle ground for the Allies. The cultural divide between Japan and the West represented far more than a gap: it was a vast chasm.

Those Westerners in Japanese hands immediately recognized that abyss, evident in matters great and small. For instance, in April

1945 a B-29 named *Mrs. Tittymouse* crashed in Tokyo's Chofu district. A group of soldiers and civilians quickly gathered to examine the remains of the giant machine. The men noted the professional-quality nose art depicting a full-figured nude, which they regarded approvingly. Women were disgusted at the men's reaction.

The Japanese response reflected an inability to absorb the nature of the enemy. As an American historian living in Japan has said, "The gawkers were less offended by the nose art itself than by the fact that they were being bombed by people who had the cocky self-assuredness to go into battle with something so cheesy painted on their plane. It was related to the fact that no Japanese servicemen would have the self-autonomy to paint something like that on his warplane. Basically it's rage along the lines of 'How dare these people take war so lightly?'"

In that brief intersection of East and West it was possible to glimpse the essential nature of the unbridgeable chasm between bitter enemies. In the mangled ruins of that magnificent machine was the tacit lesson: Japanese could only marvel at America's destructive capacity and continue suffering beneath those crushing blows.

Finally the emperor emerged from behind "the chrysanthemum curtain" to take command of his ministers, his military, and his people.

The Leaders

Strategists are essentially policy makers, and those who set policy for the air campaign over Japan resided in Washington, D.C. Once Roosevelt and Churchill had set priorities for the grand alliance in 1941, the "Germany first" strategy determined allocation of assets that lasted well into 1944. However, after Allied armies were ashore in France, the Anglo-Americans were able to focus more men and matériel against Japan. Though coincidental, the arrival of B-29s in India in June 1944 occurred within days of the Normandy invasion.

Chief architect of the air war over Japan was of course Hap Arnold. As a visionary he had few peers, building the Army Air Forces from its 1938 doldrums into the globe-spanning entity that proved the bow wave of the independent U.S. Air Force. Probably he rendered his greatest service in the three years prior to Pearl Harbor, when he set Army aviation in motion with the infrastructure, equipment, personnel, and scientific-industrial liaison essential to ultimate success.

The B-29 would not have existed without Arnold. In its massive, streamlined shape he saw the future of airpower and, assuming its performance matched its potential, Billy Mitchell's realized dream of the air arm separated from the Army. He invested wholeheartedly in the Superfortress, both personally and institutionally, and earns high credit for that risky venture.

And yet . . .

And yet Arnold came perilously close to dropping the cerulean sword from his eager hands. He permitted himself to be stampeded into prematurely committing the world's most sophisticated aircraft to combat in a primitive theater, beyond effective range of the enemy heartland. Roosevelt's urgency in involving China became the engine that drove the Superfortress into an arena where it could not be supported—a mirage almost immediately obvious to the frosty brain and discerning eye of Curtis LeMay. Yet Arnold proved unable to accept the blame for his poor decisions, and he removed subordinates who strove mightily to deliver the undeliverable. His callous handling of Kenneth Wolfe especially does him no credit.

Wolfe and then Haywood Hansell did what they could with what they had before suffering Arnold's axe. Consequently, airpower historians shudder to speculate what might have become of the program absent the saving grace of dour, taciturn Curt LeMay with his genius for innovation and a rare willingness to question conventional wisdom. From today's distant remove, LeMay remains the most competent, most thoroughly professional airman of his generation, of any service, any nation. Arnold's hysterical threat, via Lauris Norstad, to remove LeMay if he failed in the Marianas demonstrates the paucity of options available to the Army Air Forces in the opening weeks of 1945. Despite LeMay's significant improvements in the China-Burma-India Theater, the Asian B-29 project already was doomed. Without LeMay's unconventional low-level incendiary missions against Japan's urban-industrial areas, the B-29 could have proven an extremely expensive failure, and the postwar effects on the battle over a unified defense department may only be surmised.

Make no mistake—Curtis LeMay not only saved the B-29 program, he also saved Hap Arnold and, with him, perhaps the future of an independent air force.

However, even some of LeMay's admirers fault him for waiting six weeks to switch from daylight high-altitude to nighttime low-level attacks. But the successful conversion probably could not have occurred in much less time for at least three reasons.

First, LeMay had to settle into his new command, learning the players and their various strengths. Second, he needed a few missions to assess Hansell's methods and evaluate their merits. Third, having decided to commit doctrinal heresy and wager a huge gamble, LeMay wanted to load the dice as much as possible. That required stockpiling enough incendiary bombs to sustain a ten-day blitz and giving mechanics time to raise the aircraft in-commission rate to a new high. LeMay's streamlined maintenance procedures required some time to take effect. But his patience paid immense dividends, and he rode out the preparation period regardless of how it appeared in Washington.

It was typical of the man. LeMay was as vastly unconcerned with his public image as any figure in American history. Though he would turn the postwar Strategic Air Command from a four-engine flying club into a Cold War deterrent, he remains far better known for his Vietnam-era vilification as a "caveman in a bomber."

LeMay's reputation contrasts vividly with that of Admiral William Halsey, who oversaw Third Fleet operations against Japan in the final months of hostilities. As a professional airman Halsey could not begin to compete with LeMay—nor with Arnold, for that matter—and the Bull's serious lapses attending Leyte plus the December

1944 and June 1945 typhoons only reinforced his failings as a four-star commander.

Yet neither of the fast carrier commanders came up to LeMay's standards, though Marc Mitscher and John McCain both outranked him. They relied heavily upon their extremely able staffs whereas LeMay directed his commands based on an intimate knowledge of his equipment and his craft. The plain fact is that the Third and Fifth Fleet carriers likely would have performed just as well without their three-star commanders, whereas XX and XXI Bomber Command would have remained an unrealized possibility absent LeMay.

He was, in a word, indispensable.

The Mythology

After 1945 the contention arose that bombing did little or nothing to end the war, especially against Germany. Critics such as economist John Kenneth Galbraith claimed, sometimes based upon flimsy evidence, that the costs of the campaign exceeded the measurable benefits. But in truth, the D-Day landings could not have been attempted without Allied air superiority, which required reduction of Germany's aircraft and oil industries. The fact remains that a combination of strategic and tactical airpower proved crucial in Europe.

Against Imperial Japan, the opponents of airpower have even less latitude for argument. As British historian Max Hastings has written, "The myth that the Japanese were ready to surrender anyway has been so completely discredited by modern research that it is astonishing some writers continue to give it credence." Tokyo's repeated rejection of the Potsdam Declaration, and the war cabinet's pleas for Soviet assistance prior to the atomic bombings, should leave no doubt as to Tokyo's mind-set. However belatedly, only the emperor's personal intervention ended the war. And by his own admission ("a most cruel bomb") the atomic bombs prompted him to override his warlords.

In dropping 161,000 tons of conventional bombs, Superfortresses burned out 40 percent of the built-up urban areas in sixty-six cities, resulting in destruction of nearly one-third of all Japanese houses. Japan's six leading industrial cities had been marked for destruction: of their total 257 square miles, 113 had been targeted and 106 were destroyed, excluding Hiroshima and Nagasaki.

The combination of reduced imports and B-29 bombing crippled Japanese industry. Aircraft production peaked at 2,550 in November 1944, then quickly declined. The total by all manufacturers never reached 2,000 after December, dropping to barely 1,500 the following July. (In contrast, U.S. Army acceptances averaged 5,800 aircraft per month through 1944.) Unable to compete in the air, the Japanese began saving their strength to meet the impending invasion. At the end, Tokyo hoarded 10,400 aircraft (over half marked for suicide missions) and 18,000 pilots.

The naval-air campaign against the home islands tightened the noose around Tokyo's shrinking neck. With vital imports severely limited by submarines and aerial mines, the nation lacked sufficient quantities of everything from food to manganese. Allied carrier aircraft made coastal shipping a perilous enterprise, further limiting enemy transport options. Had the war lasted a few weeks longer, Japan's interior communications—especially railways—would have felt the crippling weight of American bombs. That in turn would have exerted an even greater hardship upon the badly strapped food distribution network.

Assailed from the sea and the sky—America's unmatched way of making war—Imperial Japan faced apocalyptic destruction. But the hell-bent warlords' zealous view from Tokyo surveyed their pitiful, starving subjects and determined that they had not yet suffered enough to warrant surrender.

Targeting

Other than Hiroshima and Nagasaki, the most cited criticism of U.S. bombing remains targeting urban-industrial areas. Yet because

Japanese industries relied on cottage or "shadow" factories to produce subcomponents, it was impossible to strike them specifically—if
somehow they could be identified. Small shops and even homes in
urban areas surrounding industrial plants produced a huge amount
of matériel, especially for aircraft and engine factories. The feeder
industries passed their products to component shops, which in turn
passed subassemblies to factories for completion and installation. The
variety was enormous: from simple hose clamps to airframe stringers
formed on wooden jigs to machined parts such as valves.

Therefore, area bombing remained the only option short of
returning to "precision" attacks on major factories or abandoning
the strategic air campaign. Neither the Army Air Forces, U.S. policy
makers, nor American citizens were inclined to do so—especially
against a savage enemy in the fourth year of an unrelenting war.

. LeMay's shift from "precision" attacks against specific targets has
been denigrated as "terror bombing." Certainly there was terror, but
in many cases the argument is disingenuous because it is well known
that high-altitude bombing was seldom very precise, especially with
Japan's fiercely unpredictable winds aloft that scattered ordnance far
off target. Furthermore, until nearly the end of the war, the vaunted
"pickle barrel" accuracy claimed for the Norden bombsight was more
myth than reality. Only with arrival of the Eagle radar in mid-1945
did B-29s prove consistently able to destroy precision targets.

Nevertheless, postwar analysis concluded that, absent the B-29s,
Japan's 1945 production would have run between 50 and 60 percent
of the 1944 figures, largely owing to reduced availability of raw materials. Yet in July, the last full month of hostilities, overall production
in thirty-three urban-industrial areas reached just one-third of the
1944 peak. Clearly bombing made a difference.

Whatever postwar criticism in America and the West, the Japanese acknowledged the effectiveness of area bombing. Rear Admiral
Toshitane Takata testified, "The fire bomb raids destroyed most of
the smaller factories making aircraft parts, thus causing serious losses
in production. The many small plants scattered over the cities which

were destroyed caused serious loss in other material and general production. Aircraft engine production always lagged behind a safe ratio to airframe production and was frequently numerically inferior for individual types."

Admiral Takata's view was shared by Lieutenant General Takashi Kanaoka, commanding the First Antiaircraft Division: "From the defense point of view, plane factories were your top priority, then essential war industries. Your selection of targets was excellent."

Partly because ships are more readily identified than factories, naval targeting policy was more easily defined than aerial, and the priority naval target was Japan's merchant marine. Largely due to American submarines, from 1943 onward the Empire's essential sea lanes were seriously depleted. In 1945 the eminently successful B-29 mining campaign choked off much of Japan's remaining seaborne logistics, earning often grudging admission by Army fliers that their missions represented a wholly worthwhile diversion from urban-industrial attacks.

However, the U.S. Navy's obsession with the remnants of the Imperial Navy was clearly misplaced. While the admirals' insistence in finishing off Kure's and Yokosuka's rusting warships may be understandable, it represented poor policy when those sorties could have been profitably aimed at coastal shipping. The latter work was routinely unglamorous, but there is no more superior example of its effectiveness than the destruction of Hokkaido's coal ferries.

Furthermore, carrier airpower lacked the ability to affect seriously Japanese industry—a point conceded by some admirals at the time. Therefore, the naval air strikes against aircraft plants tended to duplicate the Army effort, sometimes hitting areas already scoured by B-29s. The air admirals, being both fliers and seamen, were drawn to both target sets, and no superior was inclined to reel them in.

Conclusions

Though the campaign against the home islands was broadly dictated by the Joint Chiefs in Washington, the American effort lacked unity of command. As noted, the Army Air Forces and the Navy largely pursued their own goals, each the natural product of their respective worldviews.

Absent a single theater commander, and management of the 20th Air Force from Washington, some of America's enormous naval-air consortium was dissipated in duplication of effort and insufficient strategic focus. That lapse falls not only upon Hap Arnold of the Army Air Forces and Ernest King of the Navy, but upon Franklin Roosevelt the commander in chief, who made no effort to force a meeting of the minds. President Truman might have addressed (if not redressed) some of the Joint Chiefs' parochialism, but he was understandably concerned with the geostrategic and political problems he inherited in the final four months.

The AAF was about strategic bombardment, still linked to the Douhet-Mitchell concept of forcing the enemy's collapse by destroying his will to resist. Though that goal was only achieved by influencing Hirohito, widespread destruction of Japanese industry and transport severely crippled Tokyo's *ability* to resist.

Thus, the Allied air campaign against Japan resembled parallel train tracks—Army and Navy—each headed for the same station. Both engines might have arrived ahead of schedule had they cooperated better, allocating their specific assets to the tasks each could best perform.

But that is after the fact. The final verdict is this: airpower forced the capitulation of a desperate, tenacious enemy and thus rendered unnecessary the ghastly prospect of the bloodiest invasion in the sanguinary history of the human race.

The Bomb

What were the American alternatives to using atomic weapons against Japan? There were only three: declare victory and withdraw; maintain a blockade to await events; invade.

The first choice was dead upon arrival. America and the Allies had demanded unconditional surrender, and their populations would support nothing less, especially since Italy and Germany had been defeated under that premise. But the underlying insistence upon unconditional surrender looked beyond the war toward an unmistakable break with the past, providing the legal basis for restructuring Axis nations so they would never again initiate aggression.

An invasion would have been horrific. The Japanese correctly guessed the landing beaches and prepared accordingly. In some places the attacker-to-defender ratio would have approached one to one, a chilling prospect that Admiral Chester Nimitz opposed because of unavoidably heavy U.S. casualties. General Douglas MacArthur, likely for reasons of personal ambition, favored invasion. That left blockade.

Depending upon duration, a blockade could have inflicted more deaths upon Japan than continued bombing. Those who advocated "starving the Japs into surrender" overlooked a critical fact: the huge majority of the resultant deaths would have been civilians, especially the old, the very young, and the enfeebled. Additionally, the long-term physical and psychological effects upon the younger generation could have been immense. As in every despotic nation, in times of hunger the army eats before the civilians, be it Kim Il-sung's Korea or Saddam Hussein's Iraq.

A major factor widely ignored in the debate about the bomb is the American public. With troops redeploying from Europe to the Pacific, and the prospect of a horrific invasion of a fanatical enemy's homeland, Harry Truman the president (let alone the politician) simply could not have ignored the bomb's war-ending potential. Had the invasion proceeded without first using atomic weapons, he likely would have been impeached by politicians responding to the outraged parents of thousands of dead sons.

So the atoms would be loosed. As Truman later wrote, "The final decision had to be made by the President, and was made after a complete survey of the whole situation had been made. . . . The Japanese were given fair warning, and were offered the terms which they finally accepted, well in advance of the dropping of the bomb."

Death figures for Hiroshima vary widely, as do population estimates. The most specific sources cite from 90,000 to 140,000 deaths prior to 1946, among 320,000 to 345,000 residents. An approximate toll of 90,000 slightly exceeds the acknowledged loss in the Tokyo firebombing of March 9–10.

Figures for total radiation deaths from the two bombings vary hugely: from fewer than 800 named individuals to a claimed 100,000-plus. Partisans on both sides of the controversy have reason to manage the numbers, but scientific study leans well to the lower end—hundreds rather than thousands.

Much—perhaps most—of the criticism of 1945 U.S. military policy seems imposed by post-Vietnam attitudes rather than in context of World War II. In that regard the debate about use of the A-bomb, and bombing generally, resulted in a peculiar inversion. The Japanese, who embarked upon a brutal war of conquest, were increasingly cast as victims while the Americans who responded to that action became the aggressors. Thus was born the concept of "equivalency," with the response to the war makers somehow becoming as objectionable as the actions that launched the aggression.

The voices protesting the use of nuclear weapons spanned the political spectrum: from scientists who helped produce the bombs to some of America's most senior military leaders. Since many of the Los Alamos personnel were refugees from Occupied Europe, their prime motivation had been to produce a weapon before Hitler did. Once Nazi Germany collapsed, presumably the need for A-bombs diminished. But those opposed to using A-bombs against Japan reckoned without Tokyo's samurai zeal for national extinction.

Among the postwar critics of the bombs was Admiral Ernest King, the chief of naval operations. Widely known for his abrasive personality ("When they get into trouble they call for the sons of bitches"), his alleged moral objections to nuclear weapons appear disingenuous at best, only appearing after the fact. Certainly he had no qualms about ordering his submarines to violate international law by sinking Japanese merchant ships without warning—the only effective tactic. His seeming preference for blockade and/or invasion also falls afoul of the 5,000 kamikazes his fleet would have faced in late 1945. Far more likely he issued his statements with an eye toward the forthcoming battle over creating an independent air force rather than any queasiness about killing the enemy.

Meanwhile, the moral question about atomic weapons was shared at other rarefied levels. Former President Herbert Hoover and General Dwight D. Eisenhower believed that Tokyo was on the verge of surrender, even though Japanese documents (to say nothing of actions) clearly show otherwise. Yet the presidents' ethically based if ill-informed opposition to the bombs is still widely quoted.

Little discussed is the fact that in June 1943 Hirohito had directed his prime minister to ask the army and navy general staffs where they planned to stop the Americans. Prime Minister Hideki Tojo's adviser, General Kenryu Sato, accurately replied, "Neither the Army nor the Navy can possibly draw up a plan to stop them." Yet Japan persisted more than two years.

Nevertheless, the victims of American bombings also were heard. U.S. Army radio monitors picked up part of a Radio Tokyo broadcast in 1945: "'Blind' bombing or 'indiscriminate'—these expressions have appeared in our official communiqués but are now regarded as a gross misnomer in describing the enemy's savage attacks." Fifty years later the mayors of Hiroshima and Nagasaki compared the atomic bombings to the Holocaust. They found support among those Americans who frame the debate on behalf of Japan, an approach intellectually crippling and objectively flawed. With the war's instigators receiving a pass from the anti-atomic perspective, Tokyo is cast as victim rather than perpetrator and owner of the nation's fate.

The pattern is clear: Japan's warlords remained unconcerned about their people's suffering. Having deceived the population for years, announcing one triumph after another even as the front lines drew inexorably nearer their own shores, Japan's leaders displayed stunning indifference toward 70 million industrious, devoted subjects.

Only after the trip-hammer blows of Hiroshima, Nagasaki, and the Soviet declaration of war coming in rapid-fire sequence did the emperor intervene and override his doom-laden cabinet. One has to wonder why he did not do so five months earlier, when he sniffed the ash-strewn wind whipping round the Imperial Palace, bearing the stench of 85,000 charred corpses.

Defenders of the atomic bombings stress the lives saved on both sides in avoiding blockade or invasion. Those spared included hundreds of thousands to millions of Japanese who escaped death by starvation—let alone in an invasion—and tens of thousands of Allied POWs who almost certainly would have been killed. Moreover, those spared included an immense number of Asians—perhaps 100,000 or more *per month* in China alone—who were dying of disease, famine, and brutality.

Japan's senior civilian leaders acknowledged the primacy of airpower in forcing capitulation. Prince Konoye said, "Fundamentally the thing that brought about the determination to make peace was the prolonged bombing by the B-29s." Prime Minister Kantaro Suzuki agreed, adding, "On top of the B-29 raids came the atomic bomb, issued after the Potsdam Declaration, which was just one additional reason for giving in . . . and gave us the opportune moment to open negotiations for peace." His reference to "us" was only partly true since most of the military preferred to continue the war. But it did accurately state the position of the one human whose opinion mattered most—the emperor of Japan.

Epitaph

So the airmen had their victory, but it represented far more than the defeat of Imperial Japan. To Arnold, Spaatz, LeMay, and others, the B-29 had more than justified its $2.5 billion cost because its success set the stage for an independent air arm. Consequently, the end of World War II launched another conflict: postwar arguments about the relative effectiveness of land- and carrier-based airpower with an eye toward the emerging Army-Navy rivalry for postwar funds and missions. Looming hugely was the airmen's surging confidence that they deserved a separate service, equal to the Army and the Navy. They finally got it in 1947, with the United States Air Force.

The fliers who bombed Japan provided leadership to the Air Force and Navy for the next thirty years. LeMay and Thomas Power led the Strategic Air Command—America's primary nuclear warfighting arm—and LeMay commanded the entire Air Force from 1961 to 1965. Marc Mitscher, who led the fast carriers most of the war, earned a promotion to full admiral before dying in 1947.

Others fared less well. In 1954 physicist Robert Oppenheimer of the Manhattan Project was suspected for earlier Communist affiliations and lost his security clearance. Paul Tibbets was excoriated by leftists and pacifists for destroying Hiroshima. Harry Truman was second-guessed by two generations of historians and pundits who insist that he only permitted use of the bomb to impress the Soviets.

Some Japanese disagree. They recognize that the war cabinet was determined to go down fighting, and that an Allied invasion would have resulted in millions of Japanese deaths. Despite Hirohito's involvement in conducting the war, he did the right thing by overriding his most fanatical samurai.

In the end, the theories presented by Douhet, Mitchell, and others were alternately proven and refuted. Belief in the power of strategic bombardment to end a war quickly was clearly optimistic. So was the contention that heavy civilian casualties would force a capitulation: it was no more true in democratic Britain than in authoritarian Japan, though the scale of destruction was far different.

However, airpower's effect upon the enemy's *ability* to wage war outstripped its psychological influence. In early 1945 Japan was starving for food and fuel. The first major fire raid in March left sixteen square miles of Tokyo in ruins, with no prospect for preventing additional destruction. But five more months of even heavier bombing were required before Japan's leaders finally had enough.

Though the war ended in 1945, in a real sense it continues today. The decades-long atomic bombing debate peaked in 1993–95 when the Smithsonian Institution's National Air and Space Museum sparked enormous controversy over a fiftieth anniversary display built around the *Enola Gay*. The proposed script's treatment of bombing Hiroshima and Nagasaki largely ignored the rising toll of American casualties as the war had continued, and chose to cast the atomic bombs as revenge for Pearl Harbor. The lack of context outraged many Americans—whose taxes fund the museum—for the perception of moral equivalency in the wartime actions of the United States and Japan. Veterans and military historians were angered by the text's self-righteous tone and the reluctance of the curators responsible for the exhibit to include such objections. With increasing involvement by veterans' groups and the Air Force Association, the U.S. Senate reviewed the text and declared it "revisionist and offensive to many World War II veterans." The result was the forced resignation of the director of the National Air and Space Museum (an astronomer rather than historian) and reduction of the proposed exhibit. Though only part of the *Enola Gay* was displayed, it drew 4 million visitors in three years. Today the famous bomber is fully assembled at the museum's Dulles, Virginia, facility, testament to an air campaign unlike anything before, and never to be seen again.

Appendix A

THE UNKNOWN WAR

After the Doolittle Raid in April 1942 Japan was immune to air attack for fifteen months. When American aircraft reappeared they operated in a remote area, from an even remoter source.

The Kuril Islands comprised the northernmost portion of Japan, nearly 1,500 miles from Tokyo and therefore not considered part of the homeland. Well beyond Hokkaido, bisected by the 50th parallel, the isles were typically cold, fogbound, and of only marginal interest to American strategists. But the Kurils possessed one invaluable asset: they were within range of bombers in the Aleutians. Even then it was a long stretch—more than 700 miles across the North Pacific.

In July 1943 the Alaska-based 11th Air Force launched its first attack on the Kurils, striking Paramushiru Island. The early efforts were literally hit-and-miss affairs, as attackers necessarily dropped bombs through solid cloud layers. A large mission involved nine B-24s.

The Japanese were the least of the Aleutian airmen's problems. The weather was a perennial enemy, possessing numerous ways to kill an unwary or unlucky crew. Visibility frequently ranged from bad to zero, with mountains stuffed inside of clouds. The maritime atmosphere could choke a carburetor or overload a wing with ice, and there were few navigation aids. If a plane went down at sea, prospects for rescue were considered twofold: grim and none. Those who didn't drown would freeze to death in ten minutes.

Nevertheless, the 11th Air Force pressed ahead. With more assets dribbling into the neglected theater, the command prepared a maxi-

mum effort on September 11. A dozen Mitchells and eight Liberators attacked shipping and facilities, claiming five vessels sunk or
damaged and thirteen interceptors downed. Both figures were exaggerated, but the American losses were real enough: seven B-25s
destroyed and two B-24s lost when they landed in Russia.

An operational summary called September 11 "the most disastrous day for the Eleventh Air Force." Flying in the Aleutians weather
factory was bad enough—sometimes nearly as many missions aborted
as got through. But heavy Japanese defenses forced a rethinking. The
new air commander, Major General Davenport Johnson, suspended
Kurils missions for five months.

That summer the Japanese began paying more attention to their
northern flank. In August the Imperial Navy established the Northeast Area Fleet, responsible for Hokkaido and the Kurils. Three
months later some 260 army and navy aircraft were based in the
region but the number steadily declined. By the spring of 1945 it was
reduced to twenty army and navy aircraft with some 27,000 men.

Meanwhile, the U.S. Navy began attacking the Kurils with
"Empire Express" missions by Fleet Air Wing Four, commanded by
ascerbic, erratic Captain Leslie Gehres, who insisted on using Cata-
lina patrol planes like B-17s. In December 1943, Catalinas initiated
night bombing and reconnaissance missions over the Kurils, replaced
in February 1944 with faster, better-armed Ventura bombers.

When AAF operations resumed that month, the 11th Air Force's
offensive arm largely comprised two squadrons: B-25s on Attu and
B-24s on Shemya. Additionally, two P-38 squadrons occasionally
provided long-range escort.

Even after resuming Kurils missions, AAF emphasis was on
reconnaissance—both photographic and radar mapping. Specially
equipped Liberators periodically deployed from distant Colorado
Springs while electronic "ferret" B-24s snooped for Japanese radar
installations.

Offensive missions accelerated in the summer of 1945, with
AAF and Navy aircraft occasionally operating together. On June 9,

Army bombers covered a naval force bombarding the Kurils (almost a monthly event), but Japanese fighters intercepted the B-25s. Two Mitchells veered over Soviet territory, both being shot down with one crew killed.

The 11th Air Force logged its last bombing missions and final combat losses in June 1945. By then Fleet Air Wing Four had grown to five squadrons flying Consolidated Catalinas and Liberators plus Lockheed Venturas and Harpoons.

The fliers who made the long, perilous "Empire Express" runs possessed a special kind of motivation. They were unheralded, consigned to a secondary (some said tertiary) campaign, forced to operate with pitifully small forces. But for two years they plied their trade despite all that nature and the Japanese Empire could muster against them. In perhaps no other air operations of World War II did survival constitute such a victory.

Appendix B

JAPANESE AIRCRAFT
BY ALLIED CODE NAMES

(DATE OF FIRST FLIGHT)

Betty Mitsubishi G4M *Isshikirikkō* (Type 1 Land Attack). Navy twin-engine patrol bomber, typically with 7-man crew. 1939.

Fran/Frances Yokosuka P1Y *Ginga* (Milky Way). Navy twin-engine attack/reconnaissance bomber with 3-man crew. 1943.

Frank Nakajima Ki-84 *Hayate* (Gale). Army single-engine, single-seat fighter. 1943.

George Kawanishi N1K *Shiden* (Violet Lightning). Navy single-engine, single-seat fighter. 1942.

Irving Nakajima J1N *Gekko* (Moonlight). Navy twin-engine, two-seat night fighter. 1941.

Jack Mitsubishi J2M *Raiden* (Thunderbolt). Navy single-engine, single-seat fighter. 1942.

Nick Kawasaki Ki-45 *Toryu* (Dragon). Army twin-engine, two-seat interceptor and reconnaissance plane. 1941.

Oscar Nakajima Ki-43 *Hayabusa* (Peregrine Falcon). Army single-engine, single-seat fighter. 1939.

Tojo Nakajima Ki-44 *Shoki* (Devil Queller). Army single-engine, single-seat fighter. 1940.

Tony Kawasaki Ki-61 *Hien* (Swallow). Army single-engine, single-seat fighter. 1941.

Zeke Mitsubishi A6M *Reisen* (Zero Fighter). Navy single-engine, single-seat fighter. 1939.

Acknowledgments

VETERANS (RANKS AS OF 1945)

First Lieutenant Sandy Arnell	29th Bomb Group, Guam
Lieutenant Malcolm W. Cagle	VF-88, USS *Yorktown* (d. 2003)
Sergeant Howard Chamberlain	504th Bomb Group, Tinian
Lieutenant (jg) John H. Christiansen	VBF-16, USS *Randolph* (d. 2008)
First Lieutenant Charles M. Crawford	38th Bomb Group, Okinawa
Major Harry C. Crim	21st Fighter Group, Iwo Jima (d. 1994)
Captain Jack DeTour	38th Bomb Group, Okinawa
Sergeant Henry E. Erwin	29th Bomb Group, Guam (d. 2002)
Second Lieutenant Donald A. Gerth	39th Bomb Group, Tinian
First Lieutenant R. F. "Hap" Halloran	499th Bomb Group, Saipan
Lieutenant (jg) Willis E. Hardy	VF-17, USS *Hornet*
Lieutenant Commander Roger Hedrick	VF-84, USS *Bunker Hill* (d. 2006)
First Lieutenant Bedford M. Hertel	27th Troop Carrier Squadron, China (d. 1997)
Lieutenant Commander W. N. Leonard	Task Force 38 staff (d. 2005)
Lieutenant Hamilton McWhorter, Jr.	VF-12, USS *Randolph* (d. 2006)
Brigadier General Ernest M. Moore	VII Fighter Command, Iwo Jima (d. 1981)
Sergeant Virgil Morgan	6th Bomb Group, Tinian
First Lieutenant Harvey Phipps	21st Fighter Group, Iwo Jima
Lieutenant (jg) Robert S. Rice	VBF-3, USS Yorktown (d. 2007)

ACKNOWLEDGMENTS

Lieutenant Armistead B. Smith III	VBF-12, USS *Randolph* (d. 2000)
First Lieutenant Neil Smith, Jr.	506th Fighter Group, Iwo Jima
First Lieutenant Robert Stevens	348th Fighter Group, le Shima (d. 1994)
Colonel Clay Tice, Jr.	49th Fighter Group, Okinawa (d. 1998)

CONTRIBUTORS

All the regulars at J-Aircraft.com; Tom Behrens, 38th Bomb Group Association; Colonel Walter J. Boyne, USAF (Ret); Alan Concepcion; W. David Dickson; Robert F. Dorr; Richard L. Dunn; Edward Fahey, FDNY; Andrew Farmer; Richard B. Frank; Orland F. Gage, 38th Bomb Group Association; Phil Gentry, USS *Franklin* Association; Dennis Giangreco; C. V. Glines; Frank Grube; Dr. Richard P. Hallion; Bob Kattenheim, USS *Shangri-La* Association; Don Kehn, Jr.; Dr. Arnold Krammer; Dr. John T. Kuehn; Rich Leonard; Jim Long; Kirk Lowry, Theaerodrome.com; Chuck Lynch; Nancy Macaulay; Helen McDonald and Reagan Grau, National Museum of the Pacific War (special thanks); Roger Mansell; Donald Nijboer; Don Norton (special thanks); Seth Paridon, National WWII Museum (special thanks); Lucy Price, London Fire Brigade; Ronald W. Russell (special thanks); Henry Sakaida (special thanks); Taeko Sasamoto; Dale Sauter, East Carolina University; Dr. M. G. Sheftall; Commander Doug Siegfried, USN (Ret), Tailhook Association; Jody Smith; Joseph A. Springer; Doug Sterner, Home of Heroes; Iain Stewart; John C. Sullivan, Office of Air Force History; Osamu "Sam" Tagaya; John L. Tillman; Anthony P. Tully, Robert von Maier, *World War II Quarterly*; Sallyann Wagoner, B-29.org; and Pete Wyler, 39th Bomb Group Association.

Also, a dip of the wing to my literary agent, Jim Hornfischer, who suggested the subject, and a tip of the helmet to my patient editor, Roger Labrie.

Notes

PROLOGUE

Page

1 *something that had never been done:* In May 1938 the Chinese air force dispatched two American-built Martin bombers to drop leaflets over southern Japan, including Nagasaki. Both returned safely but no further missions were flown. Information from Richard L. Dunn, http://www.warbirdforum.com/elusive.htm.

2 *"out of the country":* http://www.njipms.org/Articles/doolittle-lawson.htm.

2 *A sub kill was claimed:* "U-boat Losses by Year," http://uboat.net/fates/index.html.

2 *Doolittle's crew:* Doolittle's copilot, Richard E. Cole, was twenty-six; bombardier Fred A. Braemer was twenty-four; navigator Henry A. Potter was twenty-three; and gunner Paul J. Leonard twenty-nine. The senior pilots were Major John A. Hilger (wings 1934) with Captains David M. Jones (1938), Edward J. York (1939), and Charles Ross Greening (1937). Of the others, four had completed pilot training in 1940; six in 1941.

4 *One observer:* Masatake Okumiya and Jiro Horikoshi with Martin Caidin, *Zero: The Story of Japan's Air War in the Pacific* (New York: Bantam, 1991), 315.

4 *"extremely satisfactory":* "The Tokyo Raid," Headquarters, Army Air Forces Director of Intelligence, October 5, 1942.

5 *the 16,700-ton* Taigei: "IJN *Ryuho*: Tabular Record of Movement," http://www.combinedfleet.com/Ryuho.htm.

5 *Tokyo reported six schools:* Conrad Black, *Franklin Delano Roosevelt, Champion of Freedom* (New York: PublicAffairs, 2003), 727.

6 *"No sir":* James H. Doolittle and Carroll V. Glines, *I Could Never Be So Lucky Again* (New York: Bantam, 1991), 12.

7 *The toll:* Jon Grinspan, "April 18, 1942: Pearl Harbor Avenged," AmericanHeritage.com, http://www.americanheritage.com/people/articles/

web/20070418-tokyo-doolittle-raid-jimmy-doolittle-pearl-harbor-battle-of-midway-world-war-II-japan.shtml.

CHAPTER ONE: BEFORE THE BEGINNING

Page

9   *"Aeronautics opened up"*: Giulio Douhet, *Command of the Air* (Dino Ferrari, translator) (New York: Coward-McCann, 1942), 3.

10 *"issuing false news"*: Philip S. Meilinger, "Giulio Douhet: The Origins of Airpower Theory," *The Paths of Heaven: Evolution of Airpower Theory* (Maxwell Air Force Base, AL: Air University Press, 1997), 10.

13 *"almost treasonable administration"*: American Airpower Biography, Maxwell Air Force Base, Alabama, http://www.airpower.maxwell.af.mil/airchronicles/cc/mitch.html.

16 *"relentless and incessant offensiveness"*: Philip S. Meilinger, "Trenchard, Slessor, and Royal Air Force Doctrine Before World War II," *The Paths of Heaven: Evolution of Airpower Theory* (Maxwell Air Force Base, AL: Air University Press, 1997), 44, 46.

18 *"the very threat"*: Lieutenant Colonel Marc A. Clodfelter, in Philip S. Meilinger, "Molding Airpower Convictions: Development and Legacy of William Mitchell's Strategic Thought," *The Paths of Heaven: Evolution of Airpower Theory* (Maxwell Air Force Base, AL: Air University Press, 1997), 96–97.

18 *In twenty years of discussion*: Lieutenant Colonel Peter R. Faber, in Philip S. Meilinger, "Interwar US Army Aviation and the Air Corps Tactical School," *The Paths of Heaven: Evolution of Airpower Theory* (Maxwell Air Force Base, AL: Air University Press, 1997), 212–21.

20 *"In view of the world situation"*: AWPD-1: The Process, Maxwell Air Force Base, AL, Air University Press, Historical Analysis: Joint Doctrine Air Campaign course, 1996, http://www.au.af.mil/au/awc/awcgate/readings/awpd-1-jfacc/awpdproc.htm.

21 *"in one blow"*: Ibid.

21 *about half of Bomber Command*: Max Hastings, *Bomber Command: The Myths and Reality of the Strategic Bombing Offensive, 1939–45* (New York: Dial, 1979), 370.

22 *By one reckoning*: Philip S. Meilinger, "Alexander P. de Seversky and American Airpower," *The Paths of Heaven: Evolution of Airpower Theory* (Maxwell Air Force Base, AL: Air University Press, 1997), 266.

22 *some of his lessons*: Alexander P. de Seversky, *Victory Through Air Power* (New York: Simon and Schuster, 1942), 120–52. Seversky's lessons:

1. No land or sea operations are possible without air superiority.
2. Navies have lost their function of strategic offensive.
3. Blockade has become a function of airpower.
4. Only airpower can defeat airpower.
5. Land-based aviation is always superior to ship-based aviation.
6. Air-striking radius must equal the maximum dimensions of the theater of operations.
7. In aviation, quality is relatively more decisive than quantity.
8. Aircraft types must be specialized for strategic and tactical concerns.
9. Destruction of enemy morale can best be accomplished by precision bombing.
10. Unity of command applies to aviation as well as land and naval operations.
11. Airpower needs its own transportation.

23 *The world's most famous bombsight:* Albert L. Pardini, *The Legendary Norden Bombsight* (Atglen, PA: Schiffer, 1999), 43–44.

23 *The first large order:* Ibid., 50–51.

25 *"A direct attack":* Meilinger, *Paths of Heaven*, 68.

25 *"the moral high ground":* Hastings, *Bomber Command*, 177.

26 *"It was preferable":* Ibid., 96.

27 *Prior to 1942:* "Heavenly Dog," *Time*, May 15, 1939; Mark Peattie, *Sunburst: The Rise of Japanese Naval Airpower* (Annapolis: Naval Institute Press, 2001), 116.

27 *"offer yourselves courageously":* "A Brief Introduction to the Shinto Religion," www.buzzle.com/articles/a-brief-introduction-to-the-shinto-religion.html.

28 *Beginning in the nineteenth century:* For the evolution (or mutation) of original samurai Bushido into the twentieth century, see Karl F. Friday, "Bushido or Bull? A Medieval Historian's Perspective on the Imperial Army and the Japanese Warrior Tradition," *InYo: Journal of Alternative Perspectives*, March 2001, http://ejmas.com/jalt/jaltart_friday_0301.htm#EN2. Regarding the lack of candor in Japanese military history, see Jonathan Parshall and Anthony Tully, *Shattered Sword: The Untold Story of the Battle of Midway* (Dulles, VA: Potomac Books, 2005), 436–32.

28 *"make money to live luxuriously":* Christopher Thone, in Max Hastings, *Retribution: The Battle for Japan, 1944–45* (New York: Knopf, 2007), 35.

29 *Nichiren Buddhism:* M. G. Sheftall, e-mails to author, April 2008.

CHAPTER TWO: CHINA SKIES

Page

31 *"an efficient guerrilla air corps"*: Alan Armstrong, *Pre-emptive Strike: The Secret Plan That Would Have Prevented the Attack on Pearl Harbor* (Guildford, CT: Lyons Press, 2006), 16.

31 *"fire fighting facilities"*: Attaché report via Dunn, 2008.

32 *A second AVG*: Daniel Ford, *Flying Tigers: Claire Chennault and His American Volunteers, 1941–1942*, revised edition (New York: HarperCollins, 2007), 85–86.

33 *"Japanese aircraft production facilities"*: Chennault to Arnold, July 16, 1942, War Plans Files, AAF, 145.95, AFHRA, cited in Guanggiu Xu, *War Wings: The United States and Chinese Military Aviation, 1929–1949* (Westport, CT: Greenwood, 2001), 173.

33 *"accomplish the downfall"*: Barbara W. Tuchman, *Stilwell and the American Experience in China, 1911–1945* (New York: Macmillan, 1970), 337.

34 *So confident*: The same month as the B-29's first flight a second very heavy bomber left the ground as Consolidated produced the B-32 Dominator as a hedge against a Boeing failure. Powered by the same engines as the Superfortress, the Dominator suffered even greater problems with various systems. Resolving the problems took time, and delivery began over two years later with only 115 being built. Ray Wagner, *American Combat Planes* (New York: Doubleday, 1968), 137.

36 *The onboard extinguisher system*: Kenneth P. Werrell, *Blankets of Fire: U.S. Bombers over Japan During World War II* (Washington, DC: Smithsonian Institution Press, 1996), 81.

36 *Flying the second prototype*: After Allen's death, workers at Boeing's Wichita plant donated $600,000 in money and labor to purchase a B-29 in his name. The *Eddie Allen* logged two dozen combat missions before sustaining serious flak damage that forced an end to its combat career.

36 *The setback*: When it became apparent that Boeing could not build enough B-29s, other manufacturers were engaged. Eventually four factories turned out Superfortresses: Boeing plants at Renton, Washington, and Wichita, Kansas; Martin at Omaha, Nebraska; and Bell at Marietta, Georgia. The program accelerated through 1943 and 1944 with production peaking at 375 in July 1945. *Army Air Forces Statistical Digest*, December 1945.

37 *"splendid record"*: Curtis E. LeMay and MacKinlay Kantor, *Mission with LeMay: My Story* (New York: Doubleday, 1965), 322.

37 *"all those college athletes"*: Werrell, *Blankets of Fire*, 72.

38 *"It is my desire"*: Ibid., 80.

38 *Crew training suffered*: Wilbur H. Morrison, *Point of No Return* (New York: Playboy, 1980), 39.

39 *"a new Boeing bomber"*: Details from Osamu Tagaya, J-Aircraft.com, http://www.j-aircraft.org/smf/index.php?topic=4470.0.

40 *Estimates of full-scale production*: Osamu Tagaya, 2007, citing *Senshi Sosho*, Volume 19.

40 *"Now the enemy"*: Richard L. Dunn, J-Aircraft.com, October 21, 2007.

42 *The man who pulled it together*: http://www.af.mil/bios/bio.asp?bioID=7545.

42 *American resources were scarce*: Wesley F. Craven and James L. Cate, *The Army Air Forces in World War II*, Vol. 7: *Services Around the World* (Chicago: University of Chicago Press, 1950), xix.

42 *"Headquarters figured"*: First Lieutenant Bedford Hertel, 27th Troop Carrier Squadron, author interview, c. 1990.

42 *Construction of XX Bomber Command bases*: http://www.cosmos=club.org/web/journals/1996/adams.html.

43 *fewer than half*: Werrell, *Blankets of Fire*, 93.

44 *"We knew basic problems"*: 462nd Bomb Group Web site, http://www.geocities.com/jr462nd/Hellbird_Stories_p7.html.

44 *Accommodations were basic*: Morrison, *Point of No Return*, 59.

46 *"We lost"*: *Wait 'Til the 58th Gets Here* (Nashville: Turner, 1999), 16.

46 *"Broken Nose Charlie"*: Bedford M. Hertel to author, c. 1975.

46 *On June 5, Wolfe's command*: XX Bomber Command mission summary, 5 June 1944; Werrell, *Blankets of Fire*, 101.

47 *"The city appeared"*: Saburo Sakai with Fred Saito and Martin Caidin, *Samurai!* (Annapolis: Naval Institute Press, 1991), 317.

50 *"acceptable number"*: Werrell, *Blankets of Fire*, 102.

51 *"I was scared!"*: Koji Takaki and Henry Sakaida, *B-29 Hunters of the JAAF* (London: Osprey, 2001), 9.

52 *In all, fifty-seven American fliers*: XX Bomber Command mission summary, 15 June 1945.

52 *"the sight of"*: Jonathon Delacour, "Japanese Remorse?", *The Heart of Things*, http://weblog.delacour.net/archives/2002/08/japanese_remorse_hardly.php; Masuo Kato, *The Lost War* (New York: Alfred A. Knopf, 1946), 8.

52 *"By the time"*: Masatake Okumiya and Jiro Horikoshi with Martin Caidin, *Zero: The Story of Japan's Air War in the Pacific* (New York: Bantam, 1991), 193.

53 *"People sat around"*: LeMay and Kantor, *Mission with LeMay*, 322.

55 *Burning wreckage*: Takaki and Sakaida, *B-29 Hunters of the JAAF*, 13, 16.

56 *From the American perspective:* During the night thirteen more bombers departed for Yawata, having been delayed by a crash on the runway. Ten bombed the primary, escaping without harm. XX Bomber Command mission summary, 20 August 1944.

57 *Beyond that, LeMay was five years younger:* The Navy's youngest two-star (rear) admiral was Harold B. Miller, who became Admiral Chester Nimitz's public relations officer in 1945 at age forty-two. AAF chief Arnold had pinned on his second star at age fifty-two in 1938, but only because of his superior's death.

58 *"If I'm going to command":* Thomas M. Coffey, *Iron Eagle* (New York: Crown, 1986), 109.

58 *"utterly absurd":* LeMay and Kantor, *Mission with LeMay,* 322.

59 *Perhaps LeMay's greatest success:* Sortie and tonnage figures computed from XX Bomber Command statistics for June to August versus October to December 1944.

59 *the "aircraft plant":* Henry Sakaida e-mail to author, December 2007; René J. Francillon, *Japanese Aircraft of the Pacific War* (London: Putnam, 1979), various entries; U.S. Strategic Bombing Survey, Aircraft Division Report No. 34, Army Air Arsenal and Navy Air Depots, Corporation Report No. XIX, February 1947, via Jim Long on J-Aircraft.com. Total production from April 1941 through 1945 was 966 aircraft and 2,100 engines.

60 *"Damage to the plane":* Brigadier General Jack Ledford (Ret) et al. *40th Bomb Group Association Memories,* July 1997. (Some accounts state that Ledford flew *20th Century Unlimited* but apparently that name was applied to the opposite side of the fuselage. *Heavenly Body's* memorable nose art was the work of a former *Esquire* magazine artist.)

61 *"negligible":* XX Bomber Command mission summary, 11 November 1944.

62 *Meanwhile, the four:* Personal papers provided by Mrs. Jody Smith, December 2007.

62 *That night of the 21st:* Dr. Frank Olynyk, USAAF (China-Burma-India Theater), *Credits for Destruction of Enemy Aircraft in Air to Air Combat, World War 2* (Privately published, 1986).

63 *"Dear Curt":* Coffey, *Iron Eagle,* 123–24.

63 *"persistent reports":* 40th Bomb Group history, 1–31 December 1944, dated 23 January 1945, 2.

63 *On December 19:* XX Bomber Command mission summary, 19 December 1944.

65 *"The barn door":* Keith Todd, *40th Bombardment Group (VH) History* (Nashville: Turner, 1989), 30–31.

65 *The nine homeland strikes:* Actual numbers of XX Bomber Command's missions to Japan were 498 of 3,058 total sorties delivering 961 of 11,244 tons of ordnance.

65 *"I've never been able":* LeMay and Kantor, *Mission with LeMay,* 322.

CHAPTER THREE: FROM THE SOUTH

Page

67 *"The Great Marianas Turkey Shoot":* See the author's detailed treatment, *Clash of the Carriers* (New York: Caliber, 2005).

68 *"There was good reason":* Masatake Okumiya and Jiro Horikoshi with Martin Caidin, *Zero: The Story of Japan's Air War in the Pacific* (New York: Bantam, 1991), 272.

68 *The Navy Seabees were so popular:* The film was *The Fighting Seabees,* 1944, script by Borden Chase, directed by Edward Ludwig. "Seabee" derived from the acronym for "construction battalion." Contrary to the film and public impression, Seabees did not all come from prewar construction crews. However, the average age was thirty-seven, well past the median twenty-six of all military personnel. Some experienced old-timers, eager to make a contribution, leveraged their experience and know-how into service at age sixty or more. "Paving the Way to Victory," https://portal.navfac.navy.mil/pls/portal/url/ITEM/130B09D8E61 041B3E0440003BA8FC471.

70 *"A world of difference":* Okumiya and Horikoshi, *Zero,* 195–96.

70 *In December 1944:* "Engineer Aviation Units," http://www.usace.army .mil/publications/misc/un21/c-14.pdf, 336, 375.

71 *"It would rain":* Howard Chamberlain, 504th Bomb Group, http:// www.444thbg.org/unithistoryinfo.htm.

71 *On Saipan:* "Paving the Way to Victory," https://portal.navfac.navy.mil/ pls/portal/url/ITEM/130B09D8E61041B3E0440003BA8FC471.

73 *"some matronly ladies":* William R. Thorsen, oral history, "World War II Through the Eyes of Cape Fear," University of North Carolina, Wilmington.

74 *The enormity of the job:* Commander Edmund L. Castillo, *The Seabees of World War II* (New York: Random House, 1963), 118, 123, 128–29.

74 *every field was completed on schedule:* Ibid., 129.

75 *some Easterners insisted:* Ibid., 118.

75 *When the Tinian complex:* Dan McNichol, *Paving the Way: Asphalt in America* (Lanham, MD: National Asphalt Paving Association, 2005), 193–95.

75 *"The lieutenant was infuriated"*: Gordon Bennett Robertson, Jr., *Bringing the Thunder* (Mechanicsburg, PA: Stackpole, 2006), 132.

76 *the centralized nature*: René J. Francillon, *Japanese Aircraft of the Pacific War* (London: Putnam, 1979), 15.

76 *"The Americans chose"*: Okumiya and Horikoshi, *Zero*, 303–4.

76 *"One of the biggest"*: Assistant Chief of Air Staff–Intelligence, HQ AAF, *Mission Accomplished: Interrogations of Japanese Industrial, Military, and Civil Leaders*, Washington, DC, 1946, 23.

77 *"Many a factory"*: Okumiya and Horikoshi, *Zero*, 304–5.

78 *In September 1941*: O'Donnell's nine-plane flight was not the first Flying Fortress deployment to the Philippine Islands, as a smaller group had preceded him. When the Japanese attacked in December 1941 there were thirty-five bombers in the Philippines, most being destroyed on the ground.

79 *Nevertheless, navigators remained*: National Museum of the Air Force Web site, http://www.nationalmuseum.af.mil/factsheets/factsheet.asp?id=1619.

80 *"a large, gray pork chop"*: Robert Leckie, *Battle for Iwo Jima* (New York: Random House, 1967).

81 *"terrible coral"*: "Guam Airfields," http://www.geocities.com/alwood.geo/B29Guam/Lairfields.html.

82 *The declining standards*: Alvin Coox, *Japan: The Final Agony* (New York: Ballantine, 1970), 60.

84 *During an interception*: Henry Sakaida, *Imperial Japanese Navy Aces, 1937–45* (London: Osprey, 1998), 88–89.

84 *The November 24 mission*: XXI Bomber Command mission summary, 24 November 1944.

84 *targets of last resort*: Ibid.

86 *later study showed*: Kenneth P. Werrell, *Blankets of Fire: U.S. Bombers over Japan During World War II* (Washington, DC: Smithsonian Institution Press, 1996), 132.

86 *Brigadier General Hansell*: Koji Takaki and Henry Sakaida, *B-29 Hunters of the JAAF* (London: Osprey, 2001), 33.

87 *The Bonin Islands*: James Bradley, *Flyboys: A True Story of Courage* (New York: Little, Brown, 2003), 190.

87 *Meanwhile, on December 3*: XXI Bomber Command mission summary, 3 December 1944.

88s *Lieutenant Hugh Mcnamer's*: 500th Bomb Group history, http://www.xmission.com/~tmathews/b29/56years/56years-4412.html. The group's mechanics repaired the plane, which eventually flew twenty-eight more missions.

88 *"I'm in sharp disagreement"*: Wilbur H. Morrison, *Point of No Return* (New York: Playboy, 1979), 167.

90 *"In my opinion"*: Wesley F. Craven and James L. Cate, *The Army Air Forces in World War II*, Vol. 5: *The Pacific: Matterhorn to Nagasaki* (Chicago: University of Chicago Press, 1958), 601.

91 *One flier survived:* http://216.219.175.113/73bw/bartlett/bartlett1.html.

92 *"About 50 lights"*: http://www.xmission.com/~tmathews/b29/56years/56years-4501a.html.

92 *Brigadier General J. H. Davies:* Sixty-three years later there was still uncertainty about Davies's given name. Social Security records and his Air Force biography state "James" but nearly all wartime documents— including some released on his authority—are "John." His nicknames were "Skippy" and "Big Jim." The urn containing his ashes in Oakland, California, is unmarked so the contradiction remains irreconcilable.

92 *"Boy that's"*: Lawrence S. Smith, *9th Bombardment Group (VH) History* (Princeton: 9th Bomb Group Association, 1995), 191.

92 *"Sergeant Owens was"*: http://www.philcrowther.com/6thBG/6bgcrewg00.html.

93 *"didn't need"*: Curtis E. LeMay and MacKinlay Kantor, *Mission with LeMay: My Story* (New York: Doubleday, 1965), 339.

93 *"This was a nail biter"*: http://www.xmission.com/~tmathews/b29/56years/56years-4501b.html.

95 *"If I ever get out"*: "Flak Alley," http://mypages.cityhighflash.com/flakalley.html. And "Now It Can Be Told," http://www.geocities.com/twincousin2334/Mission_Log.html.

95 *Irish Lassie:* Koji Takaki and Henry Sakaida, *B-29 Hunters of the JAAF* (London: Osprey, 2001), 76–77.

96 *Fifty-five years later:* "Enemies Then, Friends Now," http://home.att.net/~sallyann5/b29/enemy-friend1.html.

97 *By month's end:* Hansell's official Air Force biography at http://www.af.mil/bios/bio.asp?bioID=5693.

97 *"If you don't succeed"*: LeMay and Kantor, *Mission with LeMay*, 367.

98 *When LeMay obtained:* Ibid., 340.

98 *"a real training job"*: Ibid., 342.

99 *"a capable scientific type"*: Ibid., 345.

99 *From Guam to Tokyo:* Analysis of 8th Air Force missions to Berlin, http://www.303rdbg.com/missions.html.

100 *Nevertheless, with the new 313th Wing's:* XXI Bomber Command mission summary, 10 February 1945.

101 *"with diabolical frequency"*: LeMay and Kantor, *Mission with LeMay*, 344.

102 *McElroy was unique:* Morrison, *Point of No Return,* 187; Virgil Morgan, 6th Bomb Group Association, e-mail to author, February 2008.

102 *In all, 202 bombers:* Craven and Cate, *The Army Air Forces in World War II,* Vol. 5: *The Pacific,* 573; Coox, *Japan,* 23.

103 *"meager":* Ray Brashear diary, February 25, 1945; Ed McElroy to Virgil Morgan e-mail, February 2008.

103 *"a test incendiary mission":* Werrell, *Blankets of Fire,* 151.

103 *"a necessary preparation":* Ibid.

104 *"You know General Arnold":* LeMay and Kantor, *Mission with LeMay,* 347.

104 *"being a little unorthodox":* Ibid., 348.

CHAPTER FOUR: FROM THE SEA

Page

107 *The fleet's striking arm:* Samuel Eliot Morison, *History of U.S. Naval Operations in World War II,* Vol. 14: *Victory in the Pacific* (Boston: Little, Brown, 1960), 25.

109 *Rear Admiral William A. Moffett:* William F. Trimble, *Admiral William A. Moffett: Architect of Naval Aviation* (Washington, DC: Smithsonian Institution Press, 1993).

109 *Between 1914 and 1923:* Naval Historical Center, http://www.history.navy.mil/danfs/r4/reeves-ii.htm.

110 *Essex class carrier:* Seventeen Essexes were commissioned between December 1942 and June 1945, and despite service in three wars, none was ever sunk. Eleven of the total twenty-four served into the 1970s, including USS *Lexington* (CV-16), which remained the Navy's training carrier until 1991.

111 *"He wasn't real bright":* Rear Admiral James D. Ramage, USN (Ret), to author, 1990.

112 *Task Force 58: Location of U.S. Naval Aircraft, 20 February 1945,* distributed by U.S. Navy, copy in author's collection.

112 *"We were invited":* Barrett Tillman and Jan Jacobs, "The Wolf Gang: A History of Carrier Air Group 84," *The Hook,* August 1990, 81.

113 *"During the period 9 March 1945":* Commander, Air Group 6, report in *War History of USS Hancock,* 12 October 1945, http://www.usshancockassociation.org/wwii%20history-3.html.

113 *"The relationship":* E-mail to author from Bob Kettenheim, USS *Shangri-La* Association, 2008.

114 *"The maps":* Commander Willis E. Hardy, USN (Ret), e-mail to author, January 2008.

114 *"but plans were aborted"*: USS *Yorktown* pilot Robert S. Rice correspondence, December 6, 1976.

115 *"dark and icky"*: Jim Pearce, *A 20th Century Guy* (Goodyear, AZ: Steiner Associates, 2007), 152.

115 *"The attack of the 16th"*: Masatake Okumiya and Jiro Horikoshi with Martin Caidin, *Zero: The Story of Japan's Air War in the Pacific* (New York: Bantam, 1991), 330.

116 *"pedestrian"*: Rear Admiral Roger Hedrick (Ret), commanding officer of VF-84, to author, 1990.

117 *"a genius in the air"*: Henry Sakaida, *Winged Samurai: Saburo Sakai and the Zero Fighter Pilots* (Mesa, AZ: Champlin Museum Press, 1985), 122.

117 *"a friendly and cheerful ace"*: Ikuhiko Hata and Yasuho Izawa, *Japanese Naval Aces and Fighter Units in World War II* (Annapolis: Naval Institute Press, 1989), 250.

117 *"the toughest fighter pilot"*: Sakaida, *Winged Samurai*, 122.

117 *His wife, Kiyoko:* Ibid., 123.

118 *"The apron was packed"*: Robert S. Rice correspondence to author, December 6, 1976.

118 *"The old lesson"*: Clark G. Reynolds, *The Fast Carriers: The Forging of an Air Navy* (New York: McGraw-Hill, 1968), 333.

118 *"We, being high cover"*: Commander Willis E. Hardy, USN (Ret), e-mail to author, January 2008.

119 *But it appears:* Henry Sakaida e-mail to author, April 2008.

120 *"We appeared to be floating"*: Donald A. Pattie, *To Cock a Cannon: A Pilot's View of World War II* (Zephyrhills, FL: Pattie Properties, 1983), 111.

120 *"Looming out of the carpet"*: Ibid.

121 *"It was not"*: Ibid., 112.

121 *"We bore down"*: Ibid., 113.

122 *"On straight-deck carriers"*: Captain Wally Schirra (Ret) to author, 1995. Schirra flew off carriers from 1947 to 1958 before becoming an astronaut.

123 *In all, during two days:* Morison, *History of U.S. Naval Operations in World War II*, Vol. 14: *Victory in the Pacific*, 25. February aircraft acceptances: Barrett Tillman, *Corsair: The F4U in WW II and Korea* (Annapolis: Naval Institute Press, 1979), 203.

123 *Actual Japanese aerial losses:* Okumiya and Horikoshi, *Zero*, 330. Respective air combat claims: Hata and Izawa, *Japanese Naval Aces*, 432.

125 *some 800 men were killed: Franklin's* death toll usually is given as 724, apparently due to incomplete accounting by Captain Leslie Gehres. *Franklin* historian Joseph Springer cites 798 from 3,348 aboard.

127 *"the cream"*: VMF-123 action report, 19 March 1945.

129 *"I was armed"*: Tillman and Jacobs, "The Wolf Gang," 81.

131 *Two days' claims*: Hata and Izawa, *Japanese Naval Aces*, 432. Polmar, 474, cites 482 air and ground claims combined.

133 *"You began to realize"*: Captain Armistead B. Smith III to author, c. 1979.

CHAPTER FIVE: FIRESTORM

Page

134 *A small AAF support unit*: Kenneth P. Werrell, *Blankets of Fire: U.S. Bombers over Japan During World War II* (Washington, DC: Smithsonian Institution Press, 1996), 149.

135 *"Whenever I land"*: Samuel Eliot Morison, *History of U.S. Naval Operations in World War II*, Vol. 14: *Victory in the Pacific* (Boston: Little, Brown, 1960), 75.

135 *"We must seek"*: Wilbur H. Morrison, *Point of No Return: An Epic Saga of Disaster and Triumph* (New York: Playboy, 1979), 190.

136 *"For almost a week"*: Ralph H. Nutter, *With the Possum and the Eagle: The Memoir of a Navigator's War* (Denton: University of North Texas Press, 2005), 243.

137 *"a helluva lot worse"*: Morrison, *Point of No Return*, 191.

138 *Probably the most innovative concept*: C. V. Glines, "The Bat Bombers," *Air Force*, October 1990.

138 *In order to determine*: Stephen Budiansky, *Air Power* (New York: Viking, 2004), 336–37.

139 *Napalm was developed*: "The Man Who Invented Napalm," *Time*, January 5, 1968, http://web.archive.org/web/20050312093403/http://modern times.vcdh.virginia.edu/PVCC/mbase/docs/napalm.html.

139 *The third incendiary weapon*: John W. Mountcastle, *Flame On! U.S. Incendiary Weapons, 1918–1945* (Shippensburg, PA: White Mane, 1999), 109–111.

140 *"It made a lot of sense"*: Thomas R. Searle, "The Fire Bombing of Tokyo in March 1945," *Journal of Military History*, January 2002, 115–16.

140 *"it was necessary"*: Ronald Schaffer, *Wings of Judgment: American Bombing in World War II* (New York: Oxford University Press, 1985), 109.

140 *"The panic side"*: Ibid., 118.

141 *The first firestorm*: Francis K. Mason, *Battle over Britain* (New York: Doubleday, 1969), 473–74.

142 *That same year*: Taschenbuch f. Deutsche Polizei/Feuerwehr u. Feuerschutz-polizei, Berlin, 1941, Axis History Forum, http://forum.axishistory.com/

NOTES

viewtopic.php?f=38&t=130909&sid=706355c2f36b40c988557b27c42
864c6&p=1190967#p1190967.

143 *As was often the case:* F. J. Bradley, *No Strategic Targets Left* (Nashville:
Turner, 1999), 34.

143 *"by ritual":* John Costello, *The Pacific War* (New York: Rawson, Wade,
1981), 549.

143 *"Men were recruited":* Horatio Bond, ed., *Fire and the Air War* (Boston:
National Fire Protection Association, 1946), 152.

144 *By contrast:* "New York City 1945 Annual Report: Fire Extinguishing
Force," courtesy Ed Fahey, November 2007.

144 *"large equipment":* Bond, *Fire and the Air War*, 155.

145 *"The common portable":* Ibid., 156.

145 *As an island nation:* Ibid., 155; "Proud History: FDNY Fireboat Fleet,"
http://www.fireboat.org/history/fleetlist.asp.

146 *"totally inadequate":* Attaché Report No. 161-40, September 30, 1940,
http://209.85.173.104/search?q=cache:E_riunEJFGwJ:www.alanarm-
stronglaw.com/187.pdf+%22important+bombing+objectives%22&hl=
en&ct=clnk&cd=3&gl=us.

146 *"The reason":* Assistant Chief of Air Staff–Intelligence, HQ AAF, *Mission Accomplished: Interrogations of Japanese Industrial, Military, and Civil
Leaders*, Washington, DC, 1946, 29.

146 *"the library Obunko":* Alvin Coox, *Japan: The Final Agony* (New York:
Ballantine, 1970), 24.

147 *"once the gayest":* John Toland, *The Rising Sun: The Decline and Fall of the
Japanese Empire, 1936–1945* (New York: Random House, 1970), 834.

148 *"Night incendiary":* "56 Years Ago Today," http://www.xmission.com/
~tmathews/b29/56years/56years-4503a.html.

148 *"fiery pancakes":* "Incendiary Jelly," *Time*, April 2, 1945.

148 *"Bright flashes":* Robert Guillain, in Costello, *The Pacific War*, 550.

150 *Nearly 100 fire trucks:* Richard Frank, *Downfall: The End of the Imperial
Japanese Empire* (New York: Random House, 1999), 8.

150 *"The key to survival":* Ibid., 9.

150 *"The whole spectacle":* Martin Caidin, *A Torch to the Enemy* (New York:
Ballantine, 1961), 141.

151 *"like match sticks":* Toland, *The Rising Sun*, 836.

151 *"the hellfire began":* Frank, *Downfall*, 9.

152 *"like a cork":* Gordon Bennett Robertson, Jr., *Bringing the Thunder: The Missions of a World War II B-29 Pilot* (Mechanicsburg, PA: Stackpole, 2006), 10.

153 *"Stacked up corpses":* http://www.historylearningsite.co.uk/fire_raids_
on_japan.htm.

153 *"Red fire clouds"*: Mission Accomplished, 24.

153 *fewer than 1,300 deaths*: Frank, Downfall, 17. The actual death toll remains unknown. Authorities reckoned 83,793 dead but the uncounted missing could have raised the figure to 100,000.

154 *"The effect of incendiary bombing"*: Mission Accomplished, 73.

154 *"It was the great incendiary attacks"*: Ibid., 49.

155 *"Looked as though"*: http://www.xmission.com/~tmathews/b29/56years/56years-4503a.html.

156 *"This is a significant"*: Lawrence S. Smith, *9th Bombardment Group (VH) History* (Princeton: 9th Bomb Group Association, 1995), 133.

157 *"It became apparent"*: Mission Accomplished, 24.

157 *"After the first B-29 raid"*: John W. Mountcastle, *Flame On! U.S. Incendiary Weapons, 1918–1945* (Shippensburg, PA: White Mane, 1999), 112.

157 *In one ward alone*: Coox, Japan, 24, 28.

158 *"I felt nauseated"*: Fusako Sasaki in http://www.historylearningsite.co.uk/fire_raids_on_japan.htm.

159 *"pinpricks"*: F. J. Bradley, *No Strategic Targets Left* (Nashville: Turner, 1999), 60.

159 *"a swarm of interceptors"*: 39th Bomb Group (VH) history, http://39th.org/39TH/aerial/61st/crew34.html.

160 *"Shortly afterwards"*: 873rd Bomb Squadron history, http://www.xmission.com/~tmathews/b29/56years/56years-4504b.html.

160 *Whether the serious U.S. naval losses*: Morison, *History of U.S. Naval Operations in World War II*, Vol. 14: *Victory in the Pacific*, 233.

160 *twenty American ships*: Ship losses March 27 to May 11 compiled from ibid., 390–92. The figures for the periods before and after the B-29 strikes totaled thirty-five ships sunk or permanently disabled in eighty-seven days, or 0.4 ship per day.

161 *"These airfields"*: Bradley, No Strategic Targets Left, 60.

162 *"How they got the ships"*: Morrison, Point of No Return, 197.

164 *One crew was lost to ramming*: Koji Takaki and Henry Sakaida, *B-29 Hunters of the JAAF* (London: Osprey, 2001), 97.

165 *"One morning in mid-April"*: http://www.40thbombgroup.org/.

165 *His crew was a well-drilled team*: Author correspondence with Henry E. Erwin, Sr., 2000.

167 *He believed to the end*: Author interview with Senator Henry E. Erwin, Jr., December 2004.

167 *"We received the news"*: Robertson, Bringing the Thunder, 171.

168 *"undiscriminating bombing"*: "56 Years Ago Today," http://www.xmission.com/~tmathews/b29/56years/56years-4505a.html.

168 *"not at present"*: Toland, *The Rising Sun*, 919.

168 *"swell fires"*: Navigator's notes, 499th Bomb Group, 23–24 May 1945.

169 *"When crews returned"*: Wilbur H. Morrison, *Point of No Return: An Epic Saga of Disaster and Triumph* (New York: Playboy Press, 1979), 209.

169 *"Tokyo just isn't"*: "56 Years Ago Today," http://www.xmission.com/~tmathews/b29/56years/56years-4505b.html.

169 *"As I ran"*: http://www.historylearningsite.co.uk/fire_raids_on_japan.htm.

169 *"a netherworld scene"*: http://www.xmission.com/~tmathews/b29/56years/56years-4505b.html.

170 *"If you are shot down"*: Costello, *The Pacific War*, 548.

171 *"May 25 was"*: Halloran account, http://www.xmission.com/~tmathews/b29/56years/56years-4505b.html.

171 *subjected to vivisection*: Thomas Easton, "Japan Admits Dissecting WW II POWs," *Baltimore Sun*, May 28, 1995, http://home.comcast.net/~winjerd/Page05.htm.

172 *The most egregious sanctioned murders*: Mark Landas, *The Fallen: A True Story of American POWs and Japanese Wartime Atrocities* (Hoboken, NJ: John Wiley & Sons, 2004), 116, 167, 251. Though few Japanese were hanged for crimes committed in Japan, 920 war criminals were executed, mostly for atrocities in other areas. Some notorious offenses went unindicted because Western law had no proscriptions for cannibalism.

172 *That left 283 Americans*: Toru Fukubayashi in Takaki and Sakaida, *B-29 Hunters of the JAAF*, 114.

172 *"The time to get captured"*: Bataan Death March symposium, Arizona Military Museum, Phoenix, AZ, 1993.

173 *"considered to be futile"*: Coox, *Japan*, 36.

CHAPTER SIX: PACIFIC PONIES

Page

175 *"Mickey" Moore was typical*: Major General Ernest M. Moore (Ret) correspondence with author, 1975.

175 *"Iwo was perhaps"*: Crim correspondence with author, 1976.

176 *"When the war ended" and following*: Ibid.

177 *Taking one navy fighter squadron as an example*: Data from *Hikotai* 407, Naval Air Group 221, Luzon, November 1944, compiled from information courtesy of Richard L. Dunn.

178 *"We spotted the enemy planes"*: Henry Sakaida, *Imperial Japanese Navy Aces, 1937–45* (London: Osprey, 1998), 79.

179 *In some twenty encounters:* 343rd Air Group data compiled from Henry Sakaida and Koji Takaki, *Genda's Blade: Japan's Squadron of Aces* (UK: Surrey, 2003).

180 *"I don't believe" and following:* Major General Ernest M. Moore (Ret) correspondence with author, 1976.

181 *"I had about 500 hours":* Barrett Tillman, "The Mustangs of Iwo Jima," *Airpower Magazine*, January 1977.

181 *"We had practically":* Ibid.

181 *"the '51 with the fuselage tank full":* Ibid.

182 *"After what seemed":* Ibid.

182 *"It takes a lot":* Ibid.

183 *"You lose your radio":* Ibid.

184 *"Finding enemy aircraft":* Ibid.

185 *an American duplicating the feat:* Sakaida, *Imperial Navy Aces*, 88.

186 *After the war, U.S. investigators determined:* A war crimes tribunal imposed a forty-year sentence upon the officer responsible for releasing Scanlan to the mob. Other Japanese received from one to five years for their roles in the murder. How many of the sentences were served to completion is unknown.

187 *"I think the combat break":* Harve Phipps correspondence with author, 1976.

187 *"We dropped":* Crim correspondence, 1976.

188 *"You could really put":* Tillman, "The Mustangs of Iwo Jima."

190 *"Sure enough":* Ibid.

190 *"heavy, meager to moderate, inaccurate to accurate":* XXI Bomber Command mission summary, 26 June 1945.

191 *"Bob, get me":* http://39th.org/39th/aerial/60th/crew13a.html.

191 *"We came in sight":* Lieutenant Ernest Bonjour, USNR, letter, June 1945, via *City of Galveston* pilot Donald A. Gerth.

192 *"You don't come out":* http://39th.org/39th/bio/mundy2.htm.

193 *"Let's get the hell":* Henry Sakaida, *Pacific Air Combat* (St. Paul: Phalanx, 1993), 88.

193 *"I'm very sorry":* Ibid., 89.

CHAPTER SEVEN: THE HARBOR WAR

Page

195 *"a motivator":* Thomas M. Coffey, *Iron Eagle: The Turbulent Life of General Curtis LeMay* (New York: Crown, 1986), 153.

196 *Three nights later:* Frederick M. Sallagar, *Lessons from an Aerial Mining*

Campaign (Operation "Starvation"). RAND Corporation, April 1974, 47.

196 "an outstanding leader": http://home.att.net/~sallyann6/b29/56years-4507a.html.

196 "On 27 May": Assistant Chief of Air Staff–Intelligence, HQ AAF, Mission Accomplished: Interrogations of Japanese Industrial, Military, and Civil Leaders, Washington, DC, 1946, 30.

197 "became expert": Sallagar, Lessons from an Aerial Mining Campaign, 51.

198 "Due to the fact": Mission Accomplished, 29–30.

199 "phenomenal": Coffey, Iron Eagle, 169.

199 "About 1 April": Mission Accomplished, 30–31.

199 "a real salty old dog": Diary of Lieutenant Richard W. De Mott, VBF-85, June 9, 1945.

200 "his striking resemblance": Monsarrat, 20.

200 "I don't think": Rear Admiral William N. Leonard (Ret) to author, 1981.

200 "Working with the B-29s": Clark G. Reynolds, The Fast Carriers: The Forging of an Air Navy (New York: McGraw-Hill, 1968), 354.

202 "setting off an explosion": Fighting Squadron 6 History, 1945.

203 "second generation": "The Chippewa Chief," http://www.pequotmuseum .org/Home/CrossPaths/CrossPathsFall2003/BookReview.htm.

203 "He never got wise": "Shangri-La Horizon," USS Shangri-La (CV-38) newspaper, undated clipping, 1945.

204 "Several Japs came out": Ibid.

205 "Scapa Flow with bloody palm trees": N. M. Heckman, "England's Shadow Fleet," Sea Classics, May 2004.

205 "of the utmost importance": Admiral Sir Bruce Fraser in Nicholas E. Sarantakes, "The Short but Brilliant Life of the British Pacific Fleet," Joint Forces Quarterly, 1st quarter, 2006, 86.

205 "a very nasty": Quoted by Peter C. Smith, e-mail to author, June 2008.

206 "fully aware": Sarantakes, "The Short but Brilliant Life of the British Pacific Fleet," 88–89.

206 "were able to match us": Reynolds, The Fast Carriers, 371.

207 Additionally, the RN: Max Hastings, Retribution: The Battle for Japan, 1944–45 (New York: Alfred A. Knopf, 2008), 401.

207 In one series of strikes: Hastings, 400, 401.

207 "The kid": Rear Admiral William N. Leonard (Ret) to author, 1981.

208 "Some Neanderthals": Rear Admiral William N. Leonard (Ret) to author, 1992.

208 "a waste of time": Reynolds, The Fast Carriers, 372.

210 "I passed": "Navy Cross for an Unlikely Hero," Decatur Journal (Ala-

bama), November 24, 2005, http://legacy.decaturdaily.com/decatur-daily/news/051124/hero.shtml.

211 Essex *aviators claimed six hits:* Samuel Eliot Morison, *History of U.S. Naval Operations in World War II,* Vol. 14: *Victory in the Pacific* (Boston: Little, Brown, 1960), 316, unaccountably attributes the damage to *Yorktown* fighters, based on a report by an obscure junior officer. Morison states that all other TF 38 squadrons over Yokosuka were engaged in suppressing flak for the main effort by VF-88 Hellcats.

212 *"the toughest dogfighter":* Henry Sakaida, *Winged Samurai: Saburo Sakai and the Zero Fighter Pilots* (Mesa, AZ: Champlin Museum Press, 1985), 123–24.

213 *"almost exactly on the centerline":* http://www.combinedfleet.com/amagi .htm.

217 *"completely flooded":* U.S. Strategic Bombing Survey, *The Campaigns of the Pacific War* (Washington, D.C.: Military Analysis Division, 1946), 340.

217 *"Don't you suppose":* Rear Admiral John S. Christiansen (Ret), Tailhook reunion, Reno, NV, 2006.

217 *"If the other reasons":* William F. Halsey and J. Bryan III, *Admiral Halsey's Story* (New York: McGraw-Hill, 1947), 264–66.

219 *"Halsey is going wild":* Diary of Lieutenant Richard W. DeMott, VBF-85, July 14, 1945.

219 *"If we ever find":* Jack DeTour, e-mail to author, March 2008.

220 *"he wanted to get":* Henry Wolff, Jr., "Col. Hawes Was a Hero in Every Sense," *Victoria Advocate* (Texas), November 10, 1996.

220 *"The weather was lousy":* Colonel Jack DeTour, USAF (Ret), the Veterans History Project, http://lcweb2.loc.gov/diglib/vhp/bib/10207.

220 *"It must have caught":* Lieutenant Colonel Charles M. Crawford, USAF (Ret), e-mail to author, March 2008.

220 *Ed Hawes:* Navigator John Long also left a wife and two children. In 1946 American investigators traced the remains of Hawes's crew. Five bodies had washed ashore and were buried by the Japanese, later being returned to the States. Hawes's body was never recovered. Details courtesy of Long's nephew, Andrew H. Farmer, *Finding the Way: The Story of a Combat Navigator in World War II* (Lynchburg, VA: Warwick House, 2006).

221 *Gray was likely the last Canadian:* Stuart E. Soward, "A Brilliant Flying Spirit," CFB Esquimalt Naval and Military Museum, http://www.nava landmilitarymuseum.org/resource_pages/heroes/gray.html. Lieutenant Commander Eugene Esmonde posthumously received the VC for a torpedo attack against German cruisers in the English Channel in 1942.

CHAPTER EIGHT: "A MOST CRUEL BOMB"

Page

224 *"recent work by"*: http://hypertextbook.com/eworld/einstein.shtml.

226 *"death or worse"*: Author's father, J. H. Tillman, a wartime cadet at Naval Air Station Pasco.

227 *"was thick with experts"*: Jennet Conant, *109 East Palace* (New York: Simon & Schuster, 2005), 231.

228 *"The entire population"*: Wesley F. Craven and James L. Cate, *The Army Air Forces in World War II*, Vol. 5: *The Pacific: Matterhorn to Nagasaki* (Chicago: University of Chicago Press, 1958), 696–97.

228 *"a matter of generations"*: Alvin Coox, *Japan: The Final Agony* (New York: Ballantine, 1970), 10–11, 17.

229 *The Manhattan Project*: Program costs in 1945 dollars: B-29: $2.53 billion; Manhattan: $1.88 billion. Stephen I. Schwarz, *Atomic Audit*, Brookings Institution, 1998. Brookings Institution data cited at http://virtualology. com/MANHATTANPROJECT.COM/costs.manhattanproject.net.

229 *"His manner was reserved"*: Charles W. Sweeney with James A. Antonucci and Marion K. Antonucci, *War's End: An Eyewitness Account of America's Last Atomic Mission* (New York: Avon, 1997), 40.

230 *Into the air*: Gordon Thomas and Max Morgan Witts, *Enola Gay* (New York: Pocket, 1977), 195.

231 *"The 509 Composite Group"*: Truman to Stimson to Marshall, in Craven and Cate, *The Army Air Forces in World War II*, Vol. 5: *The Pacific*, 713–14.

231 *"of unimaginable destructive force"*: Sweeney, *War's End*, 153.

232 *"Colonel, are we"*: Thomas and Morgan Witts, *Enola Gay*, 197; "En Route on Enola Gay," http://www.2020hindsight.org/2005/08/05/1945-en-route-on-enola-gay/.

233 *"My god"*: Thomas and Morgan Witts, *Enola Gay*, 317.

233 *The actual toll*: From Hiroshima's estimated military and civilian population of 255,000 to 320,000, some 66,000 to 80,000 were killed and 69,000 to 80,000 wounded as variously determined by Manhattan Engineering District (MED), 1946; *U.S. Strategic Bombing Survey, Hiroshima and Nagasaki* (Washington, DC: Military Analysis Division, 1946), 16. And Vincent C. Jones, *Manhattan: The Army and the Atomic Bomb* (Washington, DC: Army Center of Military History, 1985), 547.

233 *"Clear cut"*: 509th Composite Group. http://www.enolagay509th.com/ groves.htm, accessed September 3, 2009.

234 *"This is the greatest thing"*: USS *Augusta* Web site, http://www.internet-esq.com/ussaugusta/truman/index.htm.

234 *General Groves did not*: Conant, *109 East Palace*, 234.

234 *"a violent, large"*: "Magic" intelligence intercept, August 7, 1945, http://www.gwu.edu/~nsarchiv/NSAEBB/NSAEBB162/61.pdf.

235 *"The hell with it"*: Sweeney, *War's End*, 211.

235 *"I've got it!"*: Ibid., 217.

236 *In bombing terms*: Apparently confusion as to Fat Man's miss distance (stated to be as much as two miles) was due to ground zero in relation to the briefed aim point versus the actual aim point. The field order specified the Mitsubishi works on the east bank of the Urakami River. But the 509th's planning summary cited a point east of the harbor in an area more likely affected by the blast.

236 *"a superbrilliant white"*: Sweeney, *War's End*, 219.

237 *"The dropping of pamphlets"*: Assistant Chief of Air Staff–Intelligence, HQ AAF, *Mission Accomplished: Interrogations of Japanese Industrial, Military, and Civil Leaders*, Washington, DC, 1946, 27. Also see Harry S. Truman Library, http://www.pbs.org/wgbh/amex/truman/psources/ps_leaflets.html.

237 *Even before Okinawa was secured*: Craven and Cate, *The Army Air Forces in World War II*, Vol. 5: *The Pacific*, 691.

238 *"appearing like magic"*: Lieutenant General George Kenney, in Ibid., 692.

239 *"quickly turned"*: Craven and Cate, *The Army Air Forces in World War II*, Vol. 5: *The Pacific*, 696.

239 *"The enemy could decide"*: Ibid., 700.

240 *"one of the most"*: Maj. Gen. Frank Armstrong, unpublished ms., *Wake the Sleeping Giant*. East Carolina Manuscript Collection, J. Y. Joyner Library, Greenville, NC.

240 *"This performance"*: Ibid.

240 *"This target destroyed"*: Ibid.

241 *By the time replacement bombers*: Osamu Tagaya, *Mitsubishi Type 1 Rikko "Betty" Units of WW 2* (London: Osprey, 2001), 97; Gordon Rottman, Akira Takizawa, et al., *Japanese Paratroop Forces of World War 2* (London: Osprey, 2005).

241 *"rain of ruin"*: Harry S. Truman Library and Museum, http://www.trumanlibrary.org/publicpapers/index.php?pid=100&st=atomic&st1=bomb.

242 *"Rumors and reports"*: Dick DeMott diary, 14 August 1945.

242 *"As we returned"*: Armstrong manuscript.

243 *"All Strike Able"*: Richard L. Newhafer, "I'll Remember," *Naval Aviation News*, December 1976.

243 *"On our way"*: DeMott diary, August 15, 1945.

244 *"all the hope"*: Newhafer, "I'll Remember."

245 *The Seafires had scored:* David Brown, *The Seafire* (U.K.: Ian Allan, 1972), 127–28, http://www.j aircraft.org/smf/index.php?topic=4522 .msg32615#msg32615.

246 *"it being far":* John Toland, *The Rising Sun: The Decline and Fall of the Japanese Empire, 1936–1945* (New York: Random House, 1970), 1038.

246 *"The Japs will never":* Barrett Tillman, *Alpha-Bravo-Delta Guide to the U.S. Air Force* (New York: Penguin, 2003), 135.

247 *"display of air power":* Craven and Cate, *The Army Air Forces in World War II*, Vol. 5: *The Pacific*, 733–34.

248 *"While Japan did agree":* Henry Sakaida, *Imperial Japanese Navy Aces* (London: Osprey, 1998), 80.

248 *"We were greeted":* Report by Lieutenant Colonel Clay Tice to 5th Air Force Headquarters, August 26, 1945; Tice interview with author c. 1985.

249 *"I started off":* http://www.aerofiles.com/tice.html.

250 *"a full throttle":* Vice Admiral Malcolm W. Cagle, USN (Ret), correspondence, 1977.

250 *In three weeks following August 27:* Craven and Cate, *The Army Air Forces in World War II*, Vol. 5: *The Pacific*, 734–35.

251 *"Now with the advent of peace":* Jefferson J. DeBlanc, *The Guadalcanal Air War* (Gretna, LA: Pelican, 2008), 168. After the war DeBlanc received the Medal of Honor for a mission in 1943. A Ph.D. educator, he died in 2007, age eighty-six.

CHAPTER NINE: LEGACY

Page

252 *The bombing of Japan:* For conflicting perspectives on bombing Japan: see Merle Miller, *Plain Speaking: An Oral Biography of Harry S. Truman* (New York: Berkley, 1974); and Fred Halstead, "Hiroshima 1945: Behind the Atom Bomb Atrocity," *The Militant*, August 14, 1995.

253 *"There was no efficient pooling":* U.S. Strategic Bombing Survey (Pacific), *Japanese Airpower: Weapons and Tactics* (Washington, DC: Military Analysis Division, July 1946), 26.

253 *In June 1944:* For joint air defense areas: U.S. Strategic Bombing Survey (Pacific): *Japanese Airpower: Weapons and Tactics* (Washington, DC: Military Analysis Division, January 1947), map, 58.

254 *A major part of the problem:* U.S. Strategic Bombing Survey (Pacific): *Japanese Airpower; Weapons and Tactics* (Washington, DC: Military Analysis Division, July 1946).

254 *"very poor"*: U.S. Strategic Bombing Survey (Pacific): Japanese Airpower, ibid., 26.

255 *"In order to overcome"*: Air Combat Regulations, Combined Fleet Ultrasecret Operation Order 86, mid-1944, via David C. Dickson, December 2007, http://indoctrine.googlepages.com/operationsordersandorders, 1941–45.

255 *"Why do we need radar?"*: Max Hastings, Bomber Command: The Myths and Reality of the Strategic Bombing Offensive, 1939–45 (New York: Dial, 1979), 47.

255 *From 1940 onward:* U.S. Strategic Bombing Survey, Japanese Air Weapons and Tactics, 71.

256 *"The Japanese fighter defense"*: Japanese Airpower, 51.

256 *"Those responsible for control"*: Assistant Chief of Air Staff–Intelligence, HQ AAF, Mission Accomplished: Interrogations of Japanese Industrial, Military, and Civil Leaders, Washington, DC, 1946, 51.

256 *Germany's toll:* Estimates for German bombing victims run from 305,000 to nearly 600,000. See John Keegan, The Second World War (New York: Penguin, 1989); and Stephen Budiansky, Air Power (New York: Viking, 2004), 330.

257 *"Day by day"*: Mamoru Shigemitsu, Japan and Her Destiny: My Struggle for Peace (London: Hutchinson, 1958).

257 *"the enemy's offensive operations"*: Onishi statement courtesy of Dr. M. G. Sheftall, 2008.

257 *"we must fight"*: Alvin Coox, Japan: The Final Agony (New York: Ballantine, 1970), 99.

258 *"The gawkers"*: E-mail to author from Dr. M. G. Sheftall, March 2008.

261 *After 1945:* For evaluations of the Anglo-American air campaign, see Alan J. Levine, The Strategic Bombing of Germany, 1940–1945 (Westport: Greenwood, 1992), 216. Also see Alfred C. Mierzejewski, The Collapse of the German War Economy, 1944–45 (Chapel Hill: University of North Carolina Press, 1988), 121.

261 *"The myth"*: Max Hastings, Retribution: The Battle for Japan, 1944–45 (New York: Alfred A. Knopf, 2008), xix. Another important factor, noted by historians such as John Dower and Richard Frank, is Hirohito's concern over domestic turmoil spurred by food shortages. That view was shared by Marquis Kido, the emperor's closest adviser, who recognized that the effects of the Allied aerial and submarine blockade would peak in the fall.

261 *"In dropping 161,000 tons"*: The Allies dropped some 2.7 million tons in Europe, with nearly half falling on Germany: http://www.anesi.com/ussbs01.htm#josp, U.S. Strategic Bombing Survey, Summary Report

(Pacific War) (Washington, DC: Military Analysis Division, July 1946), 16.

262 *targeting urban-industrial areas:* Wesley F. Craven and James L. Cate, *The Army Air Forces in World War II*, Vol. 5: *The Pacific: Matterhorn to Nagasaki* (Chicago: University of Chicago Press, 1958), 643.

263 *area bombing remained the only option:* For discussions, see Stephen Budiansky, *Air Power*; Max Hastings, *Bomber Command: The Myths and Reality of the Strategic Bombing Offensive, 1939–45* (New York: Dial, 1979); Ronald Schaffer, *Wings of Judgment: American Bombing in World War II* (New York: Oxford University Press, 1985); Kenneth P. Werrell, *Blankets of Fire: U.S. Bombers over Japan During World War II* (Washington, DC: Smithsonian Institution Press, 1996); and U.S. Strategic Bombing Survey, "Effects of Strategic Bombing on Japan's War Economy."

263 *postwar analysis concluded:* U.S. Strategic Bombing Survey, "Effects of Air Attack on Japan's Urban Economy." Washington, DC: 1946.

263 *"The fire bomb raids":* Mission Accomplished, 24.

264 *"From the defense point of view":* Ibid., 23.

266 *"The final decision":* Craven and Cate, *The Army Air Forces in World War II*, Vol. 5: *The Pacific*, 713.

267 *Death figures for Hiroshima:* Hiroshima's 1944 census listed 344,000, whereas various sources list 66,000 and 200,000 dead. In 1946 the Hiroshima police accounted for 78,000 deaths and 14,000 missing, obviously not all the latter being fatalities. The Actual Status Inventory of Atomic Bomb Survivors (*Chogoku Shimbun*, August 5, 1999) tallied almost 89,000 names of people who died before 1946. "How Many Died at Hiroshima?," http://www.warbirdforum.com/hirodead.htm.

267 *total radiation deaths:* "Is Atomic Radiation as Dangerous As We Thought?," Spiegel Online, November 2007, http://www.spiegel.de/international/world/0,1518,519043,00.html; "Radiation in Perspective: Improving comprehension of risks," International Atomic Energy Agency Bulletin 2/1995, http://www.iaea.org/Publications/Magazines/Bulletin/Bull372/37205140711.pdf.

268 *Former President Herbert Hoover and General Dwight D. Eisenhower:* As supreme Allied commander in Europe, Eisenhower's oft-cited statement that Japan sought to surrender "with a minimum loss of face" was made without knowledge of Pacific Theater intelligence. In his 1948 memoir *Crusade in Europe* (Garden City, NY: Doubleday & Co., 1948), p. 443, he admitted that his views "were not based on any analysis of the subject." That situation had not changed in 1963 when he wrote *The White House Years: Mandate for Change, 1953–1956* (Garden City,

NY: Doubleday & Co, 1963). The frequently accessed Web site http://www.doug-long.com/quotes.htm quotes a full paragraph citing Eisenhower's opposition to A-bombs, concluding, "The Secretary [Henry Stimson] was deeply perturbed by my attitude," but deletes the concluding phrase, "most angrily refuting the reasons I gave *for my quick conclusions*" (emphasis added). The site mentions p. 380 but the quote is on pp. 312–13.

Hoover's May 1945 urging of Truman to make "a short-wave broadcast to the people of Japan" reveals astonishing naïveté. It assumed that Imperial Japan was a democracy and that a majority of Japanese favored surrender. It also ignored the fact that keeping unauthorized radios was a serious offense.

268 *"Neither the Army"*: John Toland, *The Rising Sun: The Decline and Fall of the Japanese Empire, 1936–1945* (New York: Random House, 1970), 561.

268 *" 'Blind' bombing"*: *Mission Accomplished*, 25.

269 *Defenders of the atomic bombings:* Richard Frank, *Downfall: The End of the Imperial Japanese Empire* (New York: Random House, 1999), 351. For a wider discussion of the consequences of an Allied blockade, see his "Alternatives and Conclusions."

269 *"Fundamentally the thing"*: Craven and Cate, *The Army Air Forces in World War II*, Vol. 5: *The Pacific*, 756.

269 *"On top of the B-29 raids"*: *Mission Accomplished*, 39–40.

271 *"revisionist and offensive"*: "Enola Gay Archive," http://www.afa.org/media/enolagay/chrono.asp. For some revisionist views of the atomic bombings and the 1994–95 controversy over the Smithsonian Institution's *Enola Gay* exhibit, see Gar Alperovitz, *The Decision to Use the Atomic Bomb* (New York: Vintage, 1996); Robert J. Lifton and Greg Mitchell, *Hiroshima in America: Fifty Years of Denial* (New York: Putnam, 1995); Philip Noble, ed., *Judgment at the Smithsonian* (New York: Marlowe, 1995).

APPENDIX A: THE UNKNOWN WAR

Page

274 *"the most disastrous day"*: AAF *Combat Chronology*, 11 September 1943.

274 *Northeast Area Fleet:* U.S. Strategic Bombing Survey, *Campaigns of the Pacific War*. Chapter Six: The Aleutians Campaign, 83, http://www.ibiblio.org/hyperwar/AAF/USSBS/PTO-Campaigns/USSBS-PTO-6.html.

Index

About the Author

Barrett Tillman is an internationally recognized authority on air warfare and the author of more than forty books on military topics. The former managing editor of *The Hook* (the magazine of the Tailhook Association), Tillman has appeared in many television documentaries. He has received six awards for history and literature, including the Admiral Arthur Radford Award. He lives in Mesa, Arizona.